Biological
Modernism

Biological Modernism

The New Human in Weimar Culture

✦

Carl Gelderloos

NORTHWESTERN UNIVERSITY PRESS
EVANSTON, ILLINOIS

Northwestern University Press
www.nupress.northwestern.edu

Copyright © 2020 by Northwestern University Press.
Published 2020. All rights reserved.

10 9 8 7 6 5 4 3 2 1

Library of Congress Cataloging-in-Publication Data

Names: Gelderloos, Carl, author.
Title: Biological modernism : the new human in Weimar culture / Carl Gelderloos.
Description: Evanston, Illinois : Northwestern University Press, 2020. | Includes bibliographical references and index.
Identifiers: LCCN 2019027207 | ISBN 9780810141322 (paperback) | ISBN 9780810141339 (cloth) | ISBN 9780810141346 (ebook)
Subjects: LCSH: German literature—20th century—History and criticism. | Modernism (Literature)—Germany. | Human beings in literature. | Biology in literature.
Classification: LCC PT405 .G436 2020 | DDC 830.9356109042—dc23
LC record available at https://lccn.loc.gov/2019027207

CONTENTS

List of Illustrations — *vii*

Acknowledgments — *ix*

Introduction
Modern German Culture in a Life Crisis — *3*

Chapter 1
Helmuth Plessner's Eccentric Human among the Disciplines — *25*

Chapter 2
Photography's Natural Histories in the Weimar Republic — *61*

Chapter 3
Döblin's Epic Embodied — *103*

Chapter 4
Organic Modernization: Wholeness and Development in Ernst Jünger's *The Worker* — *147*

Conclusion — *175*

Notes — *185*

Index — *221*

ILLUSTRATIONS

Figure 1. August Sander, *Face of Our Time*, plate 52:
"The Composer P.H" — 71

Figure 2. August Sander, *Face of Our Time*, plate 23:
"Odd-Job Man" — 73

Figure 3. August Sander, *Face of Our Time*, plate 24:
"Communist Leader" — 73

Figure 4. August Sander, *Face of Our Time*, plate 25:
"Revolutionaries" — 74

Figure 5. August Sander, *Face of Our Time*, plate 26:
"Working Students" — 74

Figure 6. Karl Blossfeldt, *Art Forms in Nature*, plate 9:
Callicarpa dichotoma, Fraxinus ornus, Cornus pubescens — 84

Figure 7. Karl Blossfeldt, *Art Forms in Nature*, plate 17:
Cornus nuttallii, Cornus florida, Acer pennsylvanicum — 84

Figure 8. Karl Blossfeldt, *Art Forms in Nature*, plate 26:
Cucurbita — 85

Figure 9. Karl Blossfeldt, *Art Forms in Nature*, plate 27:
Cajophora lateritia, Loasaceae — 85

Figure 10. Karl Blossfeldt, *Art Forms in Nature*, plate 174:
Tritonia x crocosmiflora (Iridaceae) — 86

Figure 11. Karl Blossfeldt, *Art Forms in Nature*, plate 175:
Hordeum distichon — 86

Figure 12. Alfred Döblin, *Berge Meere und Giganten*, manuscript — 130

ACKNOWLEDGMENTS

One may write alone at a desk, but the context for this solitude is made out of conversations real and imagined, past and anticipated. This book would not have been possible without the thoughtful, generous, and supportive engagement of friends, colleagues, and mentors.

At Cornell University, I would like to thank Patrizia McBride, who is as insightful, supportive, and generous a mentor as one could hope for. Besides continuing to challenge my thinking and support my work, she remains a role model both as a scholar, showing how to combine nuanced detailed readings with incisive reorientations of the bigger picture, and as a committed, intellectually generous, and hard-working mentor. Additionally I thank Leslie A. Adelson, Paul Fleming, Peter Uwe Hohendahl, and Anette Schwarz as well for their mentorship, guidance, insightful feedback, and hard questions. In general, Cornell's Department of German Studies was a bracing, supportive place to get an education—I am grateful to other graduate students, mentors, and teachers there who asked me questions that were sometimes too difficult to answer, then or now, but which have stayed with me and helped shape this project.

Binghamton University has been an excellent place to write this book. I thank Neil Christian Pages, Harald Zils, Rosmarie Morewedge, Ingeborg Majer-O'Sickey, Sidney Dement, Nancy Tittler, Marina Zalesski, and Don Loewen for welcoming me into an invigorating, lively department, for supporting this project, for the conversations necessary to surviving late November or late March in the Southern Tier, and for helping me learn how to be faculty. Additional gratitude has been amply earned by Neil Christian, Harald, and Sidney for feedback and conversations about this project, about publishing, about teaching, and about navigating the bureaucracy. For their guidance and encouragement I thank colleagues in other departments, especially Brian Wall, Pamela Smart, Tom McDonough, and Max Pensky, who have been welcoming, gracious, and supportive since I started at Binghamton. The members of a grant-writing circle in spring 2017, particularly Kevin Boettcher and Wendy Wall, helped me to communicate the contours and interest of this project to an audience outside German Studies; I didn't get the grant, but being able to articulate what this book is actually about was much better. I am also grateful to the participants in the VizCult speaker series in Binghamton's Art History Department, where I presented an early version of part of my chapter on photography, and especially to Julia Walker for extending the invitation.

The bad thing about good readers and thoughtful interlocutors is that they make writing a book much more laborious, but this one would not have been possible without them. For taking the time to thoroughly read and comment on parts of this project amidst the pressures of the tenure track, the academic job market, and life in general, for their support and encouragement, and for their smarts and humor, I am deeply grateful to Erik Born, Paul Buchholz, Paul Dobryden, June Hwang, Jeffrey Kirkwood, Ari Linden, and Matthew Stoltz. Repeated thanks are emphatically due to Paul Buchholz and Ari Linden, who read multiple chapters and drafts, and who offered relief and real-time support by text, e-mail, and video from the beginning of this project through its final stretch. In addition to the above, I also wish to thank Anna Horakova, Katrina Nousek, and Johannes Wankhammer for their friendship and support, which has manifested itself over the years in forms ranging from conversations about literature, politics, art, life, and work to dubious forays into home karaoke. Further afield, I am grateful to the International Alfred Döblin Society, and particularly to Christina Althen, Gabriele Sander, and Sabina Becker, for their expertise, generosity, and hospitality. The two anonymous readers at Northwestern University Press provided insightful, kind, and challenging feedback—I thank them sincerely for their time, commitment, and acuity. And I thank Trevor Perri for his gracious and adroit editorial support for this project.

On the practical side of things, gratitude is owed to the institutional support that allowed me to develop and complete this project: at Binghamton, a Dean's Research Semester and an Institute for Advanced Study in the Humanities fellowship provided helpful releases from teaching to draft this manuscript; before that, an American Friends of Marbach travel grant and a Fulbright fellowship allowed me to conduct research in Germany. Parts of chapter 3 appeared in earlier form in *German Quarterly* and in *The German Historical Novel since the Eighteenth Century*, edited by Daniela Richter, and I am grateful for the permission to reprint them here.

And finally, last but most, I thank Agata and Rowan. Thanks to Rowan for being patient, for being impatient, for letting me write and for distracting me, for reenchanting the world, for reinventing language, and for reminding us to keep things in perspective. Agata has been my partner and best friend for much longer than I've been working on this project. Without her encouragement, support, good humor, tireless efforts, and belief, this project simply wouldn't exist. I dedicate this book to her.

Ithaca, New York
January 2019

Biological Modernism

Introduction

Modern German Culture in a Life Crisis

> Moreover, any beautiful object, whether a living organism or any other thing made up of parts, must have those parts not only in proper order but also on an appropriate scale. Beauty consists in scale as well as order, which is why there could not be a beautiful organism that was either minuscule or gigantic. In the first case, a glimpse that is so brief as to be close to vanishing-point cannot be distinct. In the second case—say, of an animal a thousand miles long—the impossibility of taking all in at a single glance means that unity and wholeness is lost to the viewer.
> —Aristotle, *Poetics* 7.1450b–1451a

> If a novel can't be cut up into ten pieces like an earthworm, with each part still moving on its own, then it's no good.
> —Alfred Döblin, "Comments on the Novel" (March 1917)

> The epic writer Döblin provided an excellent criterion when he said that with an epic work, as opposed to a dramatic, one can as it were take a pair of scissors and cut it into individual pieces, which remain fully capable of life.
> —Bertolt Brecht, "Theatre for Pleasure or Theatre for Instruction" (ca. 1936)

Alfred Döblin's hapless earthworm, chopped-up yet still vital, wriggles awkwardly in the space between Aristotelian unity and Brechtian montage. For Aristotle, the organic body is the emblem of unity and wholeness; Brecht, in doing away with Aristotelian unity, also dispenses with the organic body, leaving as its trace simply the attribute, "capable of life" (*lebensfähig*). The distance from Aristotle to Brecht marks the space of a well-worn paradigm shift in the idea of aesthetic form. For Aristotle, the comparison between a story and an animal pivots on the unity and wholeness of the animal body, and its relationship to a human observer. If the proportionality or size of the observed object, whether animal or story, are such that they cannot be seen or remembered as a whole, then they are not beautiful. For Brecht, by contrast, scale is no longer a relevant category, nor is beauty. Brecht's invocation of Alfred Döblin's theory of the epic hinges rather on the possibilities of montage, and indeed, Brecht's theorization of epic theater was explicitly anti-Aristotelian in its rejection of unity and emotional identification.[1]

Yet Brecht's appreciative citation of Döblin makes some crucial changes to the latter's comparison. Döblin is not speaking here of scissors (which suggest a montage or collage practice), nor is he contrasting the epic to the dramatic work, in Brecht's terms. The role of bodies, which is central to both Aristotle's and Döblin's comparisons between animals and artworks, has also dropped out of the language Brecht uses. To be sure, it is much easier to fit machine imagery—even a machine as humble as the scissors—into our picture of Weimar modernism than the lowly and abused earthworm. But what has gone missing in Brecht's reference to Döblin is the specifically biological dimension of this re-theorization of form.

So what do we do with these ten worm segments, each still moving on its own? What work is the organic doing here, in this local articulation of German modernism? If we think of the immediate context—in 1917, Döblin had been serving as a doctor near the Western Front for over two years[2]—the dissection of the worm may recall the violent disassembly of human bodies in the trenches. Or, if we anticipate somewhat and consider the better-known mobilization of organicism by the Nazis, we might want to see the worm's vital persistence as the sign of an organic unity that abides even in dismemberment, perhaps aided by the national soil (*Boden*) that is its element.

But Döblin is doing something patently different from these more familiar strategies. Elsewhere, in his novels from the early 1920s, one finds other vermiform images that represent a kind of slithery, recombinatory vitality instead of an organic unity. In Döblin's comparison, life represents a potential for growth and vitality that sidesteps any notion of wholeness. The valence of his unwillingly segmented earthworm is positive—the image does not lament a lost organic unity, but denies unity's very relevance as an aesthetic category. A novel must be modular: each piece must be able to stand on its own, effectively reconstituting itself even when removed from its context. Thus Döblin's use of the organic stands for the rejection of wholeness, for fragmentation as a positive category, rather than for wholeness and unity, in a way that seems calculated to thwart Aristotle's recipe for narrative unity.[3] Notably, Döblin's earthworm is also an image of infinite divisibility, with consequences, as we will see, not just for the artwork, but also for the *in*-dividual and for life itself.

This triple rethinking of art, the human being, and nature—what I call "biological modernism"—is the subject of this book. To identify its scope and to understand its significance, we must look backwards, not forwards:

the coherence and force of Döblin's metaphor can best be understood not against the horizon of a reactionary organicism, in the form of the looming Nazi biopolitics with its emphasis on a racialized national community, but rather as a rejection of the inheritance of bourgeois humanism, a rejection that took the form of an articulation of modernity and life that was emerging across culture and science in the 1920s, but which had roots that reached back into the late nineteenth century. What changed understanding of life enabled the shift from the "appropriate scale" of Aristotle's "beautiful organism" to the idea of the necessary modularity and divisibility of the artwork, and why does Brecht's elision of the earthworm seem so natural?

To be sure, organicism—a discourse of wholeness that relies upon metaphors of the body and of living nature more generally—has long been identified with the political Right in modern German culture and thought. From nineteenth-century vitalism to eugenics and the "blood and soil" ideology of the Nazi period, the investment of nature with spiritual meaning is often seen as an irrationalist, conservative reaction to the complex demands of modernity. In the face of rapid industrialization, the catastrophic experience of the First World War, and the social upheaval of the November Revolution, so the story goes, Weimar intellectuals who turned to images of nature did so to recover a supposedly lost unity. Yet such a narrative eclipses other uses to which organicism could be put; indeed, for many writers and intellectuals in the Weimar Republic, discourses such as organicism and vitalism, and natural sciences like biology, provided a way of theorizing modernity rather than fleeing from it.

This book seeks to restore the role played by biology, organicism, and *life* in the attempt to rethink the human being, the form and purpose of the work of art, and modernity in the period from the 1910s to the 1930s. If the turn to organic nature is commonly understood as a flight from the complexities of technological modernity, the possibility that, for Döblin, the organic could represent fragmentation rather than wholeness suggests that any presumed opposition between organic nature and technological modernity should be approached cautiously. What this book identifies in the exemplary cases of Helmuth Plessner, August Sander, Karl Blossfeldt, Alfred Döblin, and Ernst Jünger is the use of biology, organicism, and life to theorize modern experience and reformulate the human, precisely in conscious opposition to those ideas of form, organization, and subjectivity generated by the association of the organic with wholeness. This approach to life, which depended on the reception of contemporary biology as much as it stemmed from the suspicion of inherited aesthetic practices and assumptions, saw the organic as the site of fusion and growth but also, therefore, as analogous to the sense of fragmentation and possibility evoked by modern experience. What biology and organicism provided to Weimar thinkers was a field of knowledge and a trove of metaphors, concepts, and questions for theorizing the experience of modernization in self-reflexive, aspirational, proleptic, and critical ways, thereby linking different aspects of their historical moment: technological and social changes, the perceived need for aesthetic renewal, and the acutely felt insufficiency of inherited concepts of the human being. In other words, the writers and artists of the Weimar Republic who are the subject of this book did not automatically assume—as later commentators frequently have—that nature and technology, the organic and the mechanical, are contraries. Rather, they took seriously the functional and formal similarities between what was being discovered about organic life, on the one hand, and the modern, urban, technological world they saw growing up around them, on the other. They saw that both tendencies—the new science of life and the experience of technological modernity—posed insurmountable difficulties for bourgeois-era, nineteenth-century assumptions about subjective interiority, and for the received Cartesian dualism of mind and matter, soul and body, human and nonhuman nature. In order to redefine the human being for a modern, technological age, they mobilized tropes and concepts from the natural sciences and philosophies of nature. As is the case with Döblin's epic earthworm, they also frequently drew upon organic life to aspirationally define the kinds of art and theory that would correspond to this juncture. As modernists, they were not passively reacting to an experience of modernity but were, by grappling with its implications, actively constructing modernity as an idea and as a discourse.

Various crises faced by the concept of life in the early twentieth century marked the life sciences and the humanities while also raising the question of their relationship to each other. The internal restructuring of the concept of life across disciplines made it available as a field in which writers and intellectuals could also retheorize the human being and the experience of modernity. If life, as Foucault has argued, did not exist before the nineteenth century—that is, if it is a specific historical category for understanding living beings[4]—then attending to its reorganization in the early twentieth century can help us understand how contemporaries theorized and formulated the experience of modernity in self-reflexive, explicitly transdisciplinary terms, even as they never lost sight of the organic.

In biology, ideas about life were undergoing a radical expansion and revision marked by advances in empirical knowledge and experimental techniques, as well as by disciplinary formation and consolidation, with the emergence in the late nineteenth and early twentieth centuries of new subfields, disciplines, and methods. As Cathryn Carson describes the disciplinary flux within the sciences of life in the Weimar Republic,

> More, perhaps, than any other interwar science, biology seemed ripe for transformative change. It was expanding its reach on seemingly every possible front—the elucidation of cellular structures and processes, whole-organism development and behavior, species-level questions of inheritance and evolution. If there were a domain of

natural science, moreover, that promised immediate consequences for human culture, it was biology, as the pervasiveness of biological thinking in contemporary social and political discourse made clear.[5]

Freud's death drive, Spengler's organicist account of the rise and fall of civilizations, *Lebensphilosophie*, and degeneration and eugenics may well represent the best-known influences of biological thinking on the cultural imaginary of the time, yet the life sciences were proving broadly generative in the late nineteenth and early twentieth centuries for thinking about culture and the human being in various fields and diverse ways: ethology,[6] ecology,[7] embryology,[8] comparative anatomy, evolutionary theory,[9] and others. Such developments shaped ideas that went far beyond social Darwinism or pessimistic versions of biological thinking premised on antirationalist enthusiasm for strength or vitality, or on narratives of cultural decline. Beyond specific advances in biological practice, there was thus the pervasive sense that biology could grapple with larger questions that lay outside the laboratory. Indeed, given the ways in which the proliferation of disciplines and subfields both shored up and destabilized the indeterminate concept of "life," it seemed as though biology *had* to take on questions of part and whole, individual and mass, emergence, continuity, and novelty.[10]

We may take the debate between mechanism and vitalism as paradigmatic for the modern biological approach to life, because this debate in the late nineteenth and early twentieth centuries involved the latest experimental methods while also returning to philosophical questions about the relationship between matter and life that traced back to Descartes. Mechanists held that the behavior of all matter, including living matter, could be explained in purely physical terms, as the mechanical interaction of particles in motion. Vitalists, by contrast, believed that some distinctly vital force was needed to account for the behavior of living organisms, which were qualitatively different from nonliving matter. As Helmuth Plessner, writing in the mid-1920s, summarizes the impasse:

> The mechanists can point to the great strides made in identifying things in organisms that had been thought to be specifically vital with inorganic things, without however convincing the vitalists of their similarity in principle, that is, of the ability to characterize the organic in a totally mechanical way. Conversely, the vitalists assert in vain to their opponents that the complexity found in the vital character of organic processes represents an essential border between living and nonliving nature.[11]

Behind this ontological dispute lay a disciplinary conflict between reductionist and non-reductionist approaches to life. In reducing life to an instance of physical and chemical processes, mechanists effectively denied that there was an ontologically distinct realm of life in the first place, which entailed a view of biology as a subset of physics and chemistry. Vitalists, on the other hand, identified life as a distinct realm of analysis that functioned according to its own laws, and could not therefore be reduced to physics or chemistry. The mechanism/vitalism debate opened biological questions pertaining not merely to the ontological status of life, but also to the disciplinary status of biology itself.

Yet many thinkers of the time, rather than come down on one side of the mechanism/vitalism debate or the other, saw the debate itself as an impasse that was symptomatic of a broader legacy. Donna Haraway describes how mechanism and vitalism both share the premise that whatever might distinguish life from matter cannot be found in matter itself—in this reading, mechanism and vitalism constitute two sides of the same coin.[12] Helmuth Plessner frames his intervention in a similar way—his account of the human being, which similarly seeks to define the human and life as such in immanent, formal terms, sets the stage by recounting a dispute between Wolfgang Köhler and the neo-vitalist Hans Driesch in order to find a position beyond the opposition between mechanism and vitalism. The question concerned the wholeness (*Ganzheit*) of the living organism, and whether this wholeness could be explained in terms that also applied to the inorganic, or whether it was unique to life. Köhler, known for his contribution to Gestalt psychology, took the reductionist position that the same principles that made any phenomenon a whole also applied to organisms, while Driesch argued that living beings exhibited their own kind of wholeness that could not be understood with recourse to the idea of the Gestalt. Driesch showed, in experiments on the embryos of sea urchins, that it is possible for a whole organism to develop from a single embryonic cell that had been artificially isolated. These results contradicted the earlier findings of Wilhelm Roux, who had articulated a mechanistic or "mosaic" theory of development after showing that only half a frog embryo will develop if one of two cells is destroyed. For the vitalist Driesch, some other factor—which he dubbed "entelechy"—was necessary to understand the process of regulation specific to organic life, capable of generating a whole from a part. Yet precisely by positing with entelechy a factor that could not be empirically observed, he effectively recapitulated the classical vitalist option that relied on some element outside the organism in order to define organic life. The aporias of these positions help clear the ground for Plessner's own approach, which would locate the specificity of the living organism in immanent principles.[13] The mechanism/vitalism controversy represented such a problem because it was so deeply rooted in a deeper legacy of dualism, which contemporaries explicitly tied to Descartes.[14] Descartes's division of the world into *res cogitans* and *res extensa* (commonly understood as mind and matter, respectively) had the dual consequence of dematerializing the self,[15] on the one hand, and banishing both agency and the qualitative aspects from the material world,[16] on the other. For the strict mechanist materialism that largely informed post-Cartesian science this meant that animals, for example, had to be explained as machines, with far-reaching consequences that included a notion of the self as disembodied. If, as Jessica Riskin has argued, this vexed legacy continues to pose a problem for modern science, then returning to this moment when the relationships among mechanism, dualism, science, embodiment, subjectivity, and history were being interrogated so aggressively and so self-consciously can offer new insight into the bifurcated understanding of the human being that, for biological modernists, was the shadow of Descartes.[17] The very definition of life was, in the 1920s, struggling to escape from a dualist paradigm that no longer adequately contained it.

Moreover, biology was not the only domain grappling with life at the time. A more familiar association of *Leben* for present-day readers will likely be *Lebensphilosophie*, the German strain of philosophical vitalism associated chiefly with Friedrich Nietzsche, Wilhelm Dilthey, Georg Simmel, Oswald Spengler, and Ludwig Klages. While the emerging field of biology sought to understand life as a natural phenomenon, *Lebensphilosophie* questioned the Enlightenment inheritance by centering life and experience (*Erlebnis*), rather than spirit or reason, within the human realm. *Lebensphilosophie* posed questions of meaning and interpretation that went beyond the positive accumulation of facts and data. In his essay "The Use and Abuse of History for Life," for example, Nietzsche surveys different possible ways of relating to the past, ultimately criticizing the prevailing historicism and arguing instead that knowledge should be subordinated to life. For Dilthey, the human realms of history and culture were fundamentally distinct from the natural sciences, and required their own method to be properly understood, drawing on categories that come from experience and life itself.[18] In its more pronouncedly antirationalist version, exemplified by Ludwig Klages, *Lebensphilosophie* offered a trajectory that led from the early critique of the Enlightenment to Nazi biopolitics.[19] Common to all these examples is the insistence on the relationship between subjective experience and meaning, on the one hand, and the vital potential, both generative and destructive, that subtends all forms and distinctions, on the other. At heart, *Lebensphilosophie* posited a special relationship between life and meaning, and thereby exerted a powerful influence on the culture of the 1920s, in part because it offered an alternative to Enlightenment rationality and bourgeois humanism.[20]

Thus life was enmeshed in extraordinarily productive crises in both the sciences and the humanities. Both life crises, in biology and in the humanities, concerned questions of form, the emergence of novelty, and the relationship of parts and wholes. Döblin's chopped-up earthworm spans both of these domains, drawing on the specifically biological vitality of the organic body in order to make a point about the relationship between meaning and form. Yet, and this is the third life crisis, the re-theorization of life at the time did not just occur *within* different domains of science and culture, but was articulated *across* them, even questioning their very separation. Life straddled these domains and indicted the disciplinary division of labor, linked to the legacy of Cartesian dualism, that had separated them. Over and over again in texts by Plessner, Döblin, and Jünger, one finds the rejection of strict demarcations between the sciences and the humanities, and a strong critique of the view of the human being that results from only one of these domains alone. In a sense, the critique of this disciplinary bifurcation is the foundational conceit of texts like Plessner's *The Stages of the Organic and the Human Being*, Döblin's "Spirit of the Naturalistic Era," and Jünger's *The Worker*. The disciplinary division of labor between the humanities predicated on questions of interpretation and meaning, on the one hand, and natural sciences increasingly understood in terms of quantitative empiricism, on the other, was seen as a problem for understanding the human being's place in the modern world and in the natural world alike.

One consequence of this disciplinary impasse was the perceived deficit, in the 1920s, of a theory of the human being that could answer to both biology and philosophy. As a result, contemporaries sought to bridge this divide. Indeed this was, in a sense, the entire project of Philosophical Anthropology. Max Scheler points to this deficit at the beginning of his 1928 work *The Human Place in the Cosmos*, writing, "For we thus have a scientific, a philosophical, and a theological anthropology each unconcerned with the others—*but we do not possess a unified idea of the human being.*"[21] And something like a grand unified theory of the human being was the project of Plessner's magnum opus, *The Stages of the Organic and the Human Being* (*Die Stufen des Organischen und der Mensch*, 1928). Moreover, Plessner explicitly identified the disciplinary divide between the natural sciences (quantitative, empirical, objective) and the humanities (qualitative, speculative, subjective) as a direct legacy of Descartes's division of the world into *res extensa* and *res cogitans*. Plessner's project in *Stages*, therefore, was to theorize the human being not merely *despite* this disciplinary split, but in a way that would actually close it.

Advances in the experimental and empirical knowledge of living organisms meant that more was known about how life worked than ever before, yet, by the same token, this messy proliferation of knowledge and competing subfields also meant that "life" was anything but a well-delineated concept. If anything, "life" was now even more generative for thinking about realms far beyond biology proper. As Helmuth Plessner begins his first chapter:

> Every age finds its redeeming word. The terminology of the eighteenth century culminates in the concept of reason, that of the nineteenth century in the concept of development, that of the present century in the concept of life. Every age thereby designates something different, reason emphasizes the timeless and the universally binding, development emphasizes the restlessly becoming and rising, life emphasizes the demonically playing, the unconsciously creative element.[22]

Life is the "redeeming word" for the twentieth century, rather than "reason" or "development." In elaborating on the connotations of life, Plessner describes its "demonic," "creative" potential in terms that evoke aesthetic creation. In the very same year, Walter Benjamin was praising Karl Blossfeldt's magnified plant images in similar terms, also in order to link the formative potential of organic growth to a deep creative impulse behind all forms.[23] To put it mildly, life—as a concept, as a question, as a metaphor, as a field of study—was in the air, and in crisis, like never before.

These disciplinary life crises meant that contemporaries perceived the need to retheorize the human being as particularly acute. Cartesian dualism, the vitalism/mechanism debate, and the disciplinary split between the humanities and the natural sciences were manifestly unable to account for the human being as both subject and object, intellect and body, cultural and natural phenomenon. Plessner, Döblin, and Jünger all explicitly name some kind of mind/body dualism as a problematic inheritance that cannot adequately define the human being for the modern era. In place of the inherited impasses, they all proposed versions of a new human. But, beyond the merely epistemological quandaries of dualism, what were its cultural contours—what, in other words, were the characteristics of the old human that biological modernism was reacting to?

Crucially, these questions about life and the human developed in the context of a broader cultural reckoning with bourgeois humanism, specifically with prevailing conceptions of selfhood and subjectivity, and how these no longer fit within a world experienced both as more technological and more elemental. Here, too, a Cartesian legacy would be a key reference point—not because of quibbles with the details of Descartes's actual work, but because of the broader influence that Cartesian dualism was seen to have in structuring other dualisms, to the extent that Ernst Jünger could complain about "the sentiment of a decisive opposition between the mechanical and the organic world, in which we see a final flattening of the old opposition between body and soul."[24] Jessica Riskin has argued that modern selfhood and modern science "created one another" in Descartes's philosophy.[25] For Riskin, one significant consequence of the division of the world into *cogitans* and *extensa*, mind and matter, was that the assignment of intellect to a disembodied self resulted in the evacuation of life from matter: "The animal-machine, as Descartes described it in the first instance, was warm, mobile, living, responsive, sentient. The same living machinery, when measured against a disembodied, transcendent self, looked different: confined, rote, passive."[26] Plessner, Döblin, Jünger, and others addressed this dilemma from both ends, arguing against both the disembodied self and a conception of material nature as passive. Thus, a main impulse of biological modernism was to attempt to undo these dual effects of Cartesian dualism, which left a dematerialized self confronting a nature that could only be seen as passively mechanical.[27]

Furthermore, the notion of selfhood that was rejected by these thinkers was not merely disembodied, but also subjective, interior, and individual—all qualities that were seen as anachronistic. Döblin and Jünger were not alone in scornfully rejecting the idea of the artist as characterized by a privileged, protected subjectivity. Artistic subjectivity as a space of private fancy was broadly criticized as unable to confront the modern world because it clung to outmoded views of society, art, and individuality alike. Rhetorically flinging open a door, Döblin writes in an early programmatic text: "The artist works in his closed cell. His personal side is two-thirds self-deception and nonsense. The door to discussion is open."[28] In opposition to the closed garret of the inspired artist, writers in the 1920s increasingly preferred the street or the factory as symbols of public, collective, mass spaces. Yet it is also important to note that this rejection of private individuality was shaped by the larger context of the broad social division of labor between the increasingly assertive natural sciences, on the one hand, and the humanities and arts, on the other. As Lorraine Daston and Peter Galison have argued, the emergence of a modern scientific self entailed an artistic self as its counterpart: "In notable contrast to earlier views held from the Renaissance through the Enlightenment about the close analogies between artistic and scientific work, the public personas of artist and scientist polarized during this period. Artists were exhorted to express, even flaunt, their subjectivity, at the same time that scientists were admonished to restrain theirs."[29] In rejecting the artist's privileged subjectivity, Döblin— who was both a writer and a doctor, we should note—was thus also rejecting this division of knowledge and representation into two complementary opposites, and the bifurcated notion of self it necessitated.

The identification of selfhood with individuality also came in for sustained critique during the 1920s—not in the name of a uniform collectivity or a higher power, but because it was seen as insufficient for understanding the human being. To make the individual the main unit for understanding human behavior was to fixate on one level of analysis when others—such as the supra-individual level of the collective or species, or the sub-individual levels of drives, cells, organs, metabolism, and so on—were equally necessary. Rather than the individual, the type or the mass was privileged. In a similar vein, the idea of anonymity was emphasized as an antidote to the humanist notion of the centered, indivisible self. While this may be broadly familiar to readers of Brecht, for example—think of the injunction "Verwisch die Spuren!" ("Cover your tracks!") or the disassembly of individual identity in *Man Equals Man*[30]—anonymity plays an even more fundamental role in Döblin's work, where it connects his philosophy of nature to his critique of bourgeois individuality. As we will see in the various chapters that make up this book, an inherited understanding of individuality was challenged by recourse to a mass, epic poetics (Döblin), a typological photography (Sander, Blossfeldt), a positional ontology of living forms (Plessner), and even a typological cosmology (Jünger).

The turn from the individual to the mass or type had biological, technological, and social roots and connotations; more precisely, the emphasis on the mass and the type was a strategy frequently used to connect these domains in conscious objection to their dualistic separation. The goal was to imagine the human being in a way that could meet the demands of both philosophy and biology, culture and science. Nineteenth-century biology had already begun laying the groundwork for a radical critique of the idea of the individual: Rudolf Virchow's cell theory and the idea of the "Zellenrepublik" ("cell-republic"), Ernst Haeckel's consideration of the relationship between individual and organism, and Alexander Braun's description of plants as "dividuals" all destabilized the solidity and centrality of the individual body.[31] Meanwhile, the fragmentation of modern, urban, mass experience was seen to fracture both the isolation and the unity necessary for the formation of the autonomous individual. When Döblin describes the modern metropolis as a "coral stock for the human collective being,"[32] or when Jünger writes that, to the hypothetical perspective of a lunar observer, the city would offer "the image of a particular structure, and we can work out from various indications that it is nourished by the sap of a great life force,"[33] their turn from the individual to the mass proceeds through images that combine the modern, technological connotations of the metropolis with a biological, species-level view. As a result, the creative products of individual geniuses—and any version of art premised on these—seemed faded and irrelevant in the face of the elemental, mass forms unleashed by modern technologies of communication, transportation, and warfare: "The Cologne Cathedral is undoubtedly the expression of a strong, resolute spirit. The electric dynamo is a match for the Cologne Cathedral."[34] Life, in its reformulation among the disciplines, could be seen as a force both modern and elemental, both organic and technological, which could not be contained by notions of selfhood predicated on individuality or interiority (*Innerlichkeit*). If these combinations seem counterintuitive or paradoxical, this indicates the discursive, metaphorical density of the period's engagement with its own modernity; the specific constellations offered by this book's four chapters will offer a fuller picture, but for now it is necessary to underscore the extent to which these writers were consciously targeting what they saw as a bourgeois legacy that shaped available models of subjectivity, modernity, and art.

What then were the contours of the new human that emerged from this life crisis? To be clear, the "new human" was not a term used by the figures at the center of this study. Rather, it is a term of convenience I have chosen to apply to their parallel attempts to define the human being after humanism. This new human is not primarily an individual characterized by moral autonomy and psychological interiority. It is characterized by an embodied subjectivity, articulated in explicit opposition to dualisms of mind and body, self and world, inside and outside. And significantly, these characteristics derive from a reconsideration of the relationship between organisms and machines, nature and technology, rather than from one or the other. For reasons the chapters will articulate in more detail, the new human in Weimar culture is not exactly, or not only, a cyborg, a prosthetic body, or an armored body. The new human I am describing is heterogeneous. A vast difference separates Plessner's naturally artificial, "eccentric" human being from the traumatized collectivities at the end of Döblin's novel *Mountains Seas and Giants*, who in turn do not look very much like Ernst Jünger's worker. But what they all share is a skepticism of dualism, interiority, and individuality, articulated specifically in response to an experience of modernity that was undermining these inherited categories.

To the extent that the new human of biological modernism dismantled the classical traits of the liberal, humanist subject, it bears a family resemblance to the cybernetic posthuman as theorized by N. Katherine Hayles in her 1999 work *How We Became Posthuman*. Indeed, Hayles has specifically mentioned biology as a field in which she could have identified the posthuman, but contingent factors steered her in the direction of information theory and cybernetics.[35] And in large part, biology as mediated through biological modernism fits her description of the posthuman as a set of "twentieth-century developments in which an Enlightenment inheritance that emphasized autonomy, rationality, individuality and so forth, was being systematically challenged and disassembled—in a whole variety of fields."[36] Yet the dematerialization of the body in information theory, which is central to her account of posthumanism in that it causes cybernetic posthumanism (and transhumanism) to reproduce the very humanist categories they sought to transcend, does not jibe with the emphatically corporeal logics of biological modernism. Thus the biological strain of posthumanism, which Hayles invokes as a road not taken, would have a very different relationship to materiality and embodiment. This is not to say that the figures of this study completely avoided this pitfall, but I do submit that their anti-dualist engagement with the body and embodiment might amount to a more radical confrontation with this Enlightenment inheritance. Moreover, the biological modernism of the Weimar Republic can provide a useful historical concretization to current discussions of posthumanism that all too often tend to see their object as a transcendent, rather than a historical one. Seen in their own social, political, scientific, cultural, and political contexts, the motivations for revising or rejecting bourgeois humanism in the 1920s are bound up with historical conditions of knowledge production and political questions about the organization of society. The self-conscious articulation of the relationship between fields of knowledge, on the one hand, and theories of the human, on the other, aimed to prescribe different approaches to nature, in a specific reaction to disciplinary, philosophical, and cultural forms that were seen as obsolete in the 1920s. The biological modernism of the Weimar Republic can add nuance, in other words, to current ideas about a posthuman, nonhuman, or Anthropocene turn.

Moreover, the term "new" better represents the relevant temporality of this study than does "post," since the figures I discuss understood their anti-dualist reconfiguration of the human being as a specifically modern project—modern in the double sense that it was a coming to terms with a bourgeois, humanist legacy they frequently located in the nineteenth century, and that their new definitions and images of the human being corresponded to the salient features of a socially and technologically modern era. The relationship between social processes of modernization and the imagination of modernity was dense, mutual, and self-reflexive. Biological modernism, as both a reaction to and a theory of modernity, depended as much upon imaginative and aspirational projections of technology as on actual technological progress. Moreover, the suspicion of the idea that technology is a domain distinct from (or even opposed to) the natural world was at the heart of the interventions of Döblin's *Mountains Seas and Giants* (1924), Plessner's *The Stages of the Organic and the Human Being* (1928), and Ernst Jünger's *The Worker* (1932).

In linking the radical changes of technology to organic life itself, biological modernism established a counterintuitive temporality and a paradoxical relationship to modernity. On the one hand, this discourse saw itself as participating in a modernization characterized by newness, acceleration, and fragmentation. But this participation cannot simply be described as a cultural reaction to social or technological determinants: it was also the active construction of modernity on a conceptual and imaginative level.[37] In her account of the Weimar-era photographic book, Pepper Stetler has provided a suggestive model for thinking about a textual relationship to modernity. Rather than formally re-creating or reacting to an experience of fragmentation, the basic pedagogical stance of the photographic book—the goal of training the viewers to *read* in a way that would correspond to modern experience—implies an attitude towards modernity that is aspirational and proleptic.[38] Her definition of "modern vision as something imagined but never achieved"[39] informs my understanding of the relationship between modernity and modernism for biological modernism, because it suggests the tangled relationship between the experience and the imagination of modernity, and thus between the descriptive and prescriptive dimensions of these texts. One consequence of this entanglement is that, while social and technological processes and developments do matter, they matter in a way that is always mediated through their functions in a cultural imaginary. The sense is pervasive in these writers' works that inherited models of subjectivity, art, and technology cannot account for modern experience. Their texts sought not merely to describe this, but, by imagining the subjects and readers that would be adequate to the modern world, to change it.

On the other hand, in their anti-dualism and especially in seeing technological modernity as an outgrowth of organic nature, these writers thereby refuse the "work of purification" between humans and nonhumans, culture and nature that characterizes the state of being modern for Bruno Latour.[40] They thus provide an early example of the crossing of boundaries, boundaries which Elaine Graham, drawing on Latour, has characterized as an "'ontological hygiene' separating human from non-human, nature from culture, organism from machine."[41] The modernism of Weimar biological modernism consists, in this sense, of defining the modern era in terms opposed to such ontological hygiene. This twist also suggests some vexed implications for the temporalities that were important for biological modernism. Without ceasing to depend on acceleration, newness, or an aspirational, proleptic stance, it should also be clear why biological modernism might not maintain a temporality of progress or even development. Indeed, as we will see in Jünger, a technological accelerationism can coexist with an organic teleology, the goal of which is stasis. In Döblin's *Mountains Seas and Giants*, an open-ended, partly reconciled form of collectivity comes at the end of the traumatic separation and reunification of organisms and machines, technology and nature. And for Plessner, the human being is the full realization of a definition of the living organism as a border-crossing body, but this realization does not mean stasis, but rather the permanent need to regain balance, expressed for Plessner in the drive towards culture.

The fact that these texts were grappling with the construction of modernity is what constitutes their modernism. As a self-reflexive, aspirational, proleptic, and critical stance towards modernity and modernization, biological modernism cannot be described as either affirming or rejecting modernity, so much as constructing it in what might seem to us to be counterintuitive ways. Biological modernism is clearly not the same as high modernism, nor should it be understood primarily in stylistic, formal, or institutional terms. Rather, it was a cultural configuration that reacted to—and sought to define—modernity in ways that specifically and consciously reflected upon its aesthetic and epistemological constitution across disciplines, media, and forms. Looking at the Weimar Republic in this way thus draws on Marshall Berman's definition of modernism "as any attempt by modern men and women to become subjects as well as objects of modernization, to get a grip on the modern world and make themselves at home in it."[42] My emphasis would be less on the goal of making oneself "at home in a constantly changing world,"[43] since the figures of this study, each in their own way, seem to confirm Lukács's definition of the modern condition as "transcendental homelessness."[44] What Berman's definition does offer, however, is a usefully agnostic understanding of modernism as a struggle to comprehend, mediate, and form the experiences of modernity and modernization.

The methodological utility that guides the adoption of such an agnostic rather than a normative conception of modernism is provisional, pragmatic, and heuristic: what connections, lines of influence, or commonalities become visible if we view modernism as an engagement with modernity and modernization, rather than in narrower terms guided by either a stylistic, formal evaluation or by a judgment concerning the appropriateness of a writer's reaction to modernity? This is obviously not to argue that such an agnostic approach to modernism is the only approach, or even the best one. Rather, the approach is guided by my suspicion that many aspects of the various borrowings from and articulations of biology and organicism during the Weimar Republic are distorted or obscured by a normative understanding of modernism, while an agnostic, immanent approach might be able to make the similarities, resonances, and affinities among otherwise very different writers—Plessner, Döblin, and Jünger, for example—legible. Reading these figures' uses of the organic and the biological on their own terms allows me to reconstruct the contours of the critique of bourgeois humanism and Cartesian dualism during the period, illuminating, for example, the significance of how Döblin and Jünger worked with concepts of the individual, the type, and the mass. Analyzing Weimar organicism on its own terms also makes it possible to glimpse the rich internal differentiation within the various strategies of biological modernism. This latter point is especially salient—all biological thought in Weimar culture did not amount to reactionary irrationalism or a fetishization of blind nature, nor can the deployment of nature at the time be understood in the sense of a flight from the complexities of the modern world into the stable ordering systems of an earlier natural science. Biology was, and was viewed as, a set of cutting-edge knowledge practices and discourses which the figures of this book found especially fruitful for theorizing their historical moment.

What interests me is how these figures were actively constructing, and reflecting on, models of modernity. From this perspective, it is no accident that the period is full of self-diagnoses of its own modernity, self-diagnoses that cross the expected lines of nature and culture. When Döblin, considering the tendency of human society towards ever-greater complexity, asks, "What is that from a biological point of view?" he is not falling back on organicism as a compensation, but rather articulating a new configuration of nature, the human, and modernity.[45] Thus, the many self-diagnoses of the period suggest two methodological considerations: first, that the best justification for treating the Weimar Republic as a period might come from the contemporary perception of it as a period (defined against what had come before) that urgently needed to be understood, and, second, that this self-reflexivity needs to be understood as much as possible in its own terms.

Yet all too often, commentators have overlooked the extent and the specific contours of this self-reflexivity. If one problem with normative value judgments about modernism is that they overlook affinities between otherwise different writers and texts, then the problem with importing dichotomies such as nature and technology into an investigation of a period largely dedicated to undoing them is that it will find them everywhere, and often at the expense of more interesting connections. Helmut Lethen's influential 1994 book *Verhaltenslehren der Kälte: Lebensversuche zwischen den Kriegen*

(*Cool Conduct*, 2002) is a case in point. The fateful polarities he identifies at the heart of Weimar culture are shaped by the assumption of an underlying dichotomy between technology and nature, machines and organisms. Yet it matters that even the very texts upon which he bases his argument are actively and explicitly seeking to complicate or transcend such a dichotomy. Far from simply digging in behind cultural, philosophical, and political polarities, Weimar writers were self-consciously interrogating the dichotomies and dualisms that Lethen identifies as the defining feature of Weimar culture. If we actually pay attention to how and why these writers were using the organic, what we find is a rich self-awareness with important implications. Nature, as used in these texts, is richly internally differentiated and is theorized and reinvented in self-reflexive ways. The figures of this study are far more closely engaged with the insights and aporias of the natural sciences than one would guess from Lethen's account, which frequently assumes the very dichotomy between the organic and the mechanical that these writers were seeking to overturn. The complexities of the idea of life were being worked out in self-consciously transdisciplinary ways. It is only by downplaying the nuanced roles that biology, organicism, and vitalism were being asked to play in the period that Lethen can arrive at some specific, momentous missteps. He seizes, for example, on Plessner's law of natural *artificiality*, emphasizing the consequences of the second word, yet all but ignores the fact that it is a *natural* artificiality. But the origin of this human condition in the basic structure of organic life itself is essentially Plessner's entire argument in *The Stages of the Organic and the Human Being*. What we gain by being attentive to the nuanced relationship between life and modernism in the period is thus also a richer understanding of how this complex disciplinary landscape shaped the possibilities for cultural critique, aesthetic innovation, and a transdisciplinary theorization of the human being.

For example, the multifarious and unanticipated similarities between Döblin and Jünger—given their vast differences of style, politics, background, age, and temperament—suggest the rationale for bringing them together as exemplars of biological modernism, as I have here.[46] These similarities range from their multidisciplinary backgrounds (both had university training in science or medicine) to their shared reckoning with the dualisms and model of interiority they associated with the bourgeois era, to even the specific details of their imaginary constructions of modernity that resulted from this critique: Döblin's prehistoric monsters in *Mountains Seas and Giants* and Jünger's notion of the "organic construction" are both antihumanist images that fuse advanced technology with organic bodies. This suggests the contours of a broad, transdisciplinary discourse on modernity and the human being that confounds some expected categorizations, not least the association of organicism with the political Right.

There is of course a strong reason why, within German studies, the question of organicism in Weimar has been so fraught and over- or predetermined:

1933. It is, and has been, difficult to disentangle an analysis of Weimar culture and thought from the Nazi seizure of power that put an end to it. No lesser thinkers than Theodor Adorno and Helmuth Plessner, in back-to-back articles in a 1962 issue of *Merkur*, cautioned against a nostalgic celebration of the 1920s that risked ignoring where the cultural, social, and political developments of the Weimar Republic had been leading.[47] The relationship between Weimar culture and the Nazi period, as well as the ways in which features of Weimar cultural and political life might ultimately have contributed to their premature end, have profoundly shaped the scholarship of the Weimar Republic. The association of organicism with conservatism, reaction, or fascism has been pervasive, and not without reason—after all, National Socialism, even beyond "blood and soil" and "racial hygiene," would supply many images of a fusion of advanced technology with the natural landscape or the organic nation. But reducing organicism, or the role of *Leben* more generally, to its association with fascism, the Right, a nostalgic *Lebensphilosophie*, or even simply to a general "reduction of complexity in modern civil society" eclipses its status as a site of contestation and as a discursive space in which Weimar contemporaries were working out what it meant to be modern, borrowing freely from biology and shaping their conception of the human being in conscious opposition to models they saw as anachronistic.[48] There were important similarities—and differences—among these figures that are obscured if organicism is assumed at the outset to be a reactionary tendency. In thus reconstructing biological modernism as internally differentiated and contested, this book seeks to ask, in detail, *how* and *why* intellectuals and artists turned to nature to theorize and imagine modernity. The horizon that orients this study's approach to the role played by life in Weimar engagements with modernity, then, is not 1933 but rather two tendencies that predate the Weimar Republic: on the one hand, the negative reaction to the legacy of bourgeois humanism—including Cartesian dualism, the autonomous individual, and a subjectivity understood largely in terms of psychological interiority—to which these figures were deliberately responding; and, on the other, the disciplinary flux among and within the natural sciences and the humanities. This disciplinary landscape offered the tools for contemporary writers to critique the legacies of bourgeois humanism.

For despite (or perhaps in reaction to) the division of labor between the sciences and the humanities maintained by Neo-Kantianism, writers of all stripes gleefully transgressed disciplinary boundaries, in part because these boundaries were still being drawn.[49] The Weimar Republic was perhaps one of the last moments in which it would be possible to attempt to articulate a unified theory of the human being. On the one hand, this possibility resulted from the emergence of modern biology as a field that was still inchoate, indeed where the very term "biology" "suggested a unity that was hardly to be seen on the ground."[50] Methodologies and fields of study such as morphology, embryology, and anatomy had been developing within a disciplinary landscape that itself was still in formation, with the division of departments between universities' philosophical and medical faculties more a matter of historical and personnel contingency than of an a priori arrangement of knowledge.[51] And on the other hand, the possibility to define the human being across the sciences and the humanities existed at the tail end of an era not yet rigidly divided into the two cultures of what Thomas Pynchon felicitously dubbed the "Snovian Disjunction,"[52] and therefore still able to think among and between disciplines in ways that would later seem dilettantish. This disciplinary situation, aware of the growing distance between the sciences and the humanities but not yet arrived at a degree of specialization that would make this distance seem to be an unbridgeable chasm rather than a productive challenge, was as much responsible for the theorization of the new human as was the experience of modernity. Or better: this disciplinary juncture was itself a key part of the experience of modernity in the story this book tells.

A note on terminology: where it seems appropriate, I sometimes opt to use the term "transdisciplinary" instead of "interdisciplinary." The rationale for this is twofold. Historically, these disciplines and fields were in the process of formation and reconfiguration, so that using "interdisciplinary" to describe Döblin's borrowings or Plessner's attempt at a synthesis is anachronistic, and risks suggesting a disciplinary solidity that could have curtailed such projects before they had even begun.[53] Conceptually, though related to the specific disciplinary history of Weimar, the preference for the prefix "trans-" over "inter-" is inspired by Leslie A. Adelson's reading of the trope of "betweenness" as serving to keep separate what it ostensibly joins, leaving the units on either side of the "between" unaltered and further entrenched, instead of attending to the ways in which the encounter has altered the terms as well as their relationship to each other.[54]

The four chapters of this study explore paradigmatic moments of biological modernism, this historical discursive constellation that brought life and modernity to bear on each other in order to retheorize the human being. Each chapter has the dual aim of showing how we might better understand the texts and figures discussed if seen through the lens of biological modernism, on the one hand, and illuminating different aspects of biological modernism through specific readings of these texts. Thus the first chapter, on Helmuth Plessner, makes the case for the importance of his book *The Stages of the Organic and the Human Being* (1928) while also exploring the disciplinary landscape within which he was able to attempt a unified theory of the human being. The second chapter considers the relationship of biological modernism to contemporary mass media, specifically photography. By looking at key moments and texts from photographic theory and practice in the 1920s, this chapter argues that questions of modernity and aesthetic representation were necessarily theorized across media, involving specific features of photography but not narrowly limited to these—a tendency that might help us reevaluate the connotations of the "New Objectivity" under which the photography of the period tends to be organized. And chapters 3 and 4 consider two major literary articulations of this relationship between biology and modernity: Alfred Döblin's science fiction novel *Mountains Seas and Giants* (1924) and Ernst Jünger's book-length treatise *The Worker* (1932). Both texts prognosticate a future in which nature and technology have become virtually indistinguishable, in order to probe models of human subjectivity that go beyond the options of classical humanism. Yet the meaningful differences between them, particularly concerning the relationship between the organic and wholeness, show why it is necessary to take their uses of the biological and the organic seriously, and on their own terms.

The Stages of the Organic and the Human Being mobilizes contemporary discussions of biology to generate a deliberately modern theory of the human being as "naturally artificial." Crucial to Plessner's project is the way in which human specificity is grounded in a development innate to life itself, rather than being metaphysically distinct from nature. Moreover, Plessner explicitly contextualizes his project as a theory of the human being that could bridge the newly problematic divide between the humanities and the natural sciences, and thus grapple not just with the relationship between the human being and the natural world, but also with the relationship between the disciplines that dealt with these—the humanities, on the one hand, and the empirical natural sciences, on the other. By deriving human artificiality and uniqueness from nature—and, on the disciplinary and methodological levels, by situating a philosophical anthropology within biology—*Stages* is representative of biological modernism as a tendency that sought to reconcile the changed understandings of the human being and nature in a way that would be adequate to the demands of modernity. This chapter thus reads Plessner's magnum opus as paradigmatic of its intellectual and disciplinary moment, particularly with regard to his theory of human being—a creature both inside and outside its own body, suspended between artifice and nature, accountable to biology and philosophy alike.

The second chapter, on the lively debates on photographic representation conducted in the 1920s and 1930s, explores how biological modernism shaped discussions of the relationship between modernity and new media technologies. Far from serving as a mere proxy for the dynamism and speed of modern society, photography as practiced and theorized in the photobooks and writings of August Sander, Alfred Döblin, Karl Blossfeldt, and Siegfried Kracauer in fact has little to do with such hallmarks of photographic theory as the index or the fleeting moment. Instead, these photographers and writers use metaphors of nature, natural history, and the natural sciences in order to argue for a photography of types, rather than of unique individuals. From Sander's portraiture, which Döblin likened to "comparative anatomy," to Blossfeldt's meticulous attempt to make legible the "primal forms" (*Urformen*) that underlay nature and culture alike, the reality these photographers pursued was transcendent and historical, rather than instantaneous and objective. On the methodological level photography, precisely because it was so weighted with expectations in the Weimar Republic, serves as a model for discourses of modernity, modernization, and biological modernism more generally: suggestive and slippery, descriptive and aspirational alike, always about more than its putative object, inherently interdisciplinary, always suspended between nature and culture. What this broad discursive constellation meant is that theorizations of photography were never about this visual medium alone, but were able to activate broader considerations of aesthetic representation, narrative, history, experience, and modernity. Photography in the 1920s was thus a usefully polysemic field of contestation that allowed contemporaries to grapple with ideas about modernity and modernization, as well as with questions of aesthetic representation that transcend a single medium or artistic form, with important consequences for the ideas of both modernity and photographic objectivity.

The third and fourth chapters develop this relationship between biology and modernity by closely reading two literary imaginings of the future: Alfred Döblin's science fiction novel *Mountains Seas and Giants* and Ernst Jünger's treatise *The Worker*. Chapter 3 shows how *Mountains Seas and Giants* furthers Döblin's critiques both of the conventional novel form and of the inherited notion of the bourgeois subject in its plot and in its language—specifically, in scenes of the violent disarticulation and recombination of living bodies caused by monstrous organic growth. In its vast scope, its deemphasis of the development of individual characters in favor of the depiction of masses in motion, and its paratactic style, Döblin's novel is the realization of the theory of the epic that he articulated in the 1910s and 1920s. *Mountains Seas and Giants*, a sprawling global history of the future into the twenty-seventh century, fictionalizes and literalizes an important insight that Döblin was articulating elsewhere in essays and polemics on literature, modernity, and nature. To him, the inherited dualisms of mind and matter, technology and nature no longer seemed adequate in the face of modern, urban experience, on the one hand, and the current state of scientific knowledge about the body, on the other. Ultimately, I argue, Döblin's critique was directed towards closed forms, such as the classical autonomous subject predicated on psychological interiority, and the nineteenth-century novel that took this subject as its subject. Thus, the genre of science fiction provided Döblin with an imaginative space that was particularly well-suited to rupturing these closed forms in order to challenge the isolation and closure of the individual subject, dispersing subjectivity throughout nature and matter as such (an idea he would further develop in his 1927 philosophical treatise *The I above Nature*). Thus, in allowing Döblin to link three areas that were central to his work before 1930—a critique of bourgeois subjectivity, an emergent epic poetics, and a monist philosophy of nature—*Mountains Seas and Giants*, read in the broader context of biological modernism, in fact occupies a pivotal point within Döblin's thought and work in the Weimar Republic, anticipating his best-known work of epic poetics: his 1929 city novel, *Berlin Alexanderplatz*.

While the future history of Döblin's novel remains open, Jünger's vexing treatise, *The Worker*, deploys organicist and vitalist models in order to combine a logic of technological acceleration with a teleological vision of historical stasis. This deeply antidemocratic and illiberal text holds up the worker, not as a social class but as a cosmic symbol of a new era, in order to welcome the destruction of bourgeois norms, social formations, and individuality. In linking the trope of the technological body, the question of the relationship between part and whole, and a vision of history not as progress but rather as teleological fulfillment, Jünger's text draws upon specific elements of contemporary biology in order to paint a distinctly modern (albeit troubling) picture of historical and social change. While Jünger's text has been read as relying on an opposition between the organic and the mechanical, I show on the contrary that *The Worker*'s anti-dualism in fact depends on the harmonious convergence of these terms. The organic asserts itself throughout *The Worker*: as a particular vein of teleological thinking, as a means of organizing parts and wholes, as a concept of work, and as a set of rhetorical strategies. I therefore read *The Worker* as representing a technophilic vision of modernity as an organicist project. For this reason, contrasting *The Worker*'s teleological, organicist view of history to Döblin's *Mountains Seas and Giants* allows me to conclude *Biological Modernism* by showing how Weimar organicism was contested and internally nuanced, allowing contemporaries to unfold competing visions of the human being and modernity within a shared paradigm. Jünger's social vision diverged in significant ways from Döblin's; at least part of this divergence can be linked to seemingly minor distinctions, such as how they related wholeness and the idea of the organic, or how biology helped them reformulate a notion of selfhood. Thus, within the set of common terms made available by contemporary biology and organicism, there were competing and even opposing strategies for thinking about modernity, history, and the human.

Chapter 1

✦

Helmuth Plessner's Eccentric Human among the Disciplines

The year 1928 could have been an auspicious moment for a new philosophy of the human being. The same year that Helmuth Plessner, a 36-year-old professor at the University of Cologne, published *Die Stufen des Organischen und der Mensch* (*The Stages of the Organic and the Human Being*) with the De Gruyter press, the culture of the Weimar Republic was in full bloom. The violence of the war, the November Revolution, and the putsch attempts and counterrevolutions from the Right lay at least half a decade in the past; the Nazi seizure of power was still five years in the future, and by no means a certain thing. The summer elections of 1928 moved the Reichstag to the left, dealing a blow to conservatives and National Socialists, and putting an SPD-led grand coalition into office.[1] The time was also ripe for a philosophy of the human being: Max Scheler published his *The Human Place in the Cosmos* (*Die Stellung des Menschen im Kosmos*) the same year that Plessner published his work, and Heidegger's *Being and Time* had appeared just the year before. In this context, Plessner's ambitious tome, which derives human specificity from a full accounting of organic life per se, ought to have made an impact.

Yet it fizzled. There are several reasons for the lack of an enthusiastic reception by contemporaries—most notably, it was largely overshadowed by Scheler's and especially Heidegger's books. Even worse, there were murky allegations that Plessner had plagiarized his basic idea from Scheler.[2] Only in recent years has Plessner's book been getting the attention it deserves, first in Europe and, very recently, in English-language scholarship.[3] Indeed, *The Stages of the Organic and the Human Being* is both representative of intellectual currents of the time and strikingly innovative. This chapter reconstructs Plessner's definition of the human being as a paradigm of biological modernism. Plessner's work exemplifies the intense epistemological self-awareness that accompanied the re-theorization of the human being across shifting disciplinary boundaries during the 1920s, showing how intricately this revision was bound up with historical conditions of knowledge production.

By situating his analysis of human "positionality" within a broader philosophy of nature, Plessner's text arrives at a definition of the human being as "artificial by nature"—that is, the human being is both distinct and on a logical continuum with all other forms of life, such that the characteristic artifice of the human results from tendencies inherent to life itself. In his characterization of the human being as naturally artificial, Plessner's approach has features in common with other prominent versions of the emergent tradition known as Philosophical Anthropology, including Arnold Gehlen's idea of the "deficient being" (*Mängelwesen*), which holds that the specific characteristics of the human being, including language, technology, and action oriented toward the future, arise from a lack: compared to other animals, humans lack specialized organs, a specialized integration into a specific environment, and strong instincts.[4] I will argue in more detail later in this chapter why Plessner's concept of the human being should not be assimilated to a version of the *Mängelwesen* hypothesis. For the time being, we should note that a dichotomous conception of nature and technology, for example, is more likely to be supported by the idea of the human as a deficient being that has essentially fallen out of nature than by an account like Plessner's, which derives a definition of the human from basic features of organic life per se. In basing his concept of the human being on the logic of life itself, Plessner avoids positing an absolute rupture between human and nonhuman life. This is significant because Plessner's project, as we will see, grappled not just with the relationship between human being and natural world, but also with the relationship between the disciplines that dealt with these—philosophy and the humanities, on the one hand, and the empirical natural sciences, on the other. By deriving human artificiality and uniqueness from nature—and, on the disciplinary and methodological levels, by situating an anthropology within biology—*Stages* is representative of biological modernism as a tendency that sought to reconcile the changed understandings of the human being and nature in a way that would be adequate to the demands of modernity. This chapter will read Plessner's text as paradigmatic of its intellectual and disciplinary moment, particularly with regard to his theory of human being—a creature both inside and outside its own body, suspended between artifice and nature, accountable to biology and philosophy alike.

But what was Philosophical Anthropology? Joachim Fischer differentiates philosophical anthropology—as a broad field of inquiry into the human being—from Philosophical Anthropology—as a tendency or approach (if not a unified or institutionally bound school of thought) which viewed the human being as a part of nature in order to ask about the constitutive factors separating the human from nature.[5] Philosophical Anthropology in its capitalized variant is represented most prominently by Max Scheler, Helmuth Plessner, Adolf Portmann, Erich Rothacker, and Arnold Gehlen.[6] As an attempt to redefine the human being philosophically, in a way that does justice to the state of the natural sciences without being exclusively beholden to their methods, Philosophical Anthropology was fully a product of its time, sitting at the confluence of such varied intellectual currents as phenomenology, *Lebensphilosophie*, German idealism, and the fruits of recent biological research, especially embryology, developmental biology, and ethology. More broadly, this was a moment in the history of biology when the available alternatives of mechanism and vitalism had come to an impasse. Thus, even the existence of this new approach testified to the disciplinary juncture to which it was a response, indicating a precocious moment of disciplinary formation and articulation. Paraphrasing Plessner's canny historicization of his own project, in order for the philosophical question of the human to be asked anew with precision and relevance, it was first necessary for the empirical natural sciences to have established themselves and, indeed, to have triumphed over speculative or philosophical approaches.[7]

The way that Plessner posed the question, "What is the human?" is broadly representative of the contemporary intellectual context and disciplinary landscape. It is not just that *Stages of the Organic* is an intensely interdisciplinary text, drawing on fields of inquiry ranging from animal behavior to phenomenology, and involving interlocutors from Hegel to Uexküll, Dilthey to Driesch, Descartes to Buytendijk. Just as notable is the way that Plessner situates and develops his text as a self-reflexive response to a disciplinary, epistemological, and methodological impasse: the incommensurability between the quantitative, objective empiricism of the natural sciences on the one hand, and the qualitative, subjective speculation of inquiries into the human, on the other.[8] As Plessner writes in the preface to the first edition of *Stages of the Organic*, "The deep tensions between natural science and philosophy provided the decisive impetus for this book during my years studying zoology in Heidelberg, as a student of Bütschli and Herbst, Windelband and Troeltsch, Driesch and Lask."[9] Simply by asking how this chasm might be bridged, Plessner situates his inquiry at the heart of contemporary questions about science, knowledge production, and the human.

His answer to the question of the human—that the human is the being that is by nature artificial—is also paradigmatic of biological modernism in its refusal to dichotomize nature and technology, subject and object, mind and matter. Like the otherwise very different texts of Döblin and Jünger, *Stages of the Organic* situates technology within nature, seeing it as a logical outgrowth of the natural world. Plessner's approach thus differs from other definitions offered by Philosophical Anthropology, most notably from Gehlen's definition of the human as a "deficient being" (*Mängelwesen*). While Plessner's account of the human also involves a kind of compensation, as does the deficient being hypothesis, the details matter. In the case of *Stages of the Organic*, these details do not add up to a picture of human exceptionalism or a metaphysical breach between human and nature. Plessner's human being is not excluded from the logic shared by the rest of the natural world—rather, the human being's characteristic "eccentricity" is the fullest realization of the defining logic of living nature.

How Plessner arrives at this definition is the subject of this chapter. In short, his "positional" account of the stages of organic life tracks the shifting relationship between the living organism and its own bodily border (*Grenze*). In the concept of the border, which is not reducible to the skin or outer contour of an organism but is rather at once a logical abstraction and a formal necessity for the self-regulating autonomous systems that organisms are, Plessner is able to fold phenomenology and philosophical biology into an immanent critique of the Cartesian dualism between mind and matter, which he turns on its axis, recasting it as a distinction between interiority, or an inner world (*Innenwelt*), and exteriority, or an outer world (*Außenwelt*). The invocation of Descartes is important for another, disciplinary reason, as we will see: Plessner associates the epistemological rupture between quantitative sciences and qualitative humanities with the Cartesian distinction between the *res extensa* and the *res cogitans*. By bringing these distinctions into contact with a phenomenological exploration of the relationship between perceptible qualities and the substantial core that anchors those qualities, Plessner derives his definition of the living thing (which contains, as I will show, *in nuce* the definition of the human) from an intensification of an aspect of things in general—namely, their borders, which become in the case of living things an essential, functional property rather than an accidental demarcation. The living thing "realizes" its own border.[10] Each subsequent stage of the plant (open form), the animal (closed, centric form) and the human (eccentric form) marks a further realization and intensification of the relationship between the organism and its own border. Plessner's account is thus neither an evolutionary one (tracing the historical origin of the human being) nor an empirical, descriptive one. Rather, it is a question of the formal, logical possibilities that can be derived from a priori conditions in conjunction with phenomenological elucidation. For this reason, I have chosen to render the German term *Stufen* as "stages" rather than as "levels," which is also a possible translation. Although "levels" connotes spatiality better than the more temporal "stages," which might misleadingly suggest an evolutionary account, "stages" better captures the sense of qualitative difference that Plessner is describing, whereas "levels" suggests a quantitative difference. After describing in detail how Plessner arrives at the naturally artificial human, I will argue what his concept of the human is not—an armored body or a deficient being—and why it matters for our understanding of his anthropology, and for the moment of Weimar thought for which it is paradigmatic.

The Problem: Reconciling *Geist* and *Leben*

A quick glance at the table of contents of *The Stages of the Organic and the Human Being* reveals that the human being is the topic of only the last of the book's seven chapters. The bulk of Plessner's text is concerned with establishing the problem, reconstructing previous approaches and their impasses, explicating the positionality of life, and elaborating this definition for plants and animals, leaving the impression that the foundation of this work of Philosophical Anthropology far exceeds the actual edifice—that is, defining the human being. It is crucial to understand why *Stages of the Organic* is not just a major work within Philosophical Anthropology but also serves, as its subtitle ("Introduction to Philosophical Anthropology") suggests, as a kind of prolegomenon to the tradition. In order to offer a theory of the human being in terms of its eccentric positionality, and to be able to unfold the social, political, and historical implications of this eccentricity, Plessner first needs to establish a foundation in a philosophy of nature and a theory of the living organism. The reasons for this foundation say as much about the intellectual context—and the broader conditions of Weimar thought within which the human being had to be redefined—as they do about Plessner's approach to the problem. *The Stages of the Organic and the Human Being* sets out from two linked impasses, a philosophical one and a disciplinary one. Both of these concern the increasingly problematic status of *Leben*. In Plessner's contemporaneous historicization of his own project, we can clearly see the transdisciplinary ferment within which a new approach to the human being was not only possible but necessary.

One of the difficulties—and pleasures—in reading Plessner is that his account inhabits various alternative positions, ventriloquizing them and allowing them to unfold to their limits in order to bring each to a crisis point that makes it clear why a new approach is necessary. In part this is a result of necessary ground-clearing—in order to justify and elaborate his own concept of eccentric positionality, he must show why previous philosophical and biological approaches have fallen short. In this way, his book is sometimes reminiscent of another perspectival prolegomenon, Hegel's *Phenomenology of Spirit*. But it also reflects the cannily self-aware historicization that is at the heart of the way Plessner brings philosophy and biology into dialogue with each other. The approaches of German Idealism, *Lebensphilosophie*, or mechanism and vitalism in biology were not simply errors, according to Plessner, but were historically conditioned by the state of knowledge at the time. From the first pages of *Stages of the Organic* it is clear that science has a history, and that this matters. Plessner seems not to be interested in refuting other approaches so much as accounting for them. His own Philosophical Anthropology is, therefore, not merely a response to other definitions of the human but also a self-reflexive result of them, one that is only possible at a certain stage of the development of the empirical natural sciences. Thus much of the first half of *Stages of the Organic* consists of his inhabiting the approaches of others working in science or philosophy, to see where they lead.

The philosophical impasse that Plessner details at the beginning of his book concerns a crisis in the relationship between reason (*Vernunft*) and life (*Leben*). The very first sentences of the first chapter of *Stages of the Organic* establish this relationship as a temporal succession:

> Every age finds its redeeming word. The terminology of the eighteenth century culminates in the concept of reason, that of the nineteenth century in the concept of development, that of the present century in the concept of life. Every age thereby designates something different, reason emphasizes the timeless and the universally binding, development emphasizes the restlessly becoming and rising, life emphasizes the demonically playing, the unconsciously creative element.[11]

Historicizing these master tropes in this way allows Plessner to frame his contemporary epistemological moment in terms of the centrality of *Leben* and thus of biology. It also implicitly indicates the disciplinary legacies—philosophy, history, science—with which one must now grapple in order to define the human. Plessner roots this succession of keywords in specific historical contexts, yet it is also clear that reason, development, and life are also in a dialogue with each other, the broad contours of which are formed by the crisis of Idealism and the rise of *Lebensphilosophie*, or German vitalism, a tendency associated with Nietzsche, Spengler, Simmel, and Dilthey.

Much of the foundation of *Stages of the Organic* has to do with mediating between these two positions. As Joachim Fischer writes, reconstructing Plessner's argument, "The concept of 'eccentric positionality' . . . develops from the awareness of being both beyond, before the 'breach'—on the side of idealism—as well as this side of the breach, on the side of *Lebensphilosophie*, the current of thought which was increasingly decisive in Continental Europe as a result of the breach."[12] The "breach" referred to here is a historical crisis of reason, leading philosophy to turn from an autonomous subjectivity to forms of embodied experience, culminating in the watchword *Leben*. Fischer, summarizing Plessner, writes that Neo-Kantianism's restabilization of reason and *Lebensphilosophie*'s turn to the pre-rational were the two dominant reactions in the late nineteenth century to the eclipsing of Idealism.[13] For Plessner, both options were incomplete.

The problem concerns two ways of viewing the human being and the emergence of consciousness from nature. If Idealism, in this account, had overemphasized the transcendental, autonomous subject, *Geist* (spirit), and *Vernunft* (reason) over *Leben* (life), *Lebensphilosophie* had merely swung the pendulum back in the other direction. The rise of the empirical natural sciences over the course of the nineteenth century, meanwhile, had brought much-needed attention to the material and historical contingency of the human being as an animal rooted firmly in nature. The aporia arose from the increasing incompatibility of these two views. As Plessner puts it:

> Two possibilities, the only two, it seemed, had been exhausted: empirical materialism and idealist a priori philosophy. If the first theory had failed in the face of the fact of consciousness and the necessities of the laws of meaning, which cannot be derived from the physical

world and sense impressions, then the second theory had conversely failed to account for the facts of perception and the specification of physical nature. Here, the old alternative of empiricism or a priori knowledge looked like this: either the human being, with all its physical and mental characteristics, is the last link in organic development on Earth. In that case human consciousness, conscience, intellect, the system of forms in the human mind and thus human culture is a product of nature, the result of the development of the cerebrum, upright gait, certain changes in internal secretions, etc. But how it comes to this result and how intellectual dimensions arise from corporeal facts remains completely mysterious. Or the human being's own natural history in connection with the history of organisms is, like all nature, a human construction in accordance with the basic a priori forms of human intellect and in the frame of human consciousness.[14]

So rather than choose one or the other approach, Plessner's project from the beginning depends upon reconciling *Geist* and *Leben*. That is, if empirical science and *Lebensphilosophie* alike had eroded the primacy of *Geist* by various recourses to *Leben* and nature more generally, Plessner's response (and that of Philosophical Anthropology in general) will be to establish the existence of *Geist*—and human nature more generally—not in spite of but precisely through *Leben*.[15]

Yet the relationship between *Geist* and *Leben* is not just a philosophical problem, but a disciplinary one as well. The contemporary discourse of *Leben* was not exclusively biological—rather, it had been established as an important term in the self-theorization of the humanities, especially for history. It is here that Plessner builds on Dilthey's work, for Dilthey offered a definition of *Leben* that began to grapple with the epistemological status of human history as a unique subject-object of knowledge, and which was thereby distinct from the intuitive approach to *Leben* found in the vitalism of Bergson or Spengler. As Plessner describes Dilthey's contribution,

> For Dilthey, life does not mean an omnipotence that can be glimpsed by turning away from experience [*Erfahrung*], as it does for Bergson or Spengler, but rather a factor that can be experienced through contemplation and intellect and imagination and the capacity for empathy and that in turn itself enables and compels experience. All of our powers are called upon in order to discover the past in its essence and thus life in its essence, for "life comprehends life."[16]

The philosophical challenge that Plessner sets himself is how to account for the emergence of *Geist* not in opposition to *Leben* but through it, as the latter's self-consciousness.[17] The question with which *Stages of the Organic* begins is thus how, at this epistemic juncture, to account for the human being as both subject and object, immaterial and material, psychological and physical. Or, in Plessner's words, "Thus the question arose: under what conditions can the human being be viewed as the subject of intellectual-historical reality [*Subjekt geistig-geschichtlicher Wirklichkeit*], as a moral person having consciousness of responsibility *in just the same* direction that is determined by physical human phylogeny and the human's place in the whole of nature?"[18] Crucially, Plessner will frame this as a return to the question of the relationship between mind and matter, accounting for the human being both as a thinking subject and as a material object.[19]

But Plessner's use of Cartesian dualism is complex and multivalent for, among other things, he maps the distinction between *res cogitans* and *res extensa*—or, roughly, mind and matter—onto an irreconcilable split between speculative, qualitative approaches to subjectivity on the one hand, and quantitative, empirical sciences on the other: "Roughly put, this means the division of knowledge of the world [*Welterkenntnis*] into knowledge of the body and knowledge of the I or, in modern terms: physics and psychology."[20] This split arises, according to Plessner, from the identification of physicality, extension, and measurability. This identification is a problem not, in the first instance, because it denies empirical validity to questions of selfhood and mind, but because it is a reductionist view of matter and embodiment that necessarily forecloses access to nonquantifiable, nonmeasurable aspects of the physical world.

> The picture of Cartesian fundamentalism is completed by the fact that its principle demands a mathematical-mechanical representation—that is, measurement—as the sole method of knowing physical things. With the identification of physicality and extension and the concomitant equivalence of extension and measurability, the principle of the alternative of *res cogitans* and *res extensa* necessarily entails that mathematical natural science will be fundamental. To be sure, the distinction of all being into *res extensa* and *res cogitans* is originally meant ontologically. However, it automatically gains a methodologically persistent significance, which in a certain sense withdraws it from ontological critique. With the equation of physicality [*Körperlichkeit*] with extension, nature is made accessible exclusively to measuring knowledge. . . . Therefore there are only the two possibilities: either comprehending the qualitative existence and appearance of physical bodies mechanically, that is, dissolving them into quantities, or, in avoiding this kind of analysis, explaining them as the contents of cogitations, as the contents and products of our interiority.[21]

The ontological distinction between *res extensa* and *res cogitans* had become a problem of incommensurable methodologies, privileging a particular kind of quantitative, empirical natural science. This elevation of quantity causes several related problems for science. Taken together, these problems render an adequate understanding of the human being impossible. For one thing, by assimilating nature to quantifiable extension, science loses the view of the formal, nonquantifiable side of nature, including organizational questions about patterns and totalities. For another thing, the division of all that exists into physical and mental spheres eliminates cultural and historical objects—the particular realm of the human—from scientific study altogether. "The humanities, the systematic and historical study of culture, are excluded in advance by the structure of the whole. They cannot claim the validity of science once scientific rigor has been identified with mathematical verifiability."[22] And finally, the unbridgeable separation between the study of the physical and mental worlds means that the human being can be studied *either* as a mere physical object among other objects, *or* as the site of immaterial, subjective phenomena, but not as both at once, the living body that is the "subject-object" of nature and culture.[23] In other words, the Cartesian alternative as a disciplinary divide causes problems for both the natural sciences and the humanities; worse still, their absolute separation from one another renders an understanding of the human being impossible.

> Since besides the sphere of extension there is only the sphere of interiority, represented by the self, there remains no other possibility than making the sphere of interiority responsible for the qualitative characteristics of the body that cannot be measured. Thus, for the sake of the total quantification of physical bodies, all qualities are *subjectivized* and reinterpreted as merely-appearances, even further, as feelings [*Empfindungen*]. By way of Locke a direct path leads to Mach, which every naturalist still walks today.[24]

The disciplinary legacy of the Cartesian split leads, in Plessner's summary, to empirical positivism and to the loss of quality.

But qualitative, non-reductionist, and formal theories of living phenomena, from the definition of life to animal behavior, were precisely at the forefront of contemporary biology. By the early twentieth century, biology was looking for an alternative to the alternatives of mechanism and vitalism. The mechanist paradigm held that all matter (including living matter) could be explained in terms of the laws of physics and chemistry, and thus entailed a reduction of biology to a subfield of physics or chemistry. Vitalism, by contrast, posited that organic life was categorically distinct from other kinds of matter, yet by displacing the uniqueness of life onto a non-observable, nonempirical vital force, vitalism shared with mechanism the assumption that matter, and by extension the physical world, can only be treated empirically and quantitatively. This was precisely the impasse Plessner wanted to address. Thriving subfields of biology in late nineteenth- and early twentieth-century Germany, such as embryology, ethology, ecology, and animal morphology, were putting pressure on the alternatives of mechanism and vitalism, or simply moving beyond them.[25] Plessner summarizes the dispute between mechanists and (neo)vitalists in contemporary biology in a way that shows their common ground: "Depending on whether this surplus [of vitality in biological phenomena] is seen to be attributable to chemical-physical factors or not, you have mechanists or vitalists."[26] In British and American biology of the 1920s and 1930s, organicist biologists were likewise overcoming the mechanism/vitalism alternative by locating the specificity of life in observable, qualitative phenomena such as structure, form, and regulation. Donna Haraway, who like Plessner locates the origin of the mechanism/vitalism divide in Cartesian dualism, has characterized the difference between vitalism, which is still beholden to mechanist assumptions, and organicism, which moves beyond them, in this way: "Vitalists of all hues assert some nonphysical entity—either a nonquantifiable vital force like Driesch's entelechy or some basic difference between 'vital substance' and ordinary matter. Organicists insist that wholeness, directedness, and regulation can be explained fully without such notions."[27] Tellingly, Haraway could almost be describing Plessner when she writes that the organicists shifted the metaphysical dispute—where life's specificity is located—to an epistemological question—how one might approach life so that its specificity can be accounted for in a non-reductionist way.[28] The ontological and disciplinary divide that Plessner locates in Cartesian dualism had thus become an immanent problem for understanding the natural world—and this independently of the growing recognition of the insufficiency of the other side of the divide, namely, the problem of accounting for historical and cultural phenomena as the objects of a distinct kind of knowledge in their own right, and not merely as purely subjective apparitions. Simply put, quantitative empiricism was proving no longer capable of accounting even for the world of physical extension, and a new approach was needed that could move beyond the Cartesian alternative, locating selfhood and subjectivity in a physical nature that was not itself reducible to quantitative measure. "An anti-Cartesian movement must be directed against the identification of physicality [*Körperlichkeit*] and extension, physical existence and measurability, which is responsible for the fact that we have become blind to the characteristics of physical nature that cannot be measured [*die meßfremden Eigenschaften der körperlichen Natur*]."[29] The empirical natural sciences had reached an impasse that could not be resolved through empiricism alone.[30]

Besides cutting off access to such nonquantifiable aspects of nature, the methodological implications of Cartesian dualism precluded a rigorous understanding of specifically human phenomena of culture, history, and society. Plessner writes of the difficulty, described by Dilthey and Husserl, of accounting for those "cultural-historical formations, whose character does not fit into the distinction between physical and mental."[31] In contrast to the physical world of extension, which is accessible to quantitative measure, cultural and historical phenomena are characterized by a relationship to symbolic meaning, which in turn depends on finding "resonance" in the observer.[32] Matters of "state, economy, custom, art, religion, science, law" constitute meaningful unities, and cannot be understood as "conglomerates of physical, mental, and maybe a third thing besides."[33] Such cultural phenomena depend upon both sides of the Cartesian alternative, and their connection to meaning is poorly accounted for within this dualist framework.

> Within the alternatives of physical or psychological, one just cannot empirically grasp the historical, social, and cultural factors which consist of sensory matter, appealing to and saturated with the psychological dimension, which are intellectual-meaningful, valuable or valueless, and which, participating in the spheres of both extensive nature and interiority, consist of unreal semantic content.[34]

For the concept of the human being, the aporia that Plessner catalogs at the beginning of *Stages of the Organic* is the division of being and knowledge of being into two incompatible domains: the objective, measurable domain of bodily existence, on the one hand, and the subjective, immaterial, immeasurable domain of subjective experience, on the other. In itself, each side is incomplete: mind and selfhood are more than ephemeral subjectivity, and the physical world is more than quantifiable extension. But taken as a whole, the chasm between the two poses a more serious problem still, since it points to a fundamentally riven epistemology whereby the human being can be known in terms of either one domain or the other, but never as both together.

Yet for Plessner, Cartesian dualism isn't something to be merely overcome, but rather something that needs to be accounted for as a fact of human experience. In other words, if this dualism had become an epistemological and methodological impasse, it still reflected an important experiential truth. To characterize this experiential fact he uses the term "double-aspectivity" (*Doppelaspektivität*), a word that will come to have several valences and allow Plessner to shift his discussion of dualism from ontology to phenomenology, ultimately spatializing the distinction between mind and matter in a key argumentative turn. The challenge, as Plessner sets up his argument, is to account for this dualism from an epistemological position that is itself not a dualist one.[35] To do so would be to conceive of the human being "as subject-object of culture and as subject-object of nature, without dividing it up into artificial abstractions."[36] Otherwise one is left with an eviscerated concept of human subjectivity, "so that only that pale 'subject' remained, a mere wire on which the marionette that existence had become performs its dead movements."[37] Plessner's immanent critique of ontological dualism therefore proceeds from a phenomenological dualism that pertains both to the subjective experience of interiority and exteriority, and to the way that the perception of objective things seems to rely on a distinction between perceptible qualities and an anchoring essence. This immanent critique—"the beginnings of the self-overcoming of the dualism of the world according to the laws of its own perspective"[38]—sets out from the phenomenon that seems to escape the Cartesian dualism, namely, life, and the living body in particular.[39]

The Solution: Positionality from the Living Thing to the Eccentric Form

Plessner's insight is to start with the living body as a thing that is both subject and object, self and other. To anticipate somewhat, the way that Plessner initially locates the body on both sides of dualism—this rudimentary doubling of embodied existence—already signals *in nuce* the complex positionality of the human being, which exists *as* its body, *in* its body, and outside of the whole relationship as an eccentric being. Philosophical Anthropology demands, as Plessner writes, a philosophical biology.[40] But this is not because of an assumption that biology (to say nothing of evolution) contains the meaning of human experience, but rather because the project of a Philosophical Anthropology first requires an understanding of "life," understood broadly. It is because of an aporia specific to philosophy and the humanities (*Geisteswissenschaften*) that Philosophical Anthropology has to engage concretely with a philosophy of nature, according to Plessner.[41]

The first step in this project is to determine what distinguishes the living thing from the thing as such—how is a living body different from other merely physical bodies? His answer—that the living thing has an essential, necessary connection to the relationship between interiority and exteriority, which for things in general is merely an accidental connection[42]—illustrates an underlying logic of the progression of the argument in *Stages of the Organic*. Each step towards the human, from thing to living thing, plant to animal to human, depends upon the realization of a latent property of the previous stage. (In this way a core logic of Plessner's account recalls the immanent movement in Hegel's *Phenomenology of Spirit* from the in-itself to the for-itself.) Not in terms of individual consciousness but rather in terms of a formal self-fulfillment, each stage is characterized by an increasing complexity and self-reflexivity. This logic also holds true of the concept of the border, and of the "positionality" of the living organism.

To arrive at this distinction between the thing and the living thing, Plessner takes his discussion of the double-aspectivity of Cartesian dualism on a phenomenological detour, in order ultimately to recast the distinction between *cogitans* and *extensa* as a quasi-spatial relationship between *Innenwelt* (interiority, inner world) and *Außenwelt* (exteriority, outer world). The object of perception, in order to be perceived at all, is already fundamentally split: we see its perceptible attributes as its outward-facing side, but we also posit a substantial core that unifies these attributes as attributes of one and the same thing.⁴³ Thus, even in the perception of nonliving objects, Plessner identifies an interiority (substantial core) and an exteriority (perceptible attributes). This abstract, formal distinction is not identical to the spatial relationship between inside and outside, though it maps onto it, for it is precisely the increasing complexity of the border between the two realms—abstract interiority and abstract exteriority, bodily inside and environmental outside—that defines the living thing.

This complexity of the relationship between inside and outside, interiority and exteriority, is related to the ambivalent relationship between the self and the body. For Plessner, the fact that the self is commonly located *within* the body is a pervasive legacy of the Cartesian alternative, and one with far-reaching consequences. Besides the perception of a split between interior world and subjectivity on the one hand, and exterior world and objectivity on the other, Plessner identified a host of contemporary questions as the disciplinary result of this legacy, questions concerning the reality of the external world, the possibility of a psychology (even animal psychology) divorced from introspection, of the mutual relationship between organism and environment, and the connection between physical and psychological existence.⁴⁴ Yet from the perspective of the self, the body is both part of the *Innenwelt* and part of the *Außenwelt*:

> The body [*Körper*] as an extensive thing certainly already belongs to self-consciousness, and to the sphere of external perception, to be precise, but obviously at the same time communicates to the I, to the sphere of internal perception, the materials for building its ideas. In this double aspect the complete psychological-physical self presents itself, seen idealistically or non-idealistically; its outermost zone, comprising its own organs, encloses the pure here of the I in a constant bond. On the one hand one's own body [*Körper*] forms the periphery of the sphere of immanence, because it participates both in the *Außenwelt* and in the *Innenwelt*. But on the other hand the *Innenwelt*, since as self-consciousness it contains the areas of internal and external perception, encloses the *Außenwelt* in the wealth of its ideas. But how should a sphere both be held along with its borders in the *Außenwelt* and at the same time hold the *Außenwelt* in itself?⁴⁵

The answer to this question will depend on the dynamic spatiality of the living thing, its relationship to its own border in particular. By interrogating the complexity of the organic body, Plessner is also able—well before he has arrived at the definition of the human being in terms of its complex positionality—to replace the dualist notion of consciousness with an embodied consciousness that depends on the mutually constitutive relationship between body and environment. This represents an inversion of sorts, whereby the presumed interiority of consciousness is partly externalized.

In reality the matter is exactly the reverse: it is not that consciousness is in us, rather, we are "in" consciousness, i.e., we exist as bodies [*Leiber*] capable of movement in relationship to our surroundings. Consciousness can be dulled, restricted, excluded, it can change its contents, its structure depends on the organization of the body [*Leib*], but its actualization is always guaranteed wherever the unified relationship between living subject and environment exists via the body [*Leib*] in a double direction, receptive and motor. Consciousness is just this basic form and basic condition of the behavior of a living being in positioning itself vis-à-vis its surroundings.[46]

Ultimately, the spatial and formal complexity of interiority and exteriority to which he has brought his discussion of the Cartesian alternative necessitates a concept of the border as a dynamic interface. According to Plessner, where the nonliving thing simply has an edge, a *Rand* that marks the limit of its spatial extension, the living thing is characterized by the presence of a border, a *Grenze* that mediates between it and its surrounding environment. Living things, as opposed to things in general, have both their borders and the transgressions of their borders as inherent properties. For things in general, the border is merely a virtual liminality, belonging to both the thing and its environment, and to neither of them: "It is a pure crossing from the one to the other, from the other back to the one, and really only as this 'in-so-far-as' is it precisely this alternating determinacy."[47] The border marks the limit of the physical body, but does not belong to it. For living things, by contrast, the border belongs to the object demarcated, having a real rather than just a relational connection to it: "The border actually belongs to the body [*Körper*], which thus not only guarantees the crossing to the adjoining medium via its contours, as a bounded thing, but rather *carries out* this crossing in its boundedness [*Begrenzung*] and which is itself this crossing."[48] Simply put, transcending its border is an innate property of the living thing. As a "border-realizing body" (*grenzrealisierender Körper*),[49] the living thing thereby already has a dual relationship to its own body, since the living body has no way to interact with its medium other than through that body itself. This doubling of the living thing's border—both as the spatial boundary that separates inside from outside, and as the border that belongs to the living thing as one of its properties—enables and prefigures the further development of positionality in Plessner's account, including the doubling of the animal body into *Körper* and *Leib*, and the natural artificiality of the human.

The border of the living thing is therefore not just a spatial or phenomenological boundary between it and what is not it, but serves as a dynamic interface that mediates between the living body and the environment:

> What condition must be fulfilled so that, in a relative (spatial) boundedness the non-reversible border relationship between an outside and

an inside exists? The answer is, paradoxically: When a body [*Körper*] has, besides its boundedness, also the crossing of its borders as one of its own properties, then the boundedness is at the same time spatial border and aspect border and the contour gains the value of a whole form, without losing its *Gestalt*-character. It thus depends on the relationship of a bordered body to its own border [*Auf das Verhältnis des begrenzten Körpers zu seiner Grenze kommt es also an*].[50]

The living thing thus has a relationship to its own border, and it is an essential property of the living thing not just to be spatially bounded but to need to transgress its own border. The living thing is a processual phenomenon that is necessarily a becoming, and not just a being: "The existing [*seiende*] border means becoming."[51] In practical terms, this refers to organic properties that relate the organism to its environment, such as metabolism, adaptation, differentiation, and regulation, whereby an organism transgresses its border in order to maintain it.[52] Crucially, then, Plessner's account is both descriptive, drawing on contemporary biological research, and formal, reflexive. It is not merely what the border does that distinguishes the living from the nonliving thing, but has to do with a thing's relationship to its own border. For living things, there is thus a rudimentary doubling of the body. Unlike nonliving things, whose "edge" (*Rand*) is merely an indeterminate zone between the thing and its surroundings, in the case of the living thing, the body itself mediates between the body and its environment. To differentiate these two possibilities, Plessner uses the schematic Bo ← Be → M for the first, to mark the border as a "between" separating the "body" and the "medium," and Bo ← Bo → M for the second, to show that in the case of the living thing, it is the body itself that mediates between the body and its environment.[53] Because the border and the transgression of the border belong to the living thing as its properties, it is more complexly spatial and positional than nonliving things, which go as far as their physical extension and no further. The living thing, by contrast, is on either side of its border at once; and the border of the living thing, rather than being an indifferently spatial transitional zone between object and environment, both distinguishes the object from its environment and opens it up to it.

Once the border has been established as the concept that underlies the phenomenon of the living thing, the idea of positionality allows Plessner to distinguish between different stages or levels of living beings, based on their systemic relationship to their own border. For "closed" organizational forms of life such as those found in animals and humans, the body is a mediating tool between organism and environment. The fact that the border of the living thing belongs to the body, mediating between it and the external world, already indicates in germinal form the dual nature of the human body as both the seat of the self and a tool of the self, a core aspect of Plessner's anthropology. The doubling of the body is already present in every living thing; as the investigation moves from living things, to plants, to animals, to humans, the reflexivity of the border becomes even more reflexive, and ever more central to the living organism's relationship to its environment. This is the logic at the heart of Plessner's book, and it is worth noting that he locates this doubling already in the difference between things as such and living things. The doubling of the body becomes more pronounced, and more self-aware, when we make the transition from plants to animals, and again from animals to humans.

Thus, Plessner's philosophy of life and his definition of the living being clear the ground for his investigation of the human being. By locating the specificity of the living thing in a formal account of the relationship between a thing and its border, Plessner repeatedly suggests that defining traits of the human being—its eccentric positionality, natural artificiality, mediation, dislocating self-awareness, its separation, in other words, from nature—originate with life itself. The seeds even of technology can be located in the mediating function that the body itself plays for any living organism (Bo–Bo–M), a function that is further realized with the way that the animal, in contrast to the plant, must instrumentalize its own body. In this movement from spatial necessity (all things have a boundary) to heightened reflexivity (a living thing has a relationship to its own border) to realization in practice (animals instrumentalize their own bodies) to self-awareness of this realization (humans are aware of the need for this mediation) lies the developmental logic of *The Stages of the Organic and the Human Being*. This is a formal and a logical account, and not an evolutionary or historical theory. The various stages of the organic are ideal placeholders, a priori possible configurations of the relationship between organism, body, and environment. This is why Plessner characterizes the distinction between animal and plant as an absolute one,[54] and why he writes, in an intriguing aside, that the human being could theoretically take on different forms.[55] Once he has established the border as constitutive of living organisms, the increasing realization, mediation, and self-awareness of the organism with regard to its body and its border, rather than any empirical morphological or evolutionary developments, mark the movement from one possible positionality to the next, from plant to animal to human being.

The first positionality that Plessner describes is the "open form" of the plant, which constitutes a kind of logical minimum arrangement in the relationship between a "border-realizing body" and its environment. With his description of the positionality of the plant, Plessner sets the stage with a few key aspects—the relationships among a living subject (*Lebenssubjekt*), the parts of its body, its relative awareness, and its functionally and phenomenologically specific environment—that will be intensified and made increasingly reflexive in the transition to the closed form of the animal and thence to the human. While the border and its transgression are characteristics of all living things, plants are characterized by a relationship between their bodies and the surrounding medium that Plessner describes as "open"—that is, plants are integrated into their medium in an immediate way, marked by the absence of a sensorimotor center, a relative lack of differentiation in metabolic functions in discrete, localized origins in favor of their diffusion throughout the plant in the form of surfaces oriented directly towards the environment, and a kind of movement that follows the laws of organic growth rather than deliberate reactions to an objective situation.[56] Plants seem "built into" their environments, as one scholar has put it.[57]

Animals, by contrast, exemplify the closed form. The distinction between open and closed forms can be observed in differences between plant and animal bodies and behavior, but above all else it is an ontological shift to a different level of being (*Seinsniveau*). The closed form is not so much a totally separate form as an intensification of the possibilities of the open form, such that the main aspects of a living being's existence—its body, its surroundings—have taken on new meanings. Where the open form of the plant is immediately integrated into its environment (or "medium"), the closed form of the animal requires mediation.[58] This mediation is provided by its own body, so the closed form is more autonomous than the open form. Specific features of this shift include the development of internal areas into organs and organ systems without much impact on the external surface of the body, which is assigned the organs of sense and movement, resulting in a stronger division of responsibilities between the inside and the outside of the body; the presence of a sensorimotor center; and the distribution of circulation, respiration, and nutrition into discrete organ systems.[59] In these developments, Plessner identifies a broad change in the status and significance of the animal's body, compared to the possibilities available to the plant.

Plessner describes the positional result of this shift as a complication of the relationship between an organism and its own body:

> It [the living organism] is thus no longer directly in contact with the medium and the things around it, but only by means of its body [*Körper*]. The body has become the intermediate layer between the living being and the medium. . . . the living being borders the medium with its body, has gained a reality "in" the body, "behind" the body, and therefore no longer comes into direct contact with the medium. . . . Its body [*Körper*] has become its living body [*Leib*], that concrete center through which the living subject is joined to its surrounding field [*Umfeld*].[60]

Positionally, the animal's need for mediation by its own body means that the body is effectively doubled: it is a *Körper* and a *Leib*. Both *Körper* and *Leib* mean "body," but the former can also refer to physical objects in general, while the latter refers only to organic bodies, more specifically to human and animal bodies. Etymologically, *Körper* is a borrowing of the Latin *corpus*, while *Leib* is a cognate of *Leben*, and of the English word "life."⁶¹ *Körper* is also the word Plessner uses to refer to physical, nonliving bodies as such, which allows him to connect physicality per se to his consideration of the living body. It also invokes a disciplinary question: as a *Körper*, a living body is considered as physical, quantitative extension, and is thus subject to the laws of physics, for example, while as a *Leib*, the same living body also falls under the domain-specific epistemology of biology. As a *Körper*, a body is simply a physical thing that serves as the location of the living subject; as a *Leib*, it is a tool or a means interposed between the living organism and the environment. "With this *Leib*, the living thing exists as with a means, an intermediate layer that at the same time joins and separates, opens and conceals, exposes and protects, an intermediate layer that is given into the possession of the living thing."⁶² If this recalls the doubling of the body that is already implied by the border of the living thing as such (Bo–Be–M vs. Bo–Bo–M), then that is because of the developmental logic of *Stages of the Organic*, which introduces innate, structural features of living beings in general, and then charts the movement towards the human by intensifying and concretizing these features. The closed form of the animal mobilizes latent aspects of the plant's open form, while prefiguring features unique to the human being. A plant may "have" various parts, but it does not actually "have" them like an animal has its parts, as mediating organs controlled by a central instance in a way that necessarily both distances the animal from the medium and integrates it into it.⁶³ The plant's "self" is "merely a character of its living unity, but is not something that can be positionally distinguished from the body [*Körper*]," while the animal's closed form makes explicit what had already existed, albeit implicitly, for the living thing as such.⁶⁴ The animal's double body exists for the animal as well—not in a conscious way so much as in a functional one. In order for the *Leib* to be instrumentalized by the organism, there must be, Plessner posits, a kind of "central organ" or "representational organ" in which the whole body is represented, as a condition of the organic unity of the disparate parts: "Consequently, the organism has arrived at a higher level of being, which does not lie on the same plane as that taken up by its own body [*Körper*]. The organism is the unity of the body [*Körper*]—mediated through the unified representation of its parts—which precisely for that reason depends upon the central representation."⁶⁵ This doubling of the body means that the "space-like [*raumhaft*] center, the core or the self" now has a double position: within the body, if the body is not considered as a *Leib*, and outside of the body, if the body is considered as a *Leib*, so that it is dependent on the central organ.⁶⁶

As the closed form, animals thus exemplify a centric positionality. Plessner grants that there are "decentered" animals such as invertebrates, which do not rely upon such a representative center to coordinate stimulus and response. Drawing on Uexküll's theory of the "functional circuit" (*Funktionskreis*), Plessner describes such decentered, "lower" animal forms as unaware of their surrounding field (*Umfeld*) aside from the relevant sensory inputs that are channeled more or less automatically into determinate actions. Centric animals, by contrast, represent the logical fulfillment of the closed form.[67] The whole body is represented to the living subject; this in turn yields a different relationship to the surrounding field, in which things gain a relative autonomy and decisions about potential action become both possible and necessary.[68] In articulating the idea of the animal as the closed form, Plessner developed a logical schema of the possible relationships among a living subject, its body, and its border, but he was also drawing on contemporary ethology, including experiments with what was then called "animal psychology" (*Tierpsychologie*). Among others, Plessner refers to Hans Volkelt's experiments with spider perception and Wolfgang Köhler's research into the intelligence of great apes.[69] Plessner also builds here on Uexküll's theorization of the relationship between animals' *Funktionskreis* and *Umwelt*—the way that an animal species' bodily arrangement creates a corresponding environment that is unique to its sensorimotor possibilities—but he accuses Uexküll of "zoological idealism," in that Uexküll's radical subsumption of an animal's environment as part of that animal itself seems to deny the dialectical, co-constitutive relationship between organism and environment.[70]

The closed form of the animal, unlike the open form of the plant, necessitates a doubling of the body into the body that one *is*, and the body that one *has*. This is a more complex and more reflexive doubling than that represented by the border of the living thing and the scheme Bo–Bo–M. This new doubling, specific to the stage of the animal, is the differentiation of the body into *Körper* and *Leib*, and represents an intensification of tendencies inherent in Plessner's definition of life while also prefiguring the distance, mediacy, and instrumentality that characterize the human. We can see more clearly how Plessner arrives at the eccentricity of the human out of such an immanent development (deriving discontinuity from continuity, as it were) by surveying some of the differences between these two bodies. Considered as a *Körper*, a body is seen in the same terms as any other physical, nonliving body that occupies a position in space and time, while as a *Leib* it is a specifically living body. The *Körper* is in immediate contact with the medium, the *Leib* in mediated contact.[71] The *Körper* is the location of the living subject, while the *Leib* is its tool. The *Körper* is the body considered as physical body, such that it can be mechanically analyzed, while the *Leib* is a living unity that cannot be reduced to its component matter or understood in terms of mechanical laws.[72]

These accumulated layers of definitions reflect a density of meaning with perhaps surprising implications. The distinction between *Körper* and *Leib* is an ontological one, but—in the case of living organisms—it also represents two possible aspects of what is the same objective phenomenon, so that the distinction is also functional and epistemological, without ceasing to be ontological. Thus the *Körper/Leib* distinction works palimpsestically, with the properties of *Leib* layered over those of *Körper* without displacing or effacing them. After all, just because a body is subjected to the demands of life does not mean that it thereby ceases to function according to the dictates of physics and chemistry. A living body remains a physical body.

Just as the shift from things to living things depended on the relationality of the border becoming a functional characteristic of the living thing (rather than just an accidental spatial demarcation), the various doublings of the organism's body also represent a necessary mediation between organism and environment in a way that also implies a nascent subject position. Because of the close functional integration of organism and environment, this intensification of the body from *Körper* to *Leib* is accompanied by the development of the environment from medium to surrounding field (*Umfeld*). The former term represents the surroundings into which an organism is immediately integrated, while the latter takes account of the distance between an organism and its own body, necessitating a kind of rudimentary freedom vis-à-vis its field of action.[73] "In the distance to its own *Leib*, the living *Körper* has its medium as a surrounding field."[74] Just as the *Leib* and the *Körper* refer to what is objectively the same thing, *Umfeld* and *Medium* both indicate the environment that surrounds an organism, acts upon it, and upon which it must act. Specifically, *Umfeld* (like *Leib*) indicates an increased distance, a heightened reflexivity and an intensification of the immanent logic of the term upon which it is built.

Yet if the *Körper* is physical, material, immediate, and analyzable while the *Leib* is mediated, formal, instrumental, and a living unity, then some of these terms don't line up the way one might expect, were one to associate instrumentality with mechanicity. To view a body solely as a *Körper* is to take the mechanist view of life. "When I raise my arm or when the child learns to walk, the corresponding muscles are indeed innervated. And yet this only characterizes the physical [*körperlich*] process, not the bodily [*leiblich*] one. The process with the *Leib* is of a different kind."[75] To view bodily processes merely as a collection of impulses, sensations, and signals is to ignore the role that meaningful, living unities play in the behavior of organisms, missing the forest for the trees. But if a *Körper* is a mechanical way of understanding a body, this does not mean that it is instrumental, for instrumentality belongs, in Plessner's account, to the *Leib*. Plessner thus sidesteps the risk of vitalism, since the unity of the living *Leib* is explained in formally immanent terms rather than transcendent, metaphysical ones, but he also thwarts the hasty association of mechanicity and instrumentality. In the broader conceptual constellation, and in the context of other possible ways of talking about the organic and the technological, the *Leib's* connection to instrumentality is significant because it roots the characteristics of human positionality—mediation, distance, instrumentality—in a development that is immanent to organic life as such.

Thus the animal prefigures the human by concretizing latent tendencies of living things in general. Plessner describes how features that are only implicit and "present in themselves" for the living thing become explicit and "independent for themselves" in the closed form of the animal, identifying this development as a basis for consciousness:

> If one wanted to compare the essential complex of the "living thing in general" to this whole essential complex of the closed form according to the principle of stages, one would have to say that here everything is still bound, only present in-itself [*an sich*], only implied and conditioning the structure of liveliness, whereas in the closed form it is released, it has become independent for itself, explicit. Even the plant has a stalk, leaves, blossoms and fruits, but neither its self nor its having confront its *Körper* as a *Leib* in an actual opposition. The self is only a character of its living unity, but not positionally separable from the *Körper*. As soon, however, as a real difference in the *Körper* itself has appeared through the formation of a center, the whole changes positionally and the basis for all those phenomena connected to consciousness has been created.[76]

Furthermore, whereas the plant's open form is immediately integrated into its medium, the animal's mediated relationship to its surroundings means that it must actively procure its own fulfillment. The animal is characterized by the "primary unfulfilledness of the living being":

> To be primarily needy [*primär bedürftig*] means the same thing as being mediatedly incorporated into the circuit of life [*Lebenskreis*]. . . . Thus it is in essence a needy thing searching for a fulfillment that is guaranteed to it as a possibility, but which it can achieve in actuality only across a chasm. In its independence the animal is the starting point and target of its drives, which are nothing other than the immediate manifestation of its primary unfulfilledness, of its mediate incorporation into the circuit of life [*Lebenskreis*].[77]

The questing attitude often associated with an existential position is here ontologized as the result of the animal's closed form, which means that its relationship to its environment is never unmediated. Drives for Plessner, rather than constituting a kind of automatism, are in fact the manifestation of the animal's unfulfilledness and mediated incorporation into the *Lebenskreis*.[78] This conception of animal drives will prove problematic if one wishes to assimilate Plessner's philosophical anthropology to theories of the human as a deficient being lacking in instincts. Far from being the human's stable foil, the animal in this account appears as a kind of proto-human position. It is only one positional step from the animal that must seek its own fulfillment to the human being that must create its own balance.[79]

Plessner's Definition of the Human (and Why It Matters)

Plessner defines the human being as an eccentric positionality, exhibiting all of the animal features of mediation and unfulfilledness, with the added twist of self-awareness. On the one hand, this eccentricity causes the constitutive uniqueness of the human being, and is experienced by human beings as a fundamental breach in existence, a dislocating loss of naturalness. "For philosophy, this 'crosswise position' [*Querlage*] of the human being is explained by its eccentric positional form, but this doesn't help. Whoever is in this position stands under the aspect of an absolute antinomy: having to make oneself into what one already is, *leading* the life that one lives."[80] Yet on the other hand, this eccentricity is the fullest realization of the positionality of the living thing as such, and even more so, of the animal—eccentric positionality, one might say, does not mean that humans are not animals, but that they are animals that are aware that they are animals.[81] The living thing realizes its own border; the human realizes that it realizes its own border. The animal is mediated; the human is mediated, and aware of it. In this double necessity of continuity and hiatus, Plessner's definition of the human being converges and diverges with other approaches within Philosophical Anthropology. Like other texts of Philosophical Anthropology, *Stages of the Organic* grounds its account of the human's unique situatedness within nature upon an account of nature. The human being, for Philosophical Anthropology, is unnatural for natural reasons.[82] Yet Plessner's human being, far more than that of Scheler or Gehlen, is seen as the actualization of constitutive features of the living organism as such. Thus, while Plessner also emphasizes the importance of the breach and the "constitutive homelessness" of the human being,[83] it matters—for his picture of nature, for his definition of the human, and for the consequences of these—that this dislocation is immanent to his definition of life itself.

Eccentricity is the decentering of the self vis-à-vis the body and the environment, and is thus the end of the centricity of the animal in two senses: eccentricity is both the termination and the fulfillment of centricity. The closed form of the animal, its mediated integration into its environment, and its dual relationship to its own body as physical *Körper* and instrumental *Leib* all necessitate the existence of a mediating center. This center's self-awareness is also its displacement. If the animal's being is hidden from it,[84] then the human awareness of the need for mediation expels the self from the body. Yet it is important that it is not self-consciousness that causes eccentricity, but rather the other way around. Plessner begins his description of human eccentricity by asking how the living thing's positional center, present for the reader of *Stages of the Organic*, could also be present for the living thing as such.[85] In order for this to occur, the positional center would have to gain a reflexive distance from itself—not by means of another center (an impossible scenario that would threaten an infinite regress), but by the fact that the positionality of the animal becomes explicitly constitutive for the living thing. If the animal is situated (*gesetzt*) in its own middle, the human being is situated in its own situatedness in the middle: "it stands in the middle of its standing."[86] The center thereby gains distance to itself, enabling the "total reflexivity of the living system."[87] This move to the human is explicitly dialectical: the transition from a "lower" to a "higher" stage hinges upon the transformation of an implicit moment into an explicit principle, whereby the constraints of the previous stage are still preserved. "According to this law, by which the moment of the lower stage, once grasped as a principle, results in the next-higher stage and at the same time appears as a moment in it (remains 'preserved'), one can imagine a being whose organization is constituted in accordance with the positional moments of the animal."[88] The human being is centric and, aware of its centricity, thereby eccentric. Bound to the positionality of the animal, it is nevertheless no longer contained by this positionality, which has become reflexive.

> If the life of the animal is centric, then the life of the human being is, without being able to break through its centering, at the same time already outside of it, eccentric. Eccentricity is the characteristic human form of its frontal positioning vis-à-vis the surrounding field [*Umfeld*]. As an I that enables the complete reorientation of the living system to itself, the human no longer stands in the here-now, but "behind" it, behind itself, placeless, in nothing, the human is resolved into nothing, in the space-time-like nowhere-nowhen. Placelessly, timelessly, the human enables the experience [*Erlebnis*] of itself and at the same time the experience of its placelessness and timelessness as a standing-outside-of-itself, because the human is a living thing that no longer stands only in itself, but rather one for whom its "standing-in-itself" signifies the foundation of its standing. It is put into its borders and therefore beyond the borders that bound it, the living thing. The human not only lives and experiences [*lebt und erlebt*], rather, it experiences its experience. . . . Positionally there exists a threefold situation: the living thing is a body [*Körper*], is in a body (as inner life or soul), and is outside of the body as the viewpoint from which it is both of these things. . . . It is the subject of its experience, its perceptions and its actions, its initiative. It knows and it wants. Its existence truly rests upon nothing.[89]

All the components of the characteristically human eccentric positionality are there in the animal's closed form and dual body—all but consciousness, that is. As June Hwang puts it:

> Plessner claims that animals have relationships that are mediated but experienced as unmediated because animals just are; they occupy

their positions without self-awareness, and it is only with self-awareness that one can recognize mediation. That is to say, there is no "primitive" unmediated existence in animals—their relationships are mediated like those of humans; the difference lies in the ability to be aware of this mediation. Insofar as humans occupy the position that they create, they also experience this mediated immediacy. Yet they are also outside this position because they are aware of it, which means that one simultaneously occupies and is outside this position.[90]

The human for Plessner is a sort of second-order animal that experiences its experience. This constitutive self-externality of the human, although it arises from causes immanent to life itself in Plessner's account, means that human existence is distanced from the naturalness and immediacy that seem to belong to nonhuman nature. Rather than an unconscious positionality, "life" for the human is something that needs to be lived. "The human being only lives by leading a life [*Der Mensch lebt nur, indem er ein Leben führt*]. To be human is the 'withdrawal' of being alive from being, and the consummation of this withdrawal, by virtue of which the layer of liveliness [*Lebendigkeit*] appears as a quasi-independent sphere—what is a dependent moment of being in plant and animal remains as the human's characteristic."[91] Life itself, the quality of being alive, becomes for the human an independent moment, and thus a problem. If for plants and animals being alive is indistinguishable from being, the displacement involved in human eccentricity entails a recognition of contingency, and of an object-world that exists independently of the human subject.

Thus, at the highest stage of the organic, the organism's environment undergoes a corresponding shift. Where the open form of the plant had a *Medium* into which it was immediately integrated,[92] and the closed form of the animal faced an *Umfeld* upon which it needed to act, the eccentric form of the human has an external world (*Außenwelt*) made up of things that perdure independently of the living subject.[93] An external world composed of independent things corresponds to the human awareness of the need for mediation; where the animal must take action in a field of possibility, the human must do so as well, with the added insight and burden that things might be otherwise. Furthermore, the double-aspectivity that is constitutive for all life appears with the human for the first time as being both in- and for-itself, for the human, surrounded by a world of things, is aware of the double-aspectivity of these things—including itself. This awareness indexes another twist in the living subject's relationship to its own body. To recall: *Körper* is the term used to describe any physical body, living or nonliving, whereas it is only with the closed form of the animal that the *Leib* appears to the organism as an instrumental, living unity which the living subject interposes between itself and its environment. The human of course experiences its own body as a *Leib*, but the decentering transformation of the solipsistic

Umfeld into an objective *Außenwelt* means that the body is also for the human subject a *Körper*, a thing among things in an indifferent spatiotemporal field.[94]

Corresponding to the human being's *Außenwelt* are its characteristic, eccentric manifestations of the experience of self, and of other selves. Plessner dubs these two worlds the *Innenwelt* and the *Mitwelt*. The *Innenwelt* is the domain of the psychic, of *Seele* (soul) and *Erlebnis* (experience). In keeping with the consequences of eccentric positionality, the *Innenwelt* consists both of what the self is, and what it notices within itself.[95] The *Mitwelt* is the sphere of the "other I," the mutuality involved in the recognition of other selves, other persons, a mutuality that is constitutive of the awareness of the self. *Geist* emerges with the *Mitwelt*, which is itself but the fullest unfolding of the positionality of life.

> For the "other" is, regardless of its structural essential identity with me, as a person quite simply an individual reality (as I am), whose inner world is essentially completely concealed, and must first be unlocked through various kinds of interpretation. The reality of the co-world [*Mitwelt*] is guaranteed to the human being through the eccentric positional form of its self. . . . It distinguishes itself . . . from the outer world and the inner world because its elements—persons—provide no specific substrate that would materially go beyond what is already offered by the outer world and the inner world in themselves. Its specific characteristic is liveliness [*Lebendigkeit*] and, to be precise, liveliness in its highest form: eccentricity. The specific substrate of the co-world thus in fact rests only upon its own structure. Co-world is the form of the human being's own position, grasped by the human being as the sphere of other human beings.[96]

Thus, out of the intensification and total reflexivity of a development intrinsic to life itself—the increasing complexity of the relationship between a living organism and its border—arises self-consciousness and ultimately all the unique aspects of human life: technology, culture, symbolic representation. *Geist*—the social, intellectual sphere of the human that results from eccentric positionality[97]—is both the product of *Leben* and its complication. Joachim Fischer contextualizes the philosophical intervention of Plessner's eccentric positionality, in deriving *Geist* from life, as striking a middle path between German Idealism and *Lebensphilosophie*. Plessner shares with Idealism the emphasis on the autonomy of *Geist*, but, like *Lebensphilosophie*, insists on the connection between *Geist* and life: "[He] shared . . . with *Lebensphilosophie* the view that the site of *Geist* gains poignancy through its relation to the dynamic of life, which is independent of *Geist*. *Geist* is a questioning of, a challenge to the dynamic equilibrium of life."[98] Because the human being is a living organism now aware of itself and its need to live, life has become a question; the awareness of balance is at the same time the awareness of the possibility of being out of balance. For Plessner, the human being needs to actively create its own equilibrium.[99]

This recognition is formulated in terms of what Plessner calls the three basic anthropological laws: the law of natural artificiality, the law of mediated immediacy, and the law of the utopian standpoint. Natural artificiality concerns the way that the human, as an "eccentrically organized being," must make itself into what it already is. Where the animal can simply *be*, the human being must realize itself.[100] This requires, according to Plessner, an artificial complement—technology, essentially, though we will see shortly why this natural artificiality is not the same thing as a theory of the human being as deficient being. Awareness of the lack of immediacy generates a response to attempt to overcome the eccentricity by *creating* a sense of balance. The result of this is the history of human making, namely, technology and culture per se.

> This view, often stamped in mythic form, expresses a deep recognition. Because the human being is forced by its type of existence to lead the life that it lives, i.e., to make what it is—simply because the human being only is when it consummates—it needs a complement of a non-natural, non-organic [*nichtgewachsen*] kind. For that reason the human being is *artificial* [*künstlich*] by nature, for reasons of its form of existence. As an eccentric being lacking equilibrium, placeless, timeless, standing in nothingness, constitutively homeless, the human being must "become something"—and create its own equilibrium. And the human creates this only with the help of the non-natural things that spring from its work [*Schaffen*], *when* the results of this creative making receive their own weight. . . . The human being wants to escape the unbearable eccentricity of its nature [*Wesen*], it wants to compensate for the halfness [*Hälftenhaftigkeit*] of its own form of life and it can only achieve this with things that are heavy enough in order to balance the weight of the human's own existence. The eccentric form of life and the need for completion constitute one and the same fact [*Tatbestand*].[101]

Mediated immediacy refers to the way that access to the world—whether to the outer world (*Außenwelt*) of things, the inner world (*Innenwelt*) of psychological, mental experience, or the co-world (*Mitwelt*) of other human beings—is necessarily mediated by the senses, consciousness, language, and so on. Whereas for Plessner all living things exist within mediated immediacy by virtue of their complex borders, only human beings are aware of this mediated immediacy and thus must grapple with it as a basic fact of their existence.[102] The "utopian standpoint" characterizes the effect of eccentric positionality on human society and history writ large; it is connected to the recognition of the fundamental contingency of existence.

The human being, defined in terms of its eccentric positionality, is thus the culmination of the double-aspectivity with which Plessner's account begins. The human is a body and a self, a subject and an object, mind and matter. Awareness of this duality defines for Plessner what it means to be human, without thereby reconciling the divide. "For the human being, the sudden change from Being within its own body [*Leib*] to Being outside of the body is an irrevocable double-aspect of existence, a real break in human nature. The human lives both on this side of and beyond the break, as a soul and as a physical body [*Körper*] and as the psychological-physically neutral unity of these spheres."[103] In this sense, the end of Plessner's book retroactively justifies the phenomenological method chosen at its beginning, for the human being, existing in and as double-aspectivity, turns out to have the kind of perception that recognizes a double aspect of all things, composed of perceptible qualities and a substantial kernel. The human being arrived at by the end of the text is the one who can realize the constitutive double-aspectivity of perception; in that sense, the perspective at the beginning (of objects as such) is only realized by the subject generated by this account.[104]

> Strictly speaking, only that being that is manifest as a self *and* as a physical [*körperlich*] thing stands in the double-aspect; the being that acts as a physical thing like other things, but which at the same time expresses itself *as* a self and even knows of itself.... Despite all considerations of immanence and representation, I go beyond *myself* and speak of the *human* as a real genus distributed across many individuals, and for whom it is fundamental to exist in the double-aspect.[105]

Such, then, is Plessner's human being. It is eccentrically positional, constitutionally out-of-whack, ontologically unbalanced and compelled to create its own equilibrium; pulled between the promises of stability, grounding, and wholeness offered by religion, on the one hand, and *Geist*'s subversive reflexivity, on the other, which undoes all absolutes.[106] The human being, for Plessner, is both a part of nature and, in its awareness of this fact, expelled from the possibility of simply being a part of nature.

We might be tempted to assimilate Plessner's eccentric human to other, apparently similar visions of the human offered by Philosophical Anthropology, seeing in Plessner's version of the human dislocated from nature an instance of the deficient being (*Mängelwesen*) hypothesis, which defines the human being according to its apparent lack of specialization and instincts, compared to other animals. But such a move, precisely because it views the human being as a radical exception within the natural world, would elide nearly everything interesting about Plessner's project. Helmut Lethen has read Plessner's text in this way, associating it with the deficient being account of Arnold Gehlen, yet to interpret eccentric positionality in terms of the evolutionary compensation of the human as deficient being is to misread Plessner's method, emphasis, and conclusion. By stressing rupture over continuity, alienation over an immanent development, and artificiality over *natural* artificiality, Lethen is able to mobilize Plessner's theory in the service of a binary account of Weimar thought that pits culture against nature, the mechanical against the organic. By correcting this misidentification of Plessner's eccentric positionality with the deficient being, we might glimpse a different picture of Weimar thought—one that offers an interdisciplinary, post-humanist account of the human being in all its specificity, precisely as the fullest realization of a logic immanent to the definition of life itself.

Plessner plays an important role in Lethen's account of the "cold persona" of the Weimar years. Drawing on sweepingly interdisciplinary comparisons and readings of literary case studies, Lethen depicts Weimar culture as one in transition from a culture of guilt, in which the subject is guided by an internal moral compass, to one of shame, marked by an externalization of the guidelines of human conduct. The demise of the stable moral codes of the *Kaiserreich* led, according to Lethen, to the need for new codes of behavior that would guide and protect individuals in a hostile social arena destabilized by war, the loss of tradition, and rapid technological modernization. By arguing that this culture of distance was rooted in the anthropology of the 1920s—in its very picture of human nature, that is—Lethen buttresses his readings of the literary tropes and strategies of the period. In his reading of Plessner, Lethen foregrounds the importance of mediation, distance, and borders, to the extent that these concepts become consonant with the trope of the armored body.

It is important to note that Lethen reads *Stages of the Organic and the Human Being* as a result—or better, as a justification—of Plessner's social critique, rather than as an anthropology informed by recent work in the natural sciences. Lethen sees this anthropology as reflecting "a specific habitus," and continues:

> Plessner's directives are not necessarily the result of an anthropology modeled on natural science, although he makes reference to zoology, medicine, and paleontology, presumably in order to represent his code as grounded scientifically in the constitution of the individual. If we are correct in this assumption, then what we have in Plessner's most ambitious work, *Die Stufen des Organischen und der Mensch,* is the naturalization of an eccentric code of conduct.[107]

Lethen attributes Plessner's axiom that the human is artificial by nature to the "polarizing tendencies of vitalism."[108] Plessner's anthropology thus represents for Lethen the perfect example of "cool conduct" and the inscription of a historically specific cultural trope into the natural order. If the human needs armor, distance, and calculation to protect it from the risks of social contact and risibility, Lethen locates this need in Plessner's idea of natural artificiality. If Plessner defines the human being in terms of artificiality and separation from nature, Lethen wonders, why is it that he overlooks an obvious precursor for his theory of the human being—namely, the "deficient being" proposed by Johann Gottfried Herder and later developed more fully by Arnold Gehlen?

Lethen quotes the following from Herder's *Treatise on the Origin of Language* in order to suggest the proximity of Plessner's "natural artificiality" to the idea of the deficient being, and to underscore Plessner's "surprising" omission:

> Even in his very first moments this miserable creature, with no instincts, issuing forsaken from nature's lap, was a freely expressive and rational creature, bound to improve himself, as no other course lay open. All his failings and requirements as an animal set him, with all the powers at his disposal, the more urgently to prove himself as man.[109]

Compared to other animals, the human as *Mängelwesen* evidently lacks a suitable apparatus for fight or flight, and a specialized integration into a specific milieu, as well as the sureness of instincts that automatize behaviors as reactions to stimuli. Seen negatively, the human is deficient; seen positively, the human's world is open and the human is a being "that has itself as a task," as Arnold Gehlen puts it.[110] Gehlen, one of Plessner's competitors within Philosophical Anthropology, took up and developed Herder's concept of the human as deficient being as a centerpiece of his own anthropology, writing:

> Morphologically the human being, in contrast to all higher mammals, is primarily determined by *deficiencies*, which must be defined in an exact biological sense as maladaptations, as non-specializations, as primitivisms, i.e., as an undeveloped aspect: that is, essentially negative. A coat of hair is lacking and with it a natural protection from the weather; natural organs of attack are lacking, but also a bodily form suitable for flight; the human being is outdone by most animals in sensory acuity, he has an almost life-threatening lack of genuine instincts and during the whole period of infancy and childhood he is subject to a wholly incomparable long-term need of protection. In other words: living on the ground and surrounded by the most agile prey and the most dangerous predators he would, under natural, organic conditions, have been eradicated a long time ago.[111]

The theory of the *Mängelwesen* is essentially a negative anthropology that defines the human in terms of what it lacks, when compared to other animals, and tries to account for this breach between humans and nature.[112]

The most immediate rejoinder to the deficient being hypothesis is that it begs the question, for it is only coherent if one presupposes the fact that human traits such as language, tool-making, flexibility, and sociality are compensatory responses to deficiencies bestowed upon human beings by evolution, rather than as adequate evolutionary results in their own right. In this account, the human being is categorically separate from the animal world only because the theory stacks the deck in advance by fetishizing the fighty, flighty parts of animals and ignoring the social dimension. Contemporary animal researchers took issue with the way that Gehlen excised the human from evolutionary history,[113] while Plessner himself critiques negative anthropologies that see the human being as a "sick animal" for their circularity.[114] But beyond the circularity of the *Mängelwesen*'s loaded comparison between animals and humans, there are more important differences between the deficient being and eccentric positionality.

For one thing, Plessner's account depends far more on continuity than does Gehlen's (and Lethen's). If Lethen stresses the artificiality in "natural artificiality," he is giving only half the picture, for it is essential in *Stages of the Organic* that this artificiality derives from—and doesn't simply fall out of—nature. For another thing, the morphological focus of the deficient being is at odds with Plessner's formal account of positionality. For Plessner, it is not specific features of human morphology—the lack of wings or claws or other implements that give the "most agile prey and the most dangerous predators" their supposed advantage—that distinguish humans from animals, but rather the immanent development of a positional logic: it is not claws, wings, or teeth, but the nature of the relationship between an organism, its body, and its environment that matters.

Thus, not only is it irrelevant for Plessner's theory that the human being lacks claws, wings, and the like, but the same technology seen by the deficient being theory as the compensation for this lack arises, for Plessner, out of a logic of instrumentality and mediation that defines even the animal form. Instrumentality for Plessner arises not as a compensatory strategy in response to the loss of a non-deficient body and relationship to the environment, but is, in *Stages of the Organic*, already what distinguishes the animal from the plant. If the plant is characterized as an "open form," with the surface of the organism serving as the direct interface with its surrounding medium, the animal is a "closed form" that necessarily instrumentalizes its body in order to interact with its environment. Animals have a mediated relationship to their environment; humans differ in being aware of this relationship. Without the doubling of the animal body into physical *Körper* and instrumental *Leib*, human technology and artifice would not be possible. So this characteristic human artificiality is the culmination of what defines the animal, rather than arising from the mysterious absence of animal traits.

Moreover, Plessner's theory is incompatible with a theory of the deficient being if one considers that the eccentric positionality of the human is already formally presupposed in the definition of the living thing as a "border-realizing body."[115] "The foregoing analyses have tried to make clear that the living as such possesses the structure of mediated immediacy. It results from the essence of the really-posited border."[116] Because of the function of the border for the living organism, life as such possesses the structure of mediated immediacy—the human difference is that human beings represent the fullest realization of this basic definition. Thus for Plessner, technology and artifice are already latent in organic life itself, and become manifest with the human being. Put in different terms, Plessner's account is a strong challenge to the assumption that animals, plants, or nonhuman life in general are essentially harmonious and self-sufficient, and that it is only with the human being that the organism falls out of tune with its environment. A theory of the human being as deficient being would seem to entail this assumption in order to argue that, of all living species, the human being is uniquely ill-equipped by nature. The human being is different, for Plessner, but only to the extent that it fully realizes a dynamic tendency—the need to cross one's own border, the necessity of all organisms to exceed and transgress their given place—that is innate to all life.

Plessner's account from the living thing through the stages of the organic to the human is characterized by a double reflexivity, for it concerns both the living organism's relationship to its own border and its relationship to this relationship. The border as Plessner defines it is already dynamic and reflexive (unlike the spatial contour, the border both separates and joins, and thus has a functional relationship to its inside—the organism—and its outside—the environment), so that the entirety of *Stages of the Organic* portrays the full unfolding of the implications of a reflexive border. Over and over again, Plessner uses a dialectical language of latent possibilities being realized.[117] What is immediately present at one stage is realized and operationalized at the next higher stage; what is in-itself and for-us at a lower stage becomes also for-itself at a higher stage. This increasing reflexivity is also evident in the way that Plessner works with everyday language, loading simple terms like "self" and "having" with increasing complexity. One says, for example, that a living being is a system that "has" parts, and that the unitary subject of this having is a "self," even when one cannot use these terms in any psychological sense.[118] But with the increasing reflexivity of the living thing in the case of the closed, centric form of the animal, "having" becomes something that is concrete as well as structural: from the animal's perspective, its body and its organs are the means by which it interacts with its environment.[119]

Because of its emphasis on continuous development and the *natural* artificiality of the human over discontinuous rupture, because of its exploration of formal positionality rather than specific morphologies, and because of its progression through the increasingly reflexive realization of tendencies that are latent in the definition of living things as border-realizing bodies, Plessner's eccentrically positional human is not a deficient being, as understood by Gehlen and Lethen. The *Mängelwesen* is a picture of the human as a fallen creature, whose nobility lies in the response to this natural incompleteness.

The *Mängelwesen* hypothesis also necessitates an oversimplification of animal embodiment and instinct, in order for the human being to appear in greater contrast as cosmically and uniquely forlorn, tossed "naked and miserable upon the shores of this great ocean of the world."[120] Drawing on contemporary ethology and philosophical biology, Plessner advances a potent definition of the human and human artifice that does not rely on a flat definition of other forms of life.

If Lethen assimilates Plessner's concept of natural artificiality to the theory of the deficient being, his account of the culture of distance in Weimar Germany means that he reads Plessner's work more generally as a modern version of Baroque courtly behavior manuals, "cloak-and-dagger, New Objectivity-style."[121] A result of this reading is that important and nuanced concepts in Plessner's anthropology become symbols, for Lethen, of a culture of distance and calculation. In several instances, Lethen merely hypostasizes one side of a complex, dialectical concept. The border, for example, becomes in Lethen's hands a threatened frontier that separates and represses. Its maintenance requires constant vigilance. As a metaphor, it quickly accrues a martial register and bellicose connotations of all kinds:

> His central concept of the boundary now no longer designates a zone of exchange. Appearing on the scene instead is a highly reflexive individual organized internally around an ego that is strictly demarcated from the unconsciousness of physical being. It appears necessary, in order to act out embodied being correctly, to forget the body. Constantly supervising its borders, the ego exists in a state of permanent alarm.[122]

It takes Lethen all of two paragraphs to move from this description of the border to the association of the border with "armoring" (*Panzer des Ichs*).[123] Yet for Plessner, the border is necessarily a zone of exchange. The border of the living thing is the border that joins as well as separates, mediating rather than simply enclosing. Otherwise the concept would risk collapsing into the simple contour of the nonliving thing, and Plessner's entire anthropology would lose its foundation. Plessner's border is a membrane, not armor.[124] In a similar way, the concept of the mask is about expression as much as it is about concealment or protection—the complexity and interest of Plessner's theory of expression depend upon the various ways in which any attempt at immediacy is necessarily mediated, yet Lethen here as elsewhere transforms mediation into separation, isolation, and antagonism.[125]

Why does Plessner play such a central role in Lethen's account of the Weimar-era "cold persona"? Nearly twenty pages long, Lethen's discussion of Plessner's anthropology is one of the longest sections in *Cool Conduct* devoted to a single author. In Lethen's reading, Plessner becomes emblematic of a culture of distance, shame, separation, and carefully managed antagonism. Lethen needs Plessner in order to add a clear theoretical articulation, representing Weimar culture's view of the human being, to the many examples of literary types and tropes that together make up his compelling character sketch of the 1920s. Lethen sees in Plessner's anthropology a reflection of the climate of the times, the retroactive attempt to base a pessimistic social stance on a scientific footing: the ethical and social destabilization in the wake of the collapse of Wilhelmine institutions and norms called for the cold persona, as a stabilizing strategy; this strategy in turn needed, in Lethen's account of Plessner, to be projected onto nature writ large. Lethen reads *The Stages of the Organic and the Human Being* as a "naturalization of an eccentric code of conduct."[126]

Yet this is exactly backwards, and understanding this has consequences for our picture of the Weimar Republic. Lethen is right to link the social and historical contexts of the interwar period to its anthropology, literature, and political culture, yet what is obscured by the particular way he does so is much more interesting than the picture of Weimar culture that he offers. Plessner's work has little to do with "codes of conduct" (*Verhaltenslehre*), and it is a stretch to understand *Stages of the Organic* as a project of naturalization.[127] Rather, as I have tried to show, what matters about Plessner's theory of the human being is precisely the way that it derives human specificity dialectically from features that are immanent to life itself. The way that Lethen describes the disciplinary juncture in Plessner's work is telling, because Lethen is compelled to seriously underplay the role played by the natural sciences in Plessner's work.

If we extrapolate from this divergence for a moment in order to view Plessner as paradigmatic of the disciplinary flux of Weimar Germany, then we end up with two radically different pictures of the intellectual landscape of the 1920s. In Lethen's account, the natural sciences were convenient auxiliaries to justify a view of human nature—and its prescriptions for human conduct—that had already been established by the climate of the times. But a closer look at *Stages of the Organic* shows that this cannot be the case. The questions that Plessner was asking ran deeper than Lethen allows, and his answers are far more compelling. Plessner, aware that he faced a disciplinary aporia that could not satisfactorily account either for the human being as the subject-object of nature and culture or for nonquantitative aspects of the natural, material world, mobilized a phenomenological method alongside current research from various subfields of biology in order to attempt a unified theory of the human being that would meet the challenges both of biology and of philosophy.

Whether or not he succeeded, by the standards of the 1920s or of our own times, is a less relevant question than how he approached the problem. Far from being subordinate disciplines that simply gave cover to a predetermined picture of the human being, embryology, cell biology, ethology, and other fields allowed Plessner to try to bridge the disciplinary divide between the natural sciences and the humanities, between materiality and cognition, quantity and quality which he saw as a legacy of Cartesian dualism. The picture of the human being that emerged was not a *Mängelwesen*, as if acting on a terrain outside nature. The human being, for Plessner, is a being that is distinct from nature because of its embeddedness in nature; its specificity is but the fullest articulation of what constitutes life itself. Not incidentally, ethology and animal studies were important and rising fields in the Weimar Republic. Plessner's development of eccentric positionality out of the centric positionality of the animal, and his location of instrumentality already in the animal's relationship to its own body, is but a local example of a larger intellectual constellation in which the rapid advances in various subfields of biology presented generative challenges to theories of the human being that prevailed in philosophy and in the humanities more generally.[128]

Thus the modernity of Plessner's picture of the human is twofold. On the one hand, it depends on—and directly engages with—the disciplinary landscape of the 1920s. *The Stages of the Organic and the Human Being* is, at its core, an attempt to reconcile a philosophically coherent account of human existence and human experience with the current state of biological knowledge. Plessner sought to do this not merely by applying particular scientific insights or methodologies to various aspects of human existence, but from the ground up. Crucially, this project was also reciprocal, in that it sought to reclaim the possibility of understanding material nature through critical, *qualitative* analysis. To recall, Plessner was addressing what he saw as an aporia of both philosophy and the natural sciences, a double dead end which he saw as the legacy of Cartesian dualism: "An anti-Cartesian movement must be directed against the identification of physicality [*Körperlichkeit*] and extension, physical existence and measurability, which is responsible for the fact that we have become blind to the characteristics of physical nature that cannot be measured."[129]

On the other hand, and as a direct result of this disciplinary modernity, the picture of the human being that emerges in *Stages of the Organic* is strikingly modern, precisely by virtue of its entanglements with nature. Far from the trope of the armored bodies that populate a modernity characterized by technological speed and dynamism, the human being for Plessner is naturally artificial. Humanity's characteristic eccentric positionality results from human embodiment, rather than from a deficient development or a lacking naturalness. Human embodiment, understood as the complexly positional relationship among body, self, and border, is in turn merely the fullest realization of a possibility already latent within the definition of life itself. Thus, if one common view holds that technology represents a development that has fallen out of tune with nature, Plessner's theory of the living thing as a "border-realizing body" resists this dichotomy by locating the ontological dislocation within a theory of organic life. Indeed, such a dichotomy pitting technology against nature was increasingly seen by Weimar-era intellectuals as a sign of a prevailing dualism that itself belonged to an obsolescent bourgeois era, along with a mind-body dualism and the emphasis on psychological interiority and subjective autonomy as the hallmarks of the individual. As we will see with Döblin, Jünger, and in various conceptions of photography's potential, the experience of modern technology and modern urban society could no longer be understood in such dichotomous terms. Rather, the picture that emerges is of a modernity that is thoroughly technological *because* it is thoroughly elemental, natural, organic, and biological. Likewise, the modernity of Plessner's concept of the human as an eccentric being, as a life-form which realizes that the form of life is to realize its own border, is that the human is obliged to view itself and nature from the outside, without thereby falling out of nature.

Chapter 2

✦

Photography's Natural Histories in the Weimar Republic

Photography in the 1920s is paradigmatic of biological modernism because it sits at the fault line of a tectonic collision of two discursive frameworks. One of these, coeval with the medium itself, concerned photography's innate ambiguity as a practice that partakes of both nature and culture, science and art, technology and craft. Because it was a way of making images by harnessing the natural principles of light, optics, and photosensitivity, photography seemed to early practitioners to be nature's technologically mediated self-portrait—"the pencil of nature," in William Henry Fox Talbot's formulation. Photography emerged in the early nineteenth century amidst epistemological upheavals and reconfigurations prior to any firm separation between art and science, subjectivity and objectivity, so that it could be unparadoxically seen as both natural and mechanical.[1] The other discursive framework that shaped discussions of photography in the 1920s was that of modernity and modernization. The association of photography with modernity—and modernity's connotations of speed, mechanicity, objectivity, and the fragmentation of subjective experience—became especially pronounced in the early twentieth century, and central to theorizations of photography (and film) in the Weimar Republic. Yet, as Laura Saltz has suggested in arguing that photography should be seen as "unmodern," photography's putative modernity and its ambiguous place between nature and culture are but two sides of the same discursive framework. Drawing on Bruno Latour's characterization of modernity as both producing and repressing ontological hybridity, Saltz shows how photography exemplifies this concept of "the modern."[2]

By the 1920s, photography's entanglement in these two discursive frameworks—photography between nature and culture, and photography as emblematic of modernity—had become even more complex. The lines between nature and culture, science and art, objectivity and subjectivity had become more deeply entrenched, and processes of industrialization and urbanization had crystallized the associations among modernity, mechanicity, and speed. Yet, despite the enthusiasm generated by new developments in technologies of photographic production and circulation during the Weimar

Republic, the medium was never fully reduced to a symbol for technological modernity, but continued to trouble the distinctions between nature and technology, and between old and new upon which a one-sided conception of modernity depended. What this broad discursive constellation meant, for one thing, is that theorizations of photography were never about this visual medium alone, but were able to inflect broader considerations of aesthetic representation, narrative, history, experience, and modernity.

In the case of the cinematic theory of Weimar, this has long been obvious. Yet the role of still photography—so often used interchangeably with cinema by writers in the 1920s—has only belatedly been acknowledged. It is this context that can help explain why photography assumes world-historical stakes for Siegfried Kracauer in his essay "Photography," for example, or how Alfred Döblin related August Sander's portraiture both to natural history and to his own reappropriation of the epic literary form, or why Walter Benjamin and Bertolt Brecht were so allergic to the title of Albert Renger-Patzsch's photobook, *The World Is Beautiful* (*Die Welt ist schön*), and to the photographic practice it suggested to them. This interdisciplinary discursive context can also help illuminate the playful rhyming of natural and technological forms in major photobooks such as *The World Is Beautiful* and Karl Blossfeldt's *Art Forms in Nature* (*Urformen der Kunst*). Photography in the 1920s was a usefully polysemic field of contestation. Contemporaries not only were able to grapple with the pressing questions of the day by writing about photography, it often seems as though they *had* to address photography in order to think about modernity.

It may seem counterintuitive that photography, already a century old by the 1920s, should have been so closely connected to the ideas of modernization and novelty, but important changes in the production, circulation, and reception of photographic images in the Weimar Republic contributed to this association.[3] Chief among these were new genres and forms including the photobook, the photo essay, photojournalism, and the illustrated magazines. The relevant unit was no longer the individual image, but the collection of images and texts that circulated as a form of mass communication. Readily available handheld cameras and advances in semitone printing contributed to the mass production and circulation of photographs. More broadly, anxieties about modernization, experience, and representation that characterized the late nineteenth and early twentieth centuries in general and the crisis atmosphere of the Weimar Republic in particular found an outlet in photography, to the extent that it could serve both as a symbol of the speed and dynamism of modern society and as an immunization against it. In the 1920s, discussions of photography's capacity for representation blurred the boundaries between different media, discourses, and disciplines; photography and film were often described in shared terms, and considerations of photography also drew upon the representational codes and epistemological possibilities of other media and arts, or even of the natural sciences. Seen in a broader sense—not the individual image on its own but the sequence, collection, exhibition, or even the flood of images—photography promised a new way of seeing, closely linked to that of the cinema, which might be adequate to the experience of modernity.

Pepper Stetler has usefully complicated the relationship between photography and modernity in her discussion of Weimar-era photobooks. In place of a mimetic relationship between photography or cinema and the disjointed experience characteristic of modern, urban life, as argued by Tom Gunning, Stetler suggests that the photographic book evinces an aspirational, proleptic stance towards modernity. It is the very project of training an imagined "modern vision"—and not this project's actual realization—that makes Weimar photographic books modern.[4] This idea of photographic modernity, as something aspirational, proleptic, imagined and projected, pedagogical, and as necessarily existing between photographic theory and photographic practice, is what guides my readings in this chapter. The linkage between photography and modernity is not reflective or mechanical—it does not automatically follow from the speed, dynamism, and fragmentation of modern life, but rather from the very ways in which photography was *imagined* to address the perceptual and experiential rifts associated with processes of modernization.

Furthermore, the connection articulated by Lorraine Daston and Peter Galison between machines and objectivity (a connection that will be important later in this chapter) provides a useful analogy for thinking about the relationship between photography and modernity. "For the scientific atlas makers of the late nineteenth century, the machine was both a literal and a guiding ideal."[5] That is, machines actually assisted in making images that were supposedly free of the traces of a subjective will, but they also thereby came to symbolize the kind of objectivity that was defined in opposition to willful subjectivity, so that "the machine's constitutive and symbolic functions blur, for the machine seemed at once a means to and a symbol of mechanical objectivity."[6] It is a hypothesis of this chapter that Weimar-era photography stood in an analogously dual relationship to modernity for contemporaries, both constituting and symbolizing it, such that the full identity of the two (to say nothing of the coherent realization of either term) remained an aspirational and guiding ideal, subject to negotiation, conflict, and subversion.

For these reasons, photography's constitutive ambiguity between nature and culture, art and science, was not resolved by its dense association with modernity in the Weimar Republic, but only intensified by it. While many contemporaries emphasized the speed, dynamism, and mechanical exactitude of photography, thereby seeing it as an appropriate technological medium to represent a technological age, another discourse foregrounded different temporalities and different logics, ones that did not seek to disentangle ideas of nature, culture, technology, history, art, and science, but rather used photography's generative ambiguity to move among disciplines and discourses. The resulting modernist aesthetics privileged the type over the individual and complicated the facile association of photography with speed and newness.

With its emphasis on the natural and the organic, this other discourse of Weimar photography was part of the broader context of biological modernism.

In what follows I read photobooks by Karl Blossfeldt and August Sander, and essays by Alfred Döblin and Siegfried Kracauer, in order to theorize a strain within the photographic discourse of the Weimar Republic that worked against—and often explicitly rejected—the medium's associations with ideas of speed, objectivity, and other connotations of modernity. These photographers and writers complicated the punctual temporality of photography—the camera's ability to capture a fleeting moment—in order to think about its relationship to other, longer time frames. August Sander's photobook *Face of Our Time* (1929) offers a cross-section of contemporary German society in the first few decades of the twentieth century. This book's portraits are rendered legible by a variety of typological strategies that contribute to what Döblin praises as Sander's photographic realism, which was superior to the "nominalism" of other photographers who were after the individual moment or scene. By comparing Sander's photography to a kind of scientific practice, Döblin's essay "Faces, Images, and Their Truth" situates photography within natural history, thus locating photography in a longer time frame than the momentary or punctual. Karl Blossfeldt's photobook *Art Forms in Nature* (1928) deploys different strategies in the composition and arrangement of his magnified images of plants in order to train the viewer to identify primal forms that underlie nature and culture alike, yet both Sander and Blossfeldt trouble and reopen the master category of "objectivity," which guided contemporary theorizations of photography. At stake in both Sander's and Blossfeldt's work is the epistemic goal of "truth to nature" rather than mechanical objectivity (Daston and Galison), or "realism" rather than "nominalism," in Döblin's terms. Finally, Siegfried Kracauer's 1927 essay "Photography" offers a sophisticated theorization of the temporality and social circulation of photographic images, opening up important questions about the referentiality and seriality of photography—about photographs' connections to their objects, and to each other. Like Döblin, Sander, and Blossfeldt, Kracauer's essay mobilizes an idea of natural history in order to undermine claims of photographic knowledge that depend upon photography's speed and exactitude, showing how the photographic image's relationship to objective representation is in fact riven by internal contradictions. Taken together, these two photographers and two writers suggest a countervailing way of doing and thinking about photography in the Weimar Republic, one which complicates photography's automatic connection to modernity and to objectivity, or, better: this alternative photographic discourse suggests how these terms might be understood differently, in ways that seem counterintuitive unless we attend to how they were being worked out at the time.

At first glance, the contemporary discussion of photography in the Weimar Republic would certainly seem to privilege the mechanical speed and exactitude of the camera, particularly as a prophylactic against the accelerated pace of modern urban life. Much of the writing during the Weimar Republic about photography gives the impression that photography had both a symbolic and a constitutive relationship to modernity. Whether the emphasis was on the camera's dispassionate gaze or its ability to freeze the flux of dynamic time, or on ways in which viewing images was more suited to the tempo of the modern metropolis than reading text, photography came to stand as *the* modern medium. Indeed, many of the texts in praise of photography often consider it in the same terms with which the cinema was heralded as a modern way of seeing. Significantly, such praise of photography's modernity, mechanicity, objectivity, speed, and dynamism concerned both the technological possibilities of the camera and the mass media context of the illustrated magazines—both, in other words, the single image and the flood of images noted by contemporaries.

Thus, for example, Kurt Korff, editor of the *Berliner Illustrirte Zeitung* who would later go on to be an advisor at *Life* magazine, wrote in 1927 that

> it is no accident that the development of the cinema and the development of the *Berlin Illustrated Newspaper* run roughly parallel. To the extent that life became more hectic, and the individual was less prepared to leaf through a magazine in a quiet moment, to that extent it became necessary to find a sharper, more efficient form of visual representation, one which did not lose its impact on the reader even if he only glanced fleetingly at the magazine page by page.[7]

For Korff, the hectic pace of modern urban life creates a readerly need that photography, in its form in the illustrated magazine, can fill. Photography's sharpness and efficiency compensate for the impossibility of readerly contemplation, allowing the pace of reading to catch up to the celerity of modern life. Johannes Molzahn, in a piece titled "Stop Reading! Look!" declares the photograph to be the "pacesetter for the tempo of time and development,"[8] such that the eye and the psyche must work to assimilate visual information, and thereby gain a training in visual perception demanded by the spirit of the modern age.[9] The tangled causalities here—photography as alternately a response to and an initiator of a modern sense of acceleration—already begin to suggest the relationship in contemporary photographic discourse, often associative and analogical more than analytical or descriptive, among photography, speed, technology, and modernity.

What was especially crucial to the photography of the time was the identification of photography with mechanical speed and exactitude. Albert Renger-Patzsch expresses a common view when he writes:

> To a photographer who remains within the limits prescribed for photographic technique, the mechanical procedure of his medium, the

swiftness of its execution, the objectivity of its representations, and the possibility of arresting static moments of fast and even the fastest movements—these represent the greatest and most obvious advantages over every other medium of expression.[10]

Likewise, when Renger-Patzsch emphasizes that only photography is fully able to capture "the all too quickly fading formal beauty of flowers or to reproduce the dynamism in the realm of modern technology"[11] or "to do justice to modern technology's rigid linear structure, to the lofty gridwork of cranes and bridges, to the dynamism of machines operating at one thousand horsepower,"[12] he is contributing to a discourse linking photography's exactitude and speed to the modern technology it is best able to represent, effectively situating the mechanical both in and in front of the camera. To be sure, these various excerpts come from texts that are sometimes closer to enthusiastic boosterism than to cogent analysis, and it would be misguided to fault texts in this genre too severely with rhetorical imprecision. But it also matters that these claims are not as simple or straightforward as they may seem. Renger-Patzsch is not just claiming that the technical capabilities of the camera make it possible to freeze movement too quick for the human eye to see, even if this claim, though by no means new in the 1920s, was still an important part of the photographic discourse of the time. The presence of fading flowers and the suggestion that something about photography is best suited even for modern, technological subjects that are not in motion—the rigid linear structure and lofty gridwork—give a hint that more is at stake in the new ways of seeing associated with photography during the Weimar Republic.

There are other good reasons why the photography of the period continues to be associated with the categories of objectivity, precision, speed, and modernity. New Objectivity (*Neue Sachlichkeit*), a rubric under which much of the German cultural production of the mid-1920s is organized, has helped corral these associations with photography. In photography, New Objectivity is understood, in terms both of its subject matter and its style, as an unfrilled, sharply focused approach to everyday objects and views that had previously lain outside the purview of aesthetic representation or the category of the beautiful.[13] These traits are certainly exemplified by the work of August Sander and Karl Blossfeldt. But New Objectivity, which was also used to categorize paintings and literary works, cannot be understood outside of the context of contemporary crises of representation per se. Yet, as Pepper Stetler has shown in her work on Albert Renger-Patzsch and the Auriga Press and archive, the exclusive attention to the aesthetic values (such as unconventional viewing angles, the isolation of relevant details, the emphasis on significant forms) associated with the photography of New Objectivity could also sunder these values from the concrete social and institutional settings that produced them.[14] Viewed in this light, the praise of photography's speed and exactitude, and even photography's association with New Objectivity, seems at least partly fetishistic. Between the microcosmic and macrocosmic praises of photographic vision—between, that is, the isolation within the individual image of such possibilities of photographic vision as camera angle, close-up, unconventional framing, and sharpness of detail, on the one hand, and their symbolic and enthusiastic elevation to a worldview that sees the camera's possibilities and the experience of modern life as isomorphic, on the other—the whole middle ground of embedded photographic practices of production, circulation, and reception within their specific discursive, social, and institutional contexts goes missing.

The picture that emerges when we consider contexts of media, genre, and disciplinary borrowings is a different one. A closer look at some of the ways in which photographers and writers in Weimar were producing and writing about photography suggests that, in addition to serving as a symbol of speed, mechanicity, objectivity, and modernity, photography of the 1920s also often privileged biological and natural temporalities over the hurried pace of modern metropolitan life, favored the category of the type over the individual, and embraced truth-to-nature over mechanical objectivity. Scholarship over the last twenty years has done much to recover the various ways in which, theoretically and practically, the photography of the 1920s cannot be separated from other forms and fields of the period. A salutary effect of this work has been to de-fetishize photography, dispelling the New Objective aura of a purely aesthetic or stylistic stance, and linking it to other discourses, disciplines, and practices. Several studies on the Weimar-era photobook and photo essay have brought much-needed attention to the way these new forms inherited and transformed generic conventions of reading, narrative, and montage.[15] Other scholarship has demonstrated the vital interdisciplinarity of Weimar-era photography, as a field that shaped and was shaped by questions of representation, narrative, and experience as they were being posed of and by contemporary literature.[16] And finally, recent work in the history of photography has illuminated the ways in which photographic innovation in the 1920s grew out of a dialogue with modes and models of representation and perception taken from vitalism, science, and technology.[17] This work has shown that the entangled theorizations of photography that emerged during the Weimar Republic cannot be properly understood within the constraints of a single discipline or approach alone, but must be approached in a way that at least strives to approximate the disciplinary promiscuity of the period.

I wish to build on this recent contextualization of Weimar-era photography by tracing out some of the implications of the presence of biology, organicism, vitalism—in short, *life*—in Weimar photography, with an eye towards clarifying its representational assumptions and epistemological aspirations. In particular, I wish to complicate the assumptions that inhere in the association of photography with objectivity and exactitude. August Sander and Karl Blossfeldt alike were after types and forms that necessarily exceeded the frame of the individual image and the particularity of a given object of representation. Their projects consisted in representing the universal instead of the particular, the type instead of the individual, and truth instead of actuality. In this effort they were aided on the one hand by photographic practices that mobilized the compositional and juxtapositional possibilities of the photobook, and by available discourses, metaphors, and visual codes linked to the natural sciences, on the other. Conversely, in linking photography to natural history, Döblin and Kracauer identified in the medium an explosive potential for their own literary and philosophical projects, respectively. And as we will see in chapters 3 and 4, the commitment to a poetics and a vision of modernity premised on the type or the mass, coupled with an explicit rejection of the centrality of the autonomous individual, characterizes the work of Alfred Döblin and Ernst Jünger in the Weimar Republic. Recovering how the period's photography could also be interested in the typological specimen over the individual snapshot will help provide some of the broader context for this literary turn away from the individual.

The approach of this chapter thus differs from that of the other three in this book. Rather than focus on a single text or a single author, this chapter takes up key moments in the artistic and theoretical development of photography in the 1920s in order to examine photography—as medium, idea, trope, epistemological mode, social practice, and discourse of representation—from multiple sides, not in order to level all its articulations to a unified meaning, but instead to highlight the different strategies by which photographers and writers connected photographic meaning to other discourses and media, in ways that might challenge our assumptions about the identification of photography with objectivity during this period. By viewing Weimar photographic theory and practice within the larger interpretive framework of biological modernism, I want to place discussions of photography of the 1920s back into a context that has largely gone missing; it is only by doing so that we might recover the particularly interdisciplinary articulations of modernity and objectivity that photography enabled.

August Sander's Typifying Portraits

> My photographic work—"Human Beings of the Twentieth Century"—which I began in 1910 and which contains approximately 500–600 pictures from which a selection—"The Face of the Time"—appeared in 1929, is basically a declaration of faith in photography as universal language; I attempted to arrive at a physiognomic definition of the German people of the period by means of the chemical and optic, historically developed methods of photography—that is, by the creation of images through the use of light alone.[18]

In this 1931 radio lecture, August Sander declared his "faith in photography as a universal language," linking his photographic project to a physiognomy of the era.[19] The very title of Sander's 1929 photobook, *Face of Our Time* (*Antlitz der Zeit*), situates the collection within a physiognomic discourse that attributes meaning to appearance. Historically associated with figures such as Johann Casper Lavater and Cesare Lombroso, the discourse of physiognomy was premised on the idea that the appearance of individuals' faces reveals something of their character—put more broadly, that essence manifests itself through appearance.[20] Moreover, Sander's physiognomic and narrative claims are perhaps all the more striking in retrospect since they're no longer really true, as the historical conditions of the images' legibility have disappeared. As pointed out by Sabine Hake and Matthias Uecker, the physiognomic discourse that grounded the meaning of the images relied on the contemporary social consensus and representational codes that enabled the images to stand in for a type, social group, or historical narrative.[21] They are far less legible to contemporary viewers unversed in the visible signs of Weimar society. In other words, there is an unresolved tension between the aspiration to universality, on the one hand, and the particularity of the context of the images' production and reception, on the other. For Sander's portraits to be recognizable as historically specific types, the viewer already needs to be versed in the sociological, cultural, and historical contours of the era—the knowledge that was supposed to be (universally) communicated by the images is thus presupposed by them.

Yet the tension that interests me is a somewhat different one, and concerns both the ideas of history and the reading practices that might be entailed by Sander's work. Sander's radio lecture granted physiognomic photography access to historical and political knowledge, yet this knowledge is largely expressive, and fraught with moral significance.[22] "More than anything else, physiognomy means an understanding of human nature . . . When we meet a person for the first time we get an impression—that he is good or evil, that we feel attracted or repelled, that we feel spiritual kinship or do not."[23] In this understanding of physiognomy, a person's face is expressive of her or his individual moral nature. As we will see, this understanding of physiognomy can map onto a sequential, essentially Spenglerian understanding of history as organized in terms of the rises and falls of cultures. Indeed, Sander was interested in the work of Oswald Spengler, and George Baker has recovered his indebtedness to Spengler and the Spenglerian intentions behind the sequential narrative option of *Face of Our Time*. This understanding of history relies upon a narrative form that is both linear (because the sequence of images expresses a historical sequence) and cyclical (because the historical sequence is subject to repetition). Yet Sander's images could also be read according to a different understanding of physiognomy, one which reads faces not as expressive of an individual, inner moral essence but rather as bearing imprints from the outside—the marks of history and experience.

This different understanding of physiognomy, exemplified by Alfred Döblin's essay "Faces, Images, and Their Truth," in turn suggests an alternative notion of natural history beholden neither to a sequential reading practice nor to a narrative of decline. Natural history in Döblin's use depends not upon a metaphor of organic growth and decline, but rather upon a comparison between photography and comparative anatomy, a discipline concerned with the relationships between visible form, distinct types, development, and history.

After examining a few examples from Sander's book, in order to delineate how the representational strategies and ambiguities of *Face of Our Time* already generate a tension between individualizing and typifying readings, I will suggest that this tension extends to the relationship between the individual images and the book's larger narrative structure, which is produced by the images at the same time as it renders them legible as the kinds of images that would support such a structure. I will then turn to Döblin's typological realism and the comparative reading practice it requires in order to suggest why it matters that the invocation of natural history offers more than one paradigm for reading Sander's book. Ultimately, Döblin's praise of Sander's "comparative photography" and "photographic realism" has much to do with Döblin's own epic, anti-individual poetics and, more broadly, with the ways in which contemporary theories of aesthetic representation straddled disciplines and media, to the extent that Döblin could, for example, invoke biology to discuss photography in the service of a poetics that mainly unfolded in literary texts.

Just as the face of a person is, according to physiognomy, a legible text that speaks a truth about the character of the person, Sander's portraits represent types, occupations, and professions, thus revealing the deeper truths of historical and social structures. In contrast to another popular contemporary practitioner of photographic physiognomy, Hans Günther (known for works like his 1922 *Racial Science of the German People*), Sander did not draw on the comparative possibilities of the grid, nor was he interested in racial types.[24] Rather, *Face of Our Time* situates its sixty sequential plates each on its own full-page spread, grouping them according to a logic that leads the viewer through social and historical moments—farmers, rural petty bourgeoisie, small-town inhabitants, proletarians, staid middle-class families, professionals, wealthy businessmen, cultural figures, and urban poor. The people in the photographs tend to face the camera from the center of the frame. In contrast to much prior studio portrait photography with backdrops that tended to ensconce the individual, here the background is typically a neutral backdrop or a natural setting free of clutter; often, emblematic gestures or implements serve to reinforce the captions' assignment of the subjects to specific classes or professions.[25] In this project of typification, it is not just the images that de-individuate their subjects. The captions, in naming the serial images according to their profession, occupation, or class, are essential. Occasionally, as in the portrait of a masterfully dour Paul Hindemith, an

Photography's Natural Histories in the Weimar Republic

Figure 1. August Sander, *Face of Our Time*, plate 52: "The Composer P.H. Copyright © Die Photographische Sammlung / SK Stiftung Kultur – August Sander Archiv, Cologne / ARS, NY 2019

image will give the sitter's initials, but this elision only further emphasizes his profession: "The Composer P.H." (figure 1).

The subjects of *Face of Our Time* are further typified by the various relationships among multiple images, along various axes. As readers of the volume, we may page through it sequentially, noting the gradual changes that occur within and between the thematic groupings. We may flip around at random, linking distant images by virtue of thematically similar subject matter; portraits depicting mothers and children, for example. In some cases, a group photograph will foreground the otherwise implicitly multiple nature of the type, while in others an expressive abundance of gesture will carry the weight of the intended synecdochal representation of an absent group. Analogies come readily to mind, too, between sitters, implements, and backgrounds: the baker is to his bowl as the interior decorator is to his hammer, and the farmers are to their forest as the small-town couple is to their wall, as the bourgeois family is to their villa, as the doctor is to his clinic.

Sometimes the typifying narrative is carried forward by the sequence of images and the implied linkages among them. Plate 23 depicts a man carrying a load of bricks (figure 2). The connection to the idea of labor is iconic enough that the image serves not only as the cover image of the reprint of *Face of Our Time*, but also as the cover of the Penguin Classics edition of Marx's *Grundrisse*. The idea of work and the plain, confrontational stance carries over to the next image, titled simply "Communist Leader," which depicts a figure with clenched fists and a resolute mien, details corralled into significance by the image's title (figure 3). The subsequent image shows us a group of men seated on a brick stoop (figure 4). The photograph, titled simply "Revolutionaries," does not suggest any particularly revolutionary actions—the three men appear relaxed, slouching even, and their position in the lower half of the frame defies any expectations of heroic verticality one might expect from the title. The overlap of shoulder, arms, hands, and gazes conveys the sense that they are a closed unit. The frank, intelligent gaze of the middle figure manages to be both magnified and contained by the crossed gazes of the flanking figures. The brick stoop echoes the bricks carried by the bricklayer two images previous, cementing the association of labor and revolution. But without further information, the revolutionary dimension of this picture would seem to be lightly ironized by the title, composition, and position of the image, as a rebelliousness contained in its proper place in the social totality. This relativization of revolutionary as an occupation and personality type would seem to be confirmed by the following image, a group of diffidently curious "working students" in a configuration that, as in the previous image, tightens the grouping within the picture in order to suggest a group unity that is both open and closed to the images around it and the viewer facing it (figure 5). The movement of titles away from the brief political interlude (that is, from "communist leader" to "revolutionaries" to "working students") is sealed as "the herbal medicine expert" sets us off on another series consisting of roles and professions, thus both marking and dissolving the thematic coherence of this leftist grouping.

Yet the identities of some of the people in these images might complicate their assignment to a leveling framework in which all social roles, from revolutionary to herbalist, are equivalent. The communist leader is Paul Frölich, a prominent member of the German Communist Party in the 1920s, participant in the Munich Council Republic in the spring of 1919, and the biographer of Rosa Luxemburg. The middle figure in the group of revolutionaries is Erich Mühsam, an anarchist writer and activist who played a leading role in the Munich Council Republic, was arrested by the National Socialists on the night of the Reichstag fire, and was murdered by the SS in the Oranienburg concentration camp in 1934. The figures on his right and left, respectively, are Alois Lindner and Guido Kopp, leftist activists involved in revolutionary organizing at the end of the First World War in Bavaria, both of whom spent most of the 1920s in prison. The typifying captions therefore would seem to pose two difficulties. On the one hand they seem too coy, withholding what they ostensibly share. The histories of these "revolutionaries," for example, are both rich and contingent. Mühsam's expression might invoke, with generous understatement, some of the dense and tragic history of the German Left in the 1910s and 1920s, but only provided one knows who Erich Mühsam is in the first place. The other difficulty posed by these captions is that they

Figure 2. *Face of Our Time*, plate 23: "Odd-Job Man." Copyright © Die Photographische Sammlung / SK Stiftung Kultur – August Sander Archiv, Cologne / ARS, NY 2019

Figure 3. *Face of Our Time*, plate 24: "Communist Leader." Copyright © Die Photographische Sammlung / SK Stiftung Kultur – August Sander Archiv, Cologne / ARS, NY 2019

Figure 4. *Face of Our Time*, plate 25: "Revolutionaries." Copyright © Die Photographische Sammlung / SK Stiftung Kultur – August Sander Archiv, Cologne / ARS, NY 2019

Figure 5. *Face of Our Time*, plate 26: "Working Students." Copyright © Die Photographische Sammlung / SK Stiftung Kultur – August Sander Archiv, Cologne / ARS, NY 2019

level all social roles, making them equivalent to each other. The problem with this is that the selection of captions and social roles rigs the interpretive game in advance, foreclosing the narrative that the images are supposed to convey and flattening the social landscape they were to bring to life. The inclusion of "revolutionary" as a profession within a social totality whose complete dismantling and restructuring is ostensibly the revolutionary's defining function is thus both funny and sad—the revolutionaries are both honored and tamed by being included in this way. Furthermore, the various titles suggest a mutual exclusivity—why can one not be an unemployed farmer? a bricklaying revolutionary? and so on—which supports a linear, historical narrative.

This leveling movement in which all social roles are essentially equivalent thus operates within a narrative framework that intended to offer a social history. George Baker has charted Sander's interest in Oswald Spengler's theory of the growth and decline of civilizations. In this light, *Face of Our Time*, which was to be but a small preview of a much larger, never-completed project called *People of the Twentieth Century (Menschen des 20. Jahrhunderts)*, was to present the reader with a cyclical narrative of growth, decline, and decay, depicting German society's emergence from a bucolic past into the cultural flourishing of modernity, and thence down into the chaotic uncertainties of the present and the unknown future.[26] This narrative, which draws on the analogy to biological growth and decay, might seem at first glance to fit well with Döblin's claim that Sander's comparative photography offers "superb material for the cultural, class, and economic history of the last thirty years,"[27] yet, as we will see, Döblin's reading of Sander's book is far from a narrative of decline. Quite the contrary: the movement away from the individual towards the type, which Döblin sees *Face of Our Time* as exemplifying, was for Döblin a desirably modern tendency of what he elsewhere dubbed the "Naturalistic Age." Far from a discourse of cultural pessimism associated with physiognomy as the expression of an individual inner essence, Döblin will read these faces as bearing the imprints and erosions of social forces— and this inversion of physiognomy, in turn, is inseparable from Döblin's epic, mass poetics, discussed in the next chapter. My point in introducing these various assessments of Sander's typological photography is not to adjudicate between them, but rather to open the possibility of a critical wedge. I suggest that the diversity of possible appraisals of Sander's photography within the same terrain—a discourse of types—demonstrates how ambiguous, dense, and central the idea of the type was. These photographs could only enable a typified meaning because of a contemporary discursive context marked by a broad turn from the individual to the type, on the one hand, and the availability of master narratives that portrayed history as natural history, on the other.

Even in their own context the images were laden with ambiguity. The individual images and the larger narratives and discourses within which they are located may well determine each other, but they do not do so unambiguously. In drawing on a master narrative of natural history, for example, an interpretation of a photographic project inherits the ambivalences that come with this narrative, which can emphasize growth and decadence (as in Spengler) or a vital, elemental force that underlies technological modernity (as in Döblin's conception). As Döblin writes, these images provide the material for multiple narratives.[28] Moreover, the logic of typification implied by this version of physiognomy contains another ambiguity: the narrative about modern society depends on legible *differences* between the images and their assignment to different social, historical groups, but this historical narrative also aims at an aggregate effect in order to represent the face of the times; in other words, it is both the differences among the various images and their cumulative similarity as a group portrait of an era that matter. Alfred Döblin's brief, idiosyncratic essay on *Face of Our Time* can help open up some of these ambiguities surrounding the visual representation of an era. If one reads Döblin's essay in the contexts of his epic poetics and his writing on modernity, a different notion of natural history and a different practice of reading photographs suggest themselves.

Döblin on Photographic Realism and Comparative Photography

In his short prefatory essay to August Sander's book, titled "Faces, Images, and Their Truth," Döblin singles out Sander's work as an exception to the widespread mediocrity of photographers who are after the verisimilitude of visual detail. The counterintuitive terms in which Döblin praises Sander's exceptionality offer an alternative paradigm for thinking about photographic discourse in the Weimar Republic. Before even mentioning Sander's book, which he finally does about three-quarters of the way through his essay, Döblin invokes the medieval debate between realism and nominalism in order to make a point about representation. In his compact summary of the competing positions, he writes: "The Nominalists took the view that only individual objects are genuinely real and existent. The Realists, by contrast, held that only generalities, universals—a genus, for example, or an idea, were actually real and existent."[29] Where photography, with its lauded capacities to freeze the individual moment, the random detail, or the indexical trace may seem predisposed towards nominalism, Döblin's praise for Sander is actually a praise of Sander's realism—that is, his ability to exceed the depiction of individuals and particulars. Döblin's essay can help us understand some of the ways in which photography was seen as a typological form of representation akin to tendencies within the natural sciences. By the same token, reading "Faces, Images, and Their Truth" within the context of biological modernism will show how Sander's photography offered Döblin a way to link his epic poetics and critique of the individual across media and discourses.

In order to bring this distinction between nominalism and realism to bear on the question of portraiture, Döblin briefly considers a photographic collection of death masks. While Döblin does not mention the volume by name, it seems clear that he is referring to Ernst Benkard's 1927 *The Eternal Visage (Das ewige Antlitz)*.³⁰ Death, as written on the faces of figures ranging from Frederick the Great to the young girl known as "L'Inconnue de la Seine," has erased the accidental, momentary impressions, leaving a visible access to truth beyond mere particulars. Through a process that Döblin likens to erosion, the momentary expressions of the human face have been erased, leaving only the "human face *en bloc*."³¹ In Döblin's terms, the truth left after the erosive forces of death have cleared away the particulars is the triumph of realism over nominalism. "The immense burden of momentary existence, of change and alteration, has been erased from these faces. Death has carried out a massive retouching operation."³² Aside from the specifically photographic metaphor of "retouching," we should not overlook the inversion of physiognomy that Döblin introduces here—it is not an inner essence expressing itself on the face from within, but an erasure that comes from the outside. Yet it is not just death that is able to bring out the veracity of the human face. The forces of society, class, and history also share these powers of creative erosion. Turning from the death masks to Sander's book, Döblin draws a parallel between the erosive powers of death and those of social life:

> Now there is another folder in front of me, one with images of living people who have not yet fallen into the great tub in which their personalities and all activities are washed away from them [i.e., death]. The water that polishes these stones can still be seen on them. They are still rolling in the sea that rocks us all about. And while what overwhelmingly confronts us in the death masks is the one monotonous anonymity . . . , here we are looking at: individuals? Strange. You would think you were looking at individuals. But suddenly—one finds that even here one is not actually looking at individuals. . . . We are now talking about the astonishing flattening of faces and images by human society, by classes, by their level of culture.³³

This praise is flatly incompatible with any version of physiognomy that sees the face as expressive of an inner essence. What interests Döblin in Sander's faces are the erosions and imprints that come from without (the "water that polishes these stones"), rather than the essence that expresses itself from within. In a way that recalls his theory of the epic, Döblin's discussion of photographic realism makes it clear that this is a form of representation that privileges the type and the mass over the isolated, autonomous individual. Compared to what he sees as the unfortunate proliferation of nominalist photographers—those whose approach to verisimilitude seizes on personal, private, and unique details of their subjects—photographic realism as practiced by Sander is able to show the truth of the type.³⁴

As Döblin writes, Sander's "mind, his powers of observation, his knowledge, and not least his enormous photographic ability" are able to bring out the truth of an age through an aesthetic strategy that both reflects and captures the fundamental processes of that age.[35] If it is the "sea that rocks us all about" that is responsible for the anonymity of Sander's subjects, it is Sander's visual idiom that bestows this social erosion of the individual with a representative capacity. While the claim that the typical nature of these faces was brought about through the erosive, leveling vicissitudes of society, class, and history would seem to suggest that the photographer only has to record these eloquent faces for their representative potential to be made visible, Döblin's distinction between "nominalist" and "realist" photographers, and his assignment of Sander to the latter category, hints that Sander's camera itself plays a guiding role in visual typification.

And indeed, Döblin likens Sander's photographic practice to a science rather than an art: "Just as there is a comparative anatomy, through which one can arrive at a conception of the nature and history of organs, so this photographer has practiced comparative photography and has thus achieved a scientific viewpoint above the photographers of detail."[36] By likening Sander's photography to comparative anatomy, Döblin invokes a specific history of biology associated, among other things, with the Darwinian theory of evolution. In addition to describing a methodology capable of reconstructing the evolutionary history of particular organs and organisms in general (think of the beaks of Darwin's finches), comparative anatomy also had deep connections to various conceptions of taxonomy and natural history, and was indeed part of the German reception of Darwinian evolutionary theory advanced by Ernst Haeckel and Carl Gegenbaur at Jena in the 1860s and 1870s. In Haeckel's and Gegenbaur's hands, comparative anatomy linked form to development—in the dual sense of the development of individuals ("ontogeny") and the development of species ("phylogeny").[37] Döblin, who had more than a passing knowledge of contemporary biology through his medical studies at the universities of Berlin and Freiburg, thus precisely invoked *the* biological discourse that probed the visual forms of animals in order to recover the history and laws of formation and development.[38] As Lynn Nyhart writes, "the comparative anatomists sought to explain the human form by means of evolution."[39] Döblin's understanding of Sander's photography could be put in the same terms, only reversed, so that Sander's images explain evolution—that is, historical and social development—by means of the human form. Seen in this way, *Face of Our Time* is more a narrative of speciation and differentiation than a tale of rise and decline. Physiognomy understood in terms of the legible expression of an inner essence, therefore, was not the only discourse available for linking visible form to development and history, nor was an organic pattern of growth and decline the only model of natural history available for understanding history.

Moreover, Döblin's comparison suggests something important about photography as a practice of reading. The comparative photographer must be able to select and arrange his subjects—that is, he must be able to read them—in order to make their distinct features stand out, so that the "cultural, class, and economic history of the last thirty years" is rendered legible for the viewer.[40] The kind of legibility that Döblin identifies in Sander's work does not depend on the accidentals of an image or the uniqueness of its subject, which Döblin explicitly condemns as belonging to "nominalist" photography. Rather, the analogy between photography and comparative anatomy suggests that the viewer can (and must) identify the typical features that can locate a specimen within its socioeconomic and historical niche. Döblin praises Sander's work as a photography of types, not individuals.

As a typological, comparative reading practice, Döblin's notion of photography entails two interesting consequences, one pertaining to genre, the other to form. First, the need for comparison is necessarily a need for multiple images. For Döblin, the relevant generic unit of photography is not the photograph but the set of photographs. Adequate knowledge of a society which both de-individuates faces as does death and anonymizes them in class-specific ways can only be provided by the comparative collection of images—the photobook, in this case. In invoking comparative anatomy while discussing a photobook, Döblin implicitly links the photobook to visual forms and practices within the natural sciences, particularly the scientific atlas and the comparative grid. The scientific atlas traditionally both advanced an argument about classification or development in visual form, and defined the very discipline and disciplinary practices it supported. Lorraine Daston and Peter Galison define an atlas as "any compendium of images intended to be definitive for a community of practitioners"; atlases define disciplines by "aim[ing] to 'map' the territory of the sciences they serve."[41] In a similar way, the Weimar era photobook or photo essay sought to define the scope of photography while also training its reader in a certain kind of photographic vision and advancing an argument about the world. Just as comparative anatomy offered Döblin a useful methodological parallel that allowed him to allege a link between visible form and a history of development in Sander's images, so too did the genre of the scientific atlas offer a way of thinking about genre, and particularly about how collections of images work together to define a field, train a kind of vision, and make substantive claims about the world. The collection of images, bound in codex form, thus already had a well-known precedent in the scientific atlas. This lineage complicates assumptions about photography's novelty, and this context matters because it was precisely through the narrative, syntactic, and juxtapositional possibilities opened up by the form of the photo essay and photographic book that August Sander's and Karl Blossfeldt's photobooks could lay claim to a meaning that they located in types and forms that transcended the individual image.

And secondly, the idea of comparative photography raises the question of form, as something that links aesthetics, biology, and history. Döblin thereby points to an aspect that is implicit in Sander's photography, one which Blossfeldt's work will make explicit. Form or morphology in comparative anatomy is a visible difference that indicates a history of formation. We are far from the mechanical analogy that sees in the camera's speed a suitable response to the acceleration of modern life. For Döblin, Sander's photographic practice is able to access a different relationship to time—not the fleeting moment, but the history of development itself. This temporality relies upon a particular kind of interdisciplinarity that characterizes Weimar-era photographic discourse. Between scientific illustration and photography, there was a language available for making claims about the type in light of the individual specimen. The truth of the individual photograph, in this case, is less a question of its indexicality and supposed immediacy than its capacity to represent a type within the context of a complex historical narrative that aspires to the scale and scope of a natural history.

Döblin's praise allows us to understand Sander's images better, but it also shines a light on his own aesthetic project. Döblin saw in Sander's photography the kind of typifying vision that he was after in his own developing project of epic poetics, where the emphasis was not on these particular types in their own right, but as a broader project of de-individuation and de-psychologization.[42] Epic representation, in these terms, is after the historical linkages connecting individuals to the leveling forces of "human society, . . . class distinctions, . . . the cultural attainments of each class."[43] The kind of representation that would be able to locate the social and the historical in the individual face is, moreover, intermedial—because it is located among the connections between images and words, stories and pictures—as well as interdisciplinary, because comparative anatomy provides a model for comparative photography and comparative sociology, and history here takes its form from natural history.

But what kind of natural history is this, and how must it be read? Comparative anatomy, in evoking evolutionary history, does not necessarily suggest that the book be read as a linear sequence, but rather as a proliferation of morphologies whose differences from each other—rather than the passage from one to the next—is what can access historical knowledge. In other words, the idea of comparative photography does not necessarily entail a sequential reading of these images, implying a picture of modernity as a fall from bucolic grace. Rather, Döblin's conception is closer to Benjamin's and Brecht's calls for analytical photography, for photography as a visual and political aid to navigating a present that is complexly articulated and nonsynchronously layered.[44] These are two different kinds of reading, and two different kinds of natural history. On the one hand, physiognomy as the expression of an inner essence, a sequential reading, and a Spenglerian narrative of decline. On the other hand, traits shaped by external forces, a comparative, nonlinear reading, and a more complex, non-teleological, open-ended narrative of development. These are contraries, although they are also both made possible through biological metaphors and narratives. Döblin's comparison of Sander's photography to comparative anatomy can also help open up the concept of physiognomy, suggesting a way in which it might function not as the expression of an inner essence, but as the legible record of historical processes that make their mark on the subject from the outside. The ambiguities contained in Sander's project and its contemporary reception indicate the discursive space within which discussions of photography took place. What links a Spenglerian reading of *Face of Our Time* as a portrait of a society on the wane to Döblin's more optimistic assessment of Sander's "comparative photography" is that both focus on the camera's (and the photobook's) ability to typify and thus to exceed individual, particular details in order to represent a longer time frame. Karl Blossfeldt's collection of plant photographs, *Art Forms in Nature*, likewise privileges typification and classification over capturing the fleeting moment. Like Sander's work, Blossfeldt's photography complicates the very category of objectivity to which it is often consigned. Unlike Sander's portraits, however, at stake in Blossfeldt's work is not social history, rendered legible on the human face, but rather form and formative potential as such.

Karl Blossfeldt, "Ur-Forms," and Botanical Modernism

"Whether we accelerate the growth of a plant through time-lapse photography or show its form in forty-fold enlargement, in either case a geyser of new image-worlds hisses up at points in our existence where we would least have thought them possible."[45] Karl Blossfeldt's plant photographs serve Walter Benjamin in this 1928 review of *Art Forms in Nature* as a model for the idea of the "optical unconscious," a concept that would come to be important for Benjamin's understanding of the revolutionary potential of film.[46] In Benjamin's better known 1931 essay, "Little History of Photography," he would return to Blossfeldt as a model of a kind of photography capable of revealing unsuspected "image worlds, which dwell in the smallest things."[47] As one of the possibilities opened up by the technical apparatus of photography, extreme magnification made images and visual correspondences available to perception.

In the context of the photography associated with New Objectivity, during a decade when the entire world seemed to be made available by the camera, Blossfeldt's meticulous images of the previously invisible quickly came to stand in for photography's capacity for objective representation.[48] While his focus on the primal forms of nature was seen to blur the boundaries between the organic and the manmade, the capacity to locate these hidden analogies in the first place was itself understood as mechanical, objective, for it was precisely the optical abilities of the camera and the chemical potential of the light-sensitive medium that enabled these unseen views of nature to record themselves. Yet what I wish to explore in this section is the possibility that objectivity might not be the best framework for thinking about these images in their context. The identification of these plant images as *Ur-forms* depends on strategies of selection, emphasis, and syntactical arrangement, all of which require careful photographic and editorial intervention. Drawing on Lorraine Daston and Peter Galison's history of scientific objectivity, I want to suggest that truth-to-nature—an older model of scientific representation that depended on the evaluating and selecting eye of a practiced observer—better describes the project of *Art Forms in Nature* than does the idea of objectivity. More exactly, I want to ask whether truth-to-nature might help us better understand what people in the 1920s sometimes meant when they spoke of objectivity. Blossfeldt's book, located at the discursive crossroads of contemporary traffic in images, a history of scientific representation, and ideas about visual form, evinces an aesthetic commitment that was less interested in the faithful documentation of individual specimens than in the identification of shared forms that underpin these specimens. Moreover, the way of reading Blossfeldt's plant images proposed by Benjamin suggests that we should see in these magnified plant photographs not just a typology of forms, but the recapitulation of organic formative potential as such. Thus, it is not just that his pictures of plants blurred the boundaries between the organic and the artificial by evoking architectural motifs—to Benjamin, at least, they suggested a notion of aesthetic creation understood as a generative force of nature, which underlies both nature and culture.

Karl Blossfeldt was inducted into the photographic canon relatively late in his career. He began photographing in 1896, and his photographic output before the 1928 publication of *Urformen der Kunst* (misleadingly but irrevocably translated as *Art Forms in Nature*, a title I'll stick to here for the sake of simplicity) served as an aesthetic form of botanical specimen-gathering in order to provide the raw material for art instruction, informed by the idea that archetypal forms could be identified in the natural world, forms that gave both meaning to nature and impulse to culture. This conception of *Ur-Formen* was made possible most immediately by Moritz Meurer, Blossfeldt's teacher at the Berliner Kunstgewerbliche Lehranstalt, but it also hearkened back to the architect and theorist Gottfried Semper, who in the mid-nineteenth century proposed the existence, in both nature and culture, of underlying prototypical Ur-forms (*Urformen*),[49] and to the evolutionary monism of the naturalist Ernst Haeckel.[50] Indeed, Blossfeldt's title is a modification of Haeckel's well-known 1904 work *Kunstformen der Natur* (*Art Forms of Nature*). Mia Fineman has shown how, within this context, Blossfeldt's images were taken as visible evidence of the existence of "functional form," in a way that reconciled organic nature and modern technology.[51] In 1889 Blossfeldt took the academic position, newly created for him, of "Modeling from living plants."[52] The leap from the world of art pedagogy to art happened with Blossfeldt's discovery by Karl Nierendorf in 1926. The 1928 publication of *Art Forms in Nature* and Blossfeldt's inclusion in the 1929 "FiFo" ("Film and Photography") exhibition in Stuttgart cemented his status as a pioneer of New Objective photography.[53]

Art Forms in Nature draws on multiple kinds of seriality, repetition, and juxtaposition at various scales in order to teach the viewer to see these botanical photographs as instances of Ur-forms. Blossfeldt was able to isolate the desired forms in several ways: by carefully preparing his specimens, trimming interfering details, stuffing them and propping them up on dowels where necessary, by photographing them against a flat, neutral background, by magnifying the images at two to thirty-two times their original size, by carefully cropping them in order to zero in on the salient shapes and rhythms, and by arranging strong lines of the plant specimens along the major axes of the image, among other tactics. Multiple images of different plant species placed side-by-side often constitute a single numbered plate (figures 6, 7), evoking the collective resemblance of a group of family portraits or the implicit narrative of a triptych. The form is often emphasized by multiple specimens within the same image being repeated in different positions (figures 8, 9). Given the presence of distinct species within the same plate, it is clear (as has often been noted) that the goal is not botanical rigor but identifying formal possibilities. The viewer's eye is directed towards the salient formal feature by means of symmetries, triads, twists, and turns, or by carefully repetitive arrangements, as of a wallpaper pattern (figures 10, 11). The isolation of relevant forms depends not just on their insistent repetition within the single image or plate, but on the movement between plates, where the slow work of variation helps emphasize a given form by locating it in a comparative framework with other forms; as with Sander's *Face of Our Time*, the relevant unit here is not the individual image or specimen but the group, the sequence, the photobook.

The composition of individual images thus cannot be understood apart from the syntactical logics that ordered their arrangement and facilitated their comparison. This entwinement of individual form and image within the supporting context of other forms and images, in turn, has implications for the spatial and temporal aspects of reading Blossfeldt's book. In the Ur-form, the idea of vital growth itself is made visible by the vast architectonic experience of wandering, "like Lilliputians," in Walter Benjamin's phrase, among the frozen forms.[54] The arrangement of images on the page, in recalling recognizable forms such as the triptych, evokes a narrative organization, as opposed to a merely juxtapositional or serial one. In my experience, for example, students asked to write about these images have drawn on available narratives ranging from the seasons of the year to the seasons of life, with stages from birth to full vitality to death and decay, in order to try to describe the logic of the various arrangements.

But even before the syntactical and comparative elements of *Art Forms in Nature* work to identify the Ur-forms, Blossfeldt's photographic process involved careful selection and manipulation in order to make the forms

Figure 6. Karl Blossfeldt, *Art Forms in Nature*, plate 9: *Callicarpa dichotoma, Fraxinus ornus, Cornus pubescens*. Copyright © Karl Blossfeldt Archiv / Ann and Jürgen Wilde / Cologne, Germany / Artists Rights Society (ARS), NY.

Figure 7. *Art Forms in Nature*, plate 17: *Cornus nuttallii, Cornus florida, Acer pennsylvanicum*. Copyright © Karl Blossfeldt Archiv / Ann and Jürgen Wilde / Cologne, Germany / Artists Rights Society (ARS), NY.

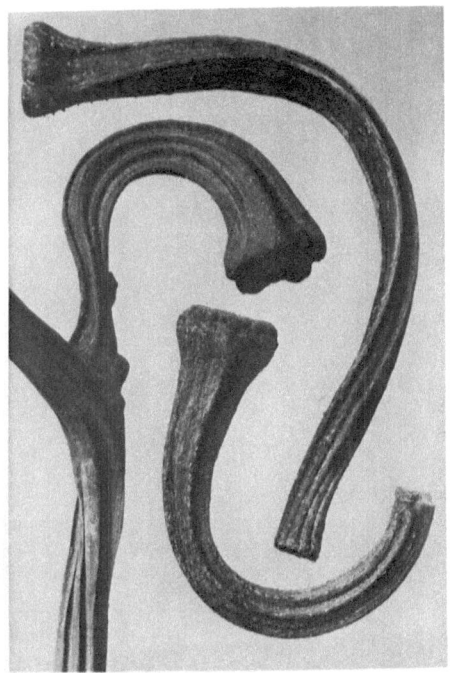

Figure 8. *Art Forms in Nature*, plate 26: *Cucurbita*. Copyright © Karl Blossfeldt Archiv / Ann and Jürgen Wilde / Cologne, Germany / Artists Rights Society (ARS), NY.

Figure 9. *Art Forms in Nature*, plate 27: *Cajophora lateritia, Loasaceae*. Copyright © Karl Blossfeldt Archiv / Ann and Jürgen Wilde / Cologne, Germany / Artists Rights Society (ARS), NY.

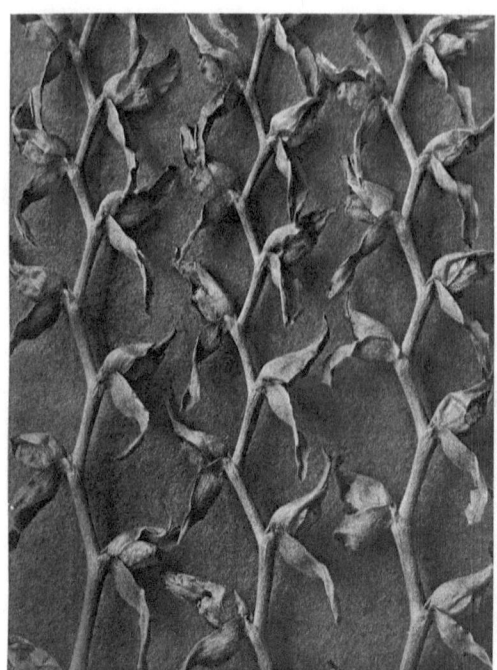

Figure 10. *Art Forms in Nature*, plate 174: *Tritonia x crocosmiflora (Iridaceae)*. Copyright © Karl Blossfeldt Archiv / Ann and Jürgen Wilde / Cologne, Germany / Artists Rights Society (ARS), NY.

Figure 11. *Art Forms in Nature*, plate 175: *Hordeum distichon*. Copyright © Karl Blossfeldt Archiv / Ann and Jürgen Wilde / Cologne, Germany / Artists Rights Society (ARS), NY.

visible in the first place. As the 2000 publication of his contact sheets under the title *Working Collages* (*Arbeitscollagen*) makes plain, Blossfeldt's botanical specimens were painstakingly selected and staged so that they would resemble the forms they were supposed to represent. Before the image was captured, the plants were often cut, trimmed, propped up on dowels, and held in place with string, modeling paste, or nails.[55] After the negative was made, the photographic prints were often retouched by hand.[56] Comparisons between the contact sheets and the photographs printed in *Art Forms in Nature* often show further enlargement, in order to isolate relevant details and eliminate undesirable branches or other elements (often marked in the working collages with an X). If the process of selection and arrangement that is apparent in *Art Forms in Nature* is not enough to dispel the association between New Objectivity (as embodied by Blossfeldt), on the one hand, and objectivity understood as verisimilitude, mimesis, or indexicality, on the other, the working process revealed in the *Working Collages* makes such an association untenable.[57]

Thus the status of objectivity, which was so central to much discussion of New Objective photography in the Weimar Republic, is fraught in Blossfeldt's work, to say the least. The camera's ability to magnify and exactly reproduce minute details is combined with the deliberate preparation and arrangement of the botanical specimens and the syntactical, narrative possibilities of the photobook, in order to demonstrate an underlying formative drive in nature that can be reclaimed for culture. Juliana Kreinik has shown how Blossfeldt's photography drew on codes of representation from the natural sciences in order to develop an evidentiary aesthetic that bolstered the argument that Ur-forms exist in nature and can be recovered for perception and cultural production.[58] While I agree with this, and with the idea that the "camera's implied objectivity" assists this representational project, it is also worth asking exactly what kind of objectivity is at play here.[59] It seems, upon closer inspection, that the density of aesthetic discourses underlying and drawing on photographic objectivity in Blossfeldt and in the period more generally run the risk of collapsing the very distinctions that the idea of objectivity needs to exist in the first place.

In charting the rise and development of the concept of objectivity in the natural sciences, Lorraine Daston and Peter Galison have contrasted the nineteenth-century idea of objectivity with the eighteenth-century ideal of truth-to-nature. Both "epistemic virtues" carried with them a particular rigor and discipline needed for the scientific subject to accurately represent the object of knowledge.[60] Where they differed was in their identification of the object of scientific knowledge—the truth discerned behind the mess of particulars, on the one hand, and the object freed from any interference on the part of the observing subject, on the other. These different objects in turn entailed different strategies of representation. Whereas truth-to-nature required the learned intervention of the subject to eliminate the accidentals of a given image in order to allow its exemplary larger truth to become apparent, mechanical objectivity sought to excise precisely this intervention in order to minimize the risk of an unconscious manipulation of the data to conform to preformed hypotheses or images.

> Truth-to-nature and objectivity are both estimable epistemic virtues, but they differ from each other in ways that are consequential for how science is done and what kind of person one must be to do it. Truth came before and remains distinct from objectivity, as the example of Linnaeus testifies. . . . To see like a naturalist required more than just sharp senses: a capacious memory, the ability to analyze and synthesize impressions, as well as the patience and talent *to extract the typical from the storehouse of natural particulars*, were all key qualifications.[61]

Both the goal of Blossfeldt's project—identifying and teaching the viewer to see typical forms—and the way he worked with images, selecting, trimming, and cropping them in order to "extract the typical from the storehouse of natural particulars," resonate with truth-to-nature more strongly than with the non-interventionism of what Daston and Galison dub mechanical objectivity.

Crucially, Daston and Galison emphasize that the difference between truth-to-nature and mechanical objectivity is not equivalent to the difference between drawing and photography.[62] Indeed, many practitioners of photography and microphotography discussed in their book *Objectivity* were after truth-to-nature, and deployed representational strategies that could also apply to Blossfeldt's own work. Wilson Bentley's photographs of snowflakes, for example, created idealized symmetries by "replacing the background, incising the object, snipping the edges, [and] improving the image," in the same way that Blossfeldt sculpted and arranged his specimens before taking their picture.[63] For scientists and image-makers committed to the epistemic virtue of truth-to-nature, such interventions were not deceptions, but necessary to produce the "reasoned images" that would enable the truth of the type to become visible through the accidents and particulars of each individual specimen.[64] Blossfeldt's images were after the clearest possible representation of the visible forms underlying the wild proliferation of actual plants in their original contexts.

By contrast, "nonintervention—not verisimilitude—lay at the heart of mechanical objectivity."[65] This distinction between nonintervention and verisimilitude usefully complicates the often all-too-calcified linkages between New Objectivity and, well, objectivity, since in Blossfeldt's case the mechanical abilities of the camera are deployed in the service of a representational project that is closer to truth-to-nature than to objectivity. The objectivity involved in the New Objectivity, at least in the cases of Blossfeldt and

Sander,[66] is not a matter of simply reproducing what is given, nor does it involve eliminating the photographer-subject from the picture. Rather, these photographers were credited with a discerning eye and a practiced skill capable of identifying, and rendering legible, the types behind the chaotic multiplicity of social or natural history. And indeed, the difference between mechanical objectivity and truth-to-nature maps onto Döblin's use of the distinction between nominalism and realism. Indeed, Daston and Galison use the term "realism" to describe the paradigm of truth-to-nature (though they opt for "naturalism" rather than "nominalism" to describe the focus on the individual object). Describing the atlas makers of the eighteenth and early nineteenth centuries, they write that they "defended the realism—the 'truth-to-nature'—of underlying types and regularities against the naturalism of the individual object, with all its misleading idiosyncrasies."[67] For Döblin too, it is not the accidentals or particulars that a good, realist photographer is able to depict, but rather the truth of the type.

Thus what connects Sander and Blossfeldt, beyond their shared canonization as photographers of New Objectivity and despite the many differences between them, is an ideal of photography that is able to see past the momentary particulars of a given subject in order to identify a salient type. It is a cataloging photographic project that drew on (and was understood by contemporaries in terms of) scientific codes of representation, but this does not mean that objectivity, much less indexicality, is the most relevant category for understanding this transdisciplinary borrowing. Rather, this typological photography bears striking similarities to Daston and Galison's truth-to-nature, in that it is after truth rather than objectivity, *Wahrheit* over *Wirklichkeit*. Both *Face of Our Time* and *Art Forms in Nature* deploy the syntactic and narrative possibilities of the form of the photobook in order to let the individual photograph represent more than it depicts, by virtue both of its difference from other images and its participation in a shared logic of classification.

Blossfeldt's work in *Art Forms in Nature*, by virtue of the processes of selection, manipulation, and arrangement that emphasize the otherwise hidden types over the accidental particulars of any given specimen, is far from views of photography premised upon verisimilitude, indexicality, or the ability to capture the fleeting moment. His realist, typological photography is not after a perfect visual rendering of the object immediately in front of the camera, but rather seeks to create a typology of forms. If one contemporary valence of *Sachlichkeit* (objectivity) hinged on the camera's mimetic capacity for precise visual representation,[68] it seems clear that, while this visual exactitude was crucial to Blossfeldt's method and mode, it alone was not the aim of *Art Forms in Nature*. Rather, this photographic book identified, produced, and trained its viewers to see forms.

Yet it is possible that these meticulous botanical images have an even more complicated relationship to mimesis. Benjamin noted, in his review of *Art Forms in Nature*, that Blossfeldt's images represent not just primal forms, but the process of formation itself. In asking what "Ur-forms" of art might be, Benjamin posits that they would necessarily be "Ur-forms"—and not just forms—of nature itself: "What can this mean, though, but originary forms of nature? Forms, that is, which were never a mere model for art but which were, from the beginning, at work as originary forms in all that was created."[69] The conception of a primal form indicates for Benjamin not just a priority of natural forms over cultural ones (not, that is, natural forms as a "mere model" [*bloßes Vorbild*] for artificial forms), but a formative potential behind everything that comes into being.

> This touches on one of the deepest, most unfathomable forms of the creative, on the variant that was always, above all others, the form of genius, of the creative collective, and of nature. This is the fruitful, dialectical opposite of invention: the *Natura non facit saltus* of the ancients. One might, with a bold supposition, name it the feminine and vegetable principle of life.[70]

Benjamin here inverts the botanical status of Blossfeldt's photographs: plants are not the photographic object or motif, but provide the formative principle of creation as such. In invoking a "feminine and vegetable principle of life," Benjamin's review necessarily complicates what it would mean to think about photographic representation or photographic mimesis. It is no longer the object that is to be represented, but its process of appearing, inasmuch as this allows access to appearance as such—to borrow a formulation from Jacques Rancière, "Miming the act of appearing instead of miming the appearance of characters to whom something happens, or who feel something, is the intoxication of art."[71]

Indeed, at this point, Rancière's essay on the dancer Loïe Fuller and the poet Stéphane Mallarmé might help us understand Blossfeldt's appeal for Benjamin, for Rancière too describes nature as a model for art—not in terms of subject material to be represented, but as the paradigm for the very capacity to produce and appear in the first place.[72] In terms resonant with Benjamin's essay on Blossfeldt, Rancière argues that a Romantic conception of art as *physis* was invoked in Fuller's dance, in Art Nouveau, and in modernism more generally:

> Such was the dream begun by romanticism . . . : that art, instead of imitating objects of physical nature or the passions of human nature, focuses on following its own potential, which is captured in the Greek notion of *physis*: its pure potential to produce and disappear in its production. . . . [Fuller's dance] is pure artifice, a pure encounter between nature and technique—nature unburdened of all the earthly or psychological heavy-handedness that this word can carry; a technique relieved of any associations with the blast furnaces and

voracious machines that the notion might invoke. The two converged during these years in the encounter between movement and light.[73]

Similarly, for Benjamin, the appeal of Blossfeldt's work is not just the way it identifies analogies between cultural and natural forms, but the fact that it makes an underlying, generative force visible, the creative form of nature, which provides a model for creation as such. Reading Benjamin's "vegetable principle of life" alongside Rancière's characterization of *physis* as the pure potential to produce and disappear in its production suggests, in the case of Blossfeldt, that the boundary between nature and culture is not just challenged by the visual analogies revealed by his typological photography, though this remains important. Rather, the fact of aesthetic production itself offers a glimpse into a deeper relationship between nature and artifice, and among modernity, modernism, and primal forms. "The intoxication of art is nature—the passage of the night into forms and the return of forms to the night—recreated by pure artifice."[74]

We seem to have arrived somewhere quite distant from the proper domain of New Objectivity, and Rancière's terms of praise are not ones in which even the most theoretically savvy photographers of the 1920s would be able to recognize their own work or ideas (which largely remained committed to the medium-specific potential of photography). Yet what is useful about Rancière's essay on dance in the context of Blossfeldt is precisely that it undermines the technological and medial fetishization that might otherwise attend to a consideration of New Objective photography. Such investment in the precision and speed of the camera, and the exactitude of lenses and photosensitive negatives and plates, was, to be sure, a major part of the enthusiasm for photography in the 1920s. But, as should be clear by now, this aspect alone cannot help us make sense of what Döblin found worthwhile in Sander's "comparative photography," nor why Blossfeldt's catalog of Ur-forms might have struck such a nerve. Photographic discourse in the 1920s inherently exceeded disciplinary and medial boundaries, and promised access to broader questions of representation, narrative, experience, and history. Blossfeldt's images suggested to Benjamin not just a catalog of forms, but a representation of an underlying process of formation. The Ur-form here moves beyond a flat conception of mimesis as verisimilitude, standing instead for a generative process that stands behind and before what is seen. This possibility—that photography might represent formation as well as reproduce forms—is also at the heart of Döblin's praise of Sander's "comparative photography." As the analogy to biological evolution suggests, Döblin sees *Face of Our Time* as the visible record of decades of social and economic history.

Blossfeldt's work thus fits within an older conception of photography that saw it as the technologically mediated process of nature recording itself. Yet by approaching photographic representation in this way in the context of a period when photographic technology, the actual practices of photographic production and circulation, and the discourse surrounding photography had changed, inextricably tying the medium to ideas of technological modernization and accelerated experience, Blossfeldt's and Sander's biological modernism shifted the terms of the debate, recalibrating the relationship among modernity, photography, and nature.

Kracauer, from Halftone Dots to the Flood of Images

While Siegfried Kracauer's 1927 essay "Photography" takes a very different approach to the medium than we have seen so far, consideration of his essay is a key part of this discussion for two reasons. On the one hand, Kracauer's sophisticated exploration of the relationship between memory and the mass circulation of photographic images also challenges optimistic assumptions about the immediacy, exactitude, and speed of photography as a mode of experience. Kracauer's essay undermines the self-evidence of the photographic image by contextualizing it within the production, circulation, and expectations of photographs, in order to get at the temporal and philosophical stakes of the photograph in a way that is not confined to the promises of the moment. And on the other hand, Kracauer elucidates the larger philosophical stakes of photography by identifying the present use of photography as a crisis point in the relationship, as old as history itself, between nature and meaning. Thus his essay, like Sander's and Blossfeldt's photography, sees photography not merely as a new mechanical medium, but locates it within a kind of natural history.

From its first section, Kracauer's essay dialectically subverts photography's apparent strengths—its capacity to exactly represent the visual, to bring the distant close, and its promise of total coverage—in order to show that these seeming strengths are actually weaknesses that obstruct understanding, and that photography's vocation is a deeper one. Kracauer develops the motif of gaps and gaplessness in order to unite—and undermine—diverse aspects of photographic production, reproduction, circulation, and consumption. Ultimately, photography's ability to create an exact and contiguous representation of the visual world is a chimera that collapses under its own weight, since it is precisely the illusory gaplessness of photography that obstructs its access to understanding, reason, and memory. Yet, and this is the dialectical turn in Kracauer's essay, it is precisely this shortcoming of photography that suggests its real potential: in a historical context of total reification, the failed promise of photography, when properly understood, might provoke cognition into a confrontation with the arbitrary social order of capitalist domination. In other words, the camera's ability to mechanically reproduce the visual does not grant the photograph inherent meaning; on the contrary, photography's strength lies in the meaninglessness of images, a meaninglessness that may ultimately make the arbitrariness, and therefore the reconfigurability, of any given social arrangement visible. Kracauer's essay, like Blossfeldt's and Sander's books, can help open up the discussion of Weimar-era photography by suggesting that photography cannot be isolated, let alone fetishized, but must be considered as an assemblage of media practices within a specific social context, in its relationship to other forms of representation and modes of experience. Moving from the fine visual details of halftone dots and an actress's eyelashes to a philosophy of history, Kracauer's essay subverts photography's promises of immediacy, exactitude, and objectivity in order to indict the historical juncture that requires such blandishments in the first place.

Kracauer begins his essay "Photography," which appeared in 1927 in the *Frankfurter Zeitung*, by comparing two photographs of young women: the diva on the Lido and the grandmother as a young woman. Where the film star is instantly recognizable, the image of the grandmother peers out at the viewer from the ancient past, and does not seem to accord with the fragmentary stories about her that had circulated through the family. Indeed, whether the woman in the photograph is in fact the grandmother at all must be taken on the parents' word: "the now-darkened appearance has so little in common with the traits still remembered that the grandchildren submit in amazement to the imperative of encountering in the photograph their fragmentarily recorded ancestor."[75] The image of the grandmother cannot be reconstituted into a meaningful whole, it seems to be arbitrary and fungible—"in reality it's any young girl in 1864"[76]—and it dissolves, lacking a connection to the present, into the archaic details of outmoded clothing. The film diva, by contrast, is fully there in her photograph, instantly recognizable, unmistakably herself.

Yet Kracauer's essay quickly complicates this picture by contrasting the effects of photographs with the workings of memory, so that what seemed at first like the strength of the photograph of the diva—its perfect reproduction of a recognizable subject—is actually a defect vis-a-vis the "memory image." Seemingly incongruous details of the way Kracauer describes the photograph of the film star already portend his critique, and his surprising praise, of the possibilities of photography. The essay's fourth and fifth sentences present the reader with what seems like an irrelevant detour. "If one were to look through a magnifying glass one could make out the grain, the millions of little dots that constitute the diva, the waves, and the hotel. The picture, however, refers not to the [dots] but to the living diva on the Lido."[77] If this is the case, one must wonder, then why draw attention to the dots in the first place, effectively handing the reader a magnifying glass that only distracts from the "[gapless] appearance" (*lückenlose Erscheinung*) of the "living diva"? Kracauer seems to be encouraging the reader to see beyond the insignificant material factors of the photographic depiction—the mass of dots—in order to really see the details that matter: her face, her hair, the scene. Yet the fact that he brings up the overlooked grid of dots (*Raster*) at all, when most readers of such a brief ekphrasis would not even think of it in the first place, alerts us to something rather more complex. By invoking the halftone dots that form the image on the printed page, a material characteristic of the medium that has to do with the relationship between marks on a page and the spaces between them, Kracauer is signaling a key motif in his essay—namely, the way that the photographic surface must be perceived as gapless (*lückenlos*) and, by extension, the idea that the photographic surface more often conceals than reveals. Conversely, the media context that informs the setting for his essay—the mass of photographs in the illustrated magazines of the day, a "flood" or "blizzard" of images without relation or gap[78]—is subtly probed at the same time.

A similarly wry subversion of the image's fullness comes further down in the opening paragraph: the diva is instantly recognizable because "everyone has already seen the original on the screen." If the original is itself already an image, then the fullness, uniqueness, and recognizability of the diva are an artifact of the medium, with the caveat that the medium of photography is here understood as a general social circulation of images among photographs, films, and illustrated magazines. This deep linkage between the individual image and the broad social context—in order to recognize the image's referent as "our demonic diva" in the first place, the viewer already must be participating in this general circulation of images—begins as an undertone, but will swell to a major theme later on. And finally, the unmistakable uniqueness of the film star is undermined by her position in a serial relation: "It is such a good likeness that she cannot be confused with anyone else, even if she is perhaps only one-twelfth of a dozen Tiller girls." Besides placing the unmistakable film star into a de-individuating chorus line,[79] the image of a dozen identical parts resonates with Kracauer's description, two sentences previously, of the diva's "twelve eyelashes right and left." The exactitude of photographic representation (twelve eyelashes) signals a mechanical seriality that effaces the individual within identical parts (twelve Tiller girls), rather than providing knowledge of its object.

In other words, the first paragraph of Kracauer's essay already insinuates that the very features of the photograph that make it full, present, and recognizable also threaten to dissolve it within a mass of indifferent details. The first word of the essay—"*This* is what the film diva looks like"—is revealed to be an ironic dodge, since the play of gaps and gaplessness, originality and repetition frustrates the photographic claim to quiddity announced by the initial "This."[80] While the photograph seems to be a solid surface, this solidity in fact melts away in multiple directions: by the mass of dots that comprise the image, by the way that the recognizability of an image is conditioned by a context that includes the circulating mass of other images, and by the seriality of parts that become mechanical. This total context will prove essential to the surprising reversal that Kracauer identifies as a possibility of photography.

In contrast to photography's attempt to present a seamless "spatial continuum" of all possible views of all possible things, memory, for Kracauer, is necessarily gappy. But it is precisely memory's gaps, blind spots, and fragmentary nature that necessitate signification as an active process of selection, whereby the remembering subject must construct a narrative of personal significance. Photography's gaplessness is deceptive, a mere "surface coherence,"[81] and is actually a hindrance to meaning, memory, and critical reflection. As Miriam Bratu Hansen writes, "Understanding is prevented above all by the contiguous arrangement of the images—'without any gaps'—thereby systematically occluding reflection on things in their relationality (*Zusammenhang*) and history, which would require the work of consciousness."[82] In another twist in Kracauer's argument, we learn that photography is not simply incapable of the process of selection, and *forgetting*, that enables any meaning or memory at all, but that photographs have come to play the role of the disjecta necessary to any process of signification: "The truth content of the original is left behind in its history; the photograph captures only the residuum that history has discharged."[83] Such residua would include the grandmother's clothes, now comically archaic in their arbitrary modishness and lack of connection to the present.

The essay's interest in clothing is not incidental, since we now learn that photographs partake of a temporality of fashion, wherein the past is not just past, but is outmoded and thus, paradoxically, liberated. Because history has moved on from these past "orders of existence," their entire context is rendered both meaningless and thereby redeemable. Put differently, the obvious arbitrariness of outmoded styles, which photography makes visible, can also lead to the recognition that any current social configuration is equally arbitrary. "This ghost-like reality is *unredeemed*. It consists of elements in space whose configuration is so far from necessary that one could just as well imagine a different organization of these elements. Those things once clung to us like our skin, and this is how our property still clings to us today."[84] Thus, a recognition of photography's contingency becomes the photographic insight into the historical and political contingency of the capitalist order as such.

This is a surprising and paradoxical potency to attribute to photography, and it is one rendered all the more urgent by photography itself, which at the same time continues to promise an illusory access to the world that only has the effect of obstructing understanding.

> Never before has an age been so informed about itself, if being informed means having an image of objects that resembles them in a photographic sense. . . . The flood of photos sweeps away the dams of memory. . . . Never before has a period known so little about itself. In the hands of the ruling society, the invention of illustrated magazines is one of the most powerful means of organizing a strike against understanding. . . . The contiguity of these images systematically excludes their contextual framework available to consciousness.[85]

By now it is clear that, for Kracauer, the surface coherence of photography pertains not just to the individual image but especially to the mass of images circulating in photographs, films, and illustrated newspapers and magazines that marked the contemporary media context of Weimar Germany. The opposition between the spatial figure of contiguity, on the one hand, and understanding or consciousness, on the other, is illuminated by the earlier contrast between the photograph and the artwork, which indicates the problem with a focus on exact visual depiction.

> In order for history to present itself, the mere surface coherence offered by photography must be destroyed. For in the artwork the meaning of the object takes on spatial appearance, whereas in photography the spatial appearance of an object is its meaning. The two spatial appearances—the "natural" one and that of the object permeated by cognition—are not identical. By sacrificing the former for the sake of the latter, the artwork also negates the likeness achieved by photography.[86]

Yet, as Patrizia McBride has shown, this is not a simple argument for depth over surface, nor is it a "traditional distrust of mimesis."[87] Rather, the use of the term "spatial appearance" (*Raumerscheinung*) must be read in the context of the motif of gaplessness. An object's "spatial appearance" thus connects the idea of contiguity invoked (and undermined) by the images of the halftone dots and the twelve eyelashes at the beginning of the essay to the notion of a social order or arrangement (*Ordnung, Organisation*) at the end of the essay. Within the essay's metaphorical matrix of gaps, contiguity, and fragments, photography's rigid devotion to depicting the spatial arrangement of an object or a scene echoes the apparent immutability of a given social order. Compared to this, art's freer use of subjective decision in arranging a scene in the service of meaning (*Bedeutung*) shows what photography loses in the pursuit of exactitude.

This historically specific crisis of representation is tied, for Kracauer, to the history of nature and to the nature of history as such. The stakes are nothing less than consciousness's ability to liberate itself from nature. In the penultimate section of his essay Kracauer sketches something like a dialectic of enlightenment, according to which consciousness and spirit come into being by extricating themselves from nature. Consciousness emerges from natural contingency and necessity into self-awareness, yet a second nature—explicitly capitalism and the domination of human activity by property relations and human-made necessities—presents consciousness with the very compulsion and impenetrability it thought it had left behind in first nature.

But precisely because photography, as the mass of sediment that falls away in order to construct meaning, is able to make meaninglessness visible to consciousness, it can also therefore provide a critical distance and reflection on the second nature of capitalism.

A consciousness caught up in nature is unable to see its own material base. It is the task of photography to disclose this previously unexamined *foundation of nature*. For the first time in history, photography brings to light the entire natural cocoon; for the first time, the inert world presents itself in its independence from human beings. Photography shows cities in aerial shots, brings crockets and figures down from Gothic cathedrals. All spatial configurations are incorporated into the central archive in unusual combinations which distance them from human proximity. Once the grandmother's costume has lost its relationship to the present, it will no longer be funny; it will be peculiar, like a submarine polyp. This is how the elements crumble, since they are not held together. The photographic archive assembles in effigy the last elements of a nature alienated from meaning.

This warehousing of nature promotes the confrontation of consciousness with nature.... It is therefore incumbent on consciousness to establish the *provisional status* of all given configurations, and perhaps even to awaken an inkling of the right order of the inventory of nature.[88]

If all given configurations of the social order are as provisional, as contingent, and ultimately as fleeting as the grandmother's costume, this means that the present is provisional as well, and can be changed. Photography's vocation, for Kracauer, is ultimately to defamiliarize, effectively to denaturalize the present, in order to show that this configuration can be changed. Such a recognition of contingency opens the way for an active consciousness—precisely that which photography's gaplessness otherwise obstructs—to reflect on different configurations, "perhaps even to awaken an inkling of the right order of the inventory of nature."

The logic of fragmentation and reassembly that Kracauer develops in "Photography" is elucidated by a brief look at an essay he had published the previous year. In "Calico World," Kracauer describes a visit to the UFA film studio in Babelsberg. The welter of props and sets draws his critical scrutiny, and provides a model for the "warehousing of nature" that he describes in his photography essay. It is not just that the scattered props, sets, and live animals coexist in a provisional arrangement dictated by the hasty needs of concurrent film productions, presenting a wild juxtaposition of "periods, peoples, and styles," and mixing cultural references and physical scales.[89] Beyond the theme of provisionality, the language that Kracauer uses to describe this fragmentation of the world echoes his description of the photographic archive, with the "ruins of the universe stored in warehouses for sets," "remnants of the natural ... put into storage [*einmagaziniert*]," and the fragments reassembled over the course of filming and editing: "Instead of leaving the world in its fragmented state, one reconstitutes a world out of these pieces. The objects that have been liberated from the larger context are now reinserted into it, their isolation effaced and their grimace smoothed over."[90] Furthermore, even the connections between this logic of fragmentation and the visual motifs of dots and gaps can be found here as well: "Life is constructed in a pointillist manner. It is a speckling of images [*ein Getüpfel von Aufnahmen*] that stem from numerous locations and initially remain unconnected."[91] We should note in passing that the logic of fragmentation, reassembly, and montage that Kracauer develops here in order to characterize the relationship between film sets and film editing also allows him to talk about the circulation of photographic, non-filmic images in a mass media context. Just as Benjamin's concepts of the optical unconscious and the aura were articulated in essays about film and photography alike, the resonances between "Calico World" and "Photography" demonstrate the ways in which real differences between photography and cinema were elided by Weimar writers in the service of deeper, intermedial theorizations of representation and experience.

While the logic of fragmentation and recombination that Kracauer explores in the two essays is thus necessarily multimedial, it is also distinctly photographic, provided one understands photography in its broader, social context as a totality of production and circulation. The chaos that Kracauer identifies in the film studio corresponds to the messy adjacency of illustrated magazines—in both cases, it is photography that is able to excise such fragmentary images out of their original contexts and weave them back into new ones, without the sense of recombination thereby being fully obscured. "This warehousing of nature promotes the confrontation of consciousness with nature"[92]—photography is necessary for this Herculean task, because of the very pretension to totality that makes it unable to comprehend historical reality in the same way as memory or art. This totalizing claim of being able to bring the whole world close is photography's failure, but in true dialectical fashion, the total scope of this failure of a totalizing claim is necessary in order for recognition to confront its own situation. For Kracauer, the recognition that photography might make possible is not a recognition of the objects and views of the world, but a second-order recognition of recognition itself.

Furthermore, the contemporary media context of photographic circulation—"the flood of photos" that "sweeps away the dams of memory"—does not exhaust the philosophical importance Kracauer sees in photography, but it is not incidental either. In order for the totalizing fragments of nature—the "sediment" that constitutes photography's meaninglessness[93]—to constitute a "central archive" (*Hauptarchiv*) and clear the way for a recognition of recognition, and of the "provisional status of all given configurations," a photographic practice is needed that joins the disparate and brings the distant close. And such a practice is exactly what characterized the photography of the 1920s, particularly the photobooks, photo essays, and illustrated magazines. Kracauer's examples of aerial photographs of cities and details of Gothic architecture are certainly well-chosen stand-ins for the moment. Not only do they suggest a comprehensive spread from medieval architecture to modern urbanism, craft to industry, and detail view to panorama, but they also refer to two specific ways in which photography was bringing hitherto impossible views into the purview of the kinds of vision a mass public was being trained in during the 1920s. Several prominent photographic books of the time, including Moholy-Nagy's *Painting Photography Film* (1925) and Roh and Tschichold's *Photo-Eye* (1929), featured aerial shots. As for the details of Gothic architecture, Pepper Stetler (2011) has shown how the lauded objectivity of Albert Renger-Patzsch's photography—especially its use of unconventional angles, close-ups, and deliberate lighting in order to isolate significant details—emerged in part from commissioned work he did with the Auriga Press and archive, including the 1925 book *The Choir Stalls of Cappenberg*, work which had the pedagogical goal of "introduc[ing] works of art and cultural artefacts to a mass audience."[94] Thus, Kracauer's examples of photography's capacity for making the world visible, beyond evoking the medium's claims to totality, very precisely refer to the contours of photographic circulation in the 1920s.

The broader point concerns photography's circulation among media, forms, discourses, and disciplines at the time. While one might object that Kracauer's essay, in quickly linking photography to a dialectic of enlightenment that extends from the beginning of linguistic signification to the present day, fails to do justice to photography as a specific medium with its specific constraints and possibilities, this objection would miss one of the more interesting aspects of the contemporary understanding of photography: Kracauer is able to identify philosophical, historical stakes in photography, broadly conceived, because photography was in fact broadly conceived at the time. It was seen, lauded, and criticized as a generalized circulation of images, and drew so much enthusiasm and so many expectations in part because of its medial, discursive, and disciplinary polyvalency, functioning as a promise of truth, a promise of objectivity, and a promise of modernity. There was a contemporary discourse that joined photographs, exhibitions, camera practices, visual styles, photo essays, photobooks, cinema, and urban experience, and it is this discourse that Kracauer's essay addresses, and dialectically subverts, in order to identify photography as the all-or-nothing game of history itself.[95]

What Kracauer's essay thus also shows is a paradox of photographic discourse of the 1920s. If this discourse was always about more than the camera and the image—and I believe that it was—then this polymorphous lack of specificity undermines the very photographic fetishism that encouraged such sweeping claims for photography in the first place. Kracauer's essay and, in their own ways, Sander's and Blossfeldt's work amount to a critique of photographic objectivity from within. For Kracauer, photography's strength lies not in showing the world as it really is, but in showing that photography renders this task impossible. Sander and Blossfeldt were also after something other than an objective representation of an individual subject. Their photographic projects, each typological in its own way, frustrate attempts to understand them in terms of verisimilitude, indexicality, objectivity, or the glimpse of the fleeting moment. Their subjects are not just what one sees in their images, but concern types and forms that have histories and depth. This does not mean that they should be considered any less modern, or as being outside the scope of New Objectivity. Rather, they challenge us to understand the conceptual nuances and paradoxes of New Objectivity and modernity alike, as these unfolded during the period. What one can say of the photography of August Sander and Karl Blossfeldt is true of the photography of the 1920s more generally: it is more than just an exact visual representation of the given world, and more than one can see in the image alone.

In their strategic deemphasis of the individual and the particular, these photobooks and essays about photography suggest that New Objectivity might be seen as a particular juncture in the history of photography, though not in the way that it has commonly been described. Rather than serving as either a dispassionate aestheticization or evidentiary documentation of unadorned reality, photography's function in this case was to reveal underlying forms and types that are inaccessible to unaided vision by virtue of their transcendence. In light of the averred connections between the camera's speed and that of the experience of mechanical, urban modernity, therefore, this shift in the temporalities ascribed to the camera also suggests that we must be attentive to alternative temporalities and logics used to characterize modernity. Photography thus fits into, and furthers, a paradigm of biological modernism that located modernity within nature (and vice versa), rather than opposing the two terms. We have seen how Plessner develops the human being's characteristic "natural artificiality" immanently, from his definition of life itself. In the two remaining chapters, we will see how Alfred Döblin articulates a modernist, epic theory of the novel in conjunction with a monist philosophy of nature, and how Ernst Jünger's vision of a post-bourgeois future depends upon the perfect integration of organism and machine, on the one hand, and a teleological understanding of history derived from a theory of organic development, on the other.

Indeed, a closer look at the novels and essays of Alfred Döblin and Ernst Jünger will flesh out the conception of modernity delineated by my discussion of photography in this chapter. Modernity is expressed in terms of biological, geological, and other natural temporalities rather than the acceleration of technological progress alone. On the one hand, this historical discourse about modernity was an important factor in shaping the ways in which images were produced, circulated, and received; attention to it can thus help recover some of the complexity of Weimar-era photographic theory in ways that might contribute to available ways of theorizing the medium. On the other hand, this historical discourse suggests that organicism, which is commonly associated in scholarship with the political Right in Germany, was in fact a much more complex discourse that also provided terms for thinking about technology and modernity in ways that cannot be assimilated to political reaction. The theory and practice of photography in Germany in the 1920s, which explored the relationships between visual representation, history, and knowledge in dense and often surprising ways, thus indicates a new way into the vexed and contested visions of modernity that marked the period.

Chapter 3

✦

Döblin's Epic Embodied

In May 1913, the cover of Herwarth Walden's journal *Der Sturm* featured a programmatic article by the thirty-four-year-old writer and doctor Alfred Döblin. The manifesto, titled "To Novelists and Their Critics: Berlin Program," begins with a short paragraph ridiculing the figure of the artist: "The artist works in his closed cell. His personal side is two-thirds self-deception and nonsense. The door to discussion is open."[1] By situating the artist's subjectivity—his "personal side"—between two spaces that are either closed or just recently opened—the "closed cell" and the open door to discussion—Döblin's essay implies by analogy that conventional artistic subjectivity is also a closed space that must be opened. Between the closed cell and the opened door, the reader of Döblin's essay is invited to peek at and critique, as if over an artist's shoulder, private spaces of literary production, literary subjectivity, and literary reception. The short text proceeds to weave these spaces together, criticizing inherited notions of art and subjectivity alike by rejecting the aesthetic, psychological, and social premises on which these are based. The conception of individuality as a closed, private domain is thus seen to mirror artistic production as a private, closed activity. By connecting the ideas of closure, privacy, and individuality, Döblin's essay rejects a notion of individuality and of art, implying that both are too closed, too individualistic, and too private; too bourgeois. Drawing the same parallel seventeen years later, Siegfried Kracauer will write: "The closed construction of the old novel form mirrors the presumed closure of personality."[2] In its use of a spatial imagery of closure and openings to link a kind of artistic production to a conception of subjectivity, Döblin's paragraph signals a tactic that he will use over the following decades to develop a theory of the epic that draws upon a critique of bourgeois subjectivity and a philosophy of nature. These persistent and complex linkages in Döblin's writing among a poetics, a theory of the subject, and a philosophy of nature—Döblin's biological modernism—are the focus of this chapter.

As I will show, Döblin's largely neglected 1924 novel *Mountains Seas and Giants* (*Berge Meere und Giganten*) mobilizes the imaginative possibilities of science fiction and the author's dense, paratactic style in order to advance his theory of the novel, his monist philosophy of nature, and his critique of bourgeois subjectivity in tandem. Where Döblin's essays of the period reject the closure and interiority of the autonomous subject, *Mountains Seas and Giants* renders this critique literal by depicting bodies being ruptured open and recombined. Where Döblin's programmatic poetic statements called for a new epic form that would overcome the individual focus of the inherited novel form, his science fiction novel enacts this program by depicting history as a mass process and by decentering subjective agency in its very style. And where Döblin would elsewhere articulate a philosophy of nature that sees all nature partaking of selfhood, his radical exploration of natural cataclysm and runaway organic growth in *Mountains Seas and Giants* give this vision vivid contours. Central to the biological modernism of Döblin's 1924 novel is the refusal of any distinction between the organic and mechanical realms, between nature and technology. The new human that emerges over the several centuries of global human history narrated in *Mountains Seas and Giants* is generated precisely at this ambiguous juncture of the natural and the technological by the tight linkage among the philosophical, psychological, and poetic aspects of Döblin's critique of closed forms.

The self-deceiving artist in his closed room is no longer adequate, "To Novelists and Their Critics" continues, because the modern era demands new working methods for art: "The world has grown deeper and broader; the old Pegasus has been outstripped [*überflügelt*] by technology, it has let itself be baffled and has transformed into a stubborn ass."[3] Yet in the face of a changed world that calls for art as a "public affair,"[4] contemporary novelists still hold on to a psychological reduction of human behavior by focusing on private interiority and legible affects and motives, rather than being open to the "living totality" of human subjectivity. In his dual role as a doctor and a writer, Döblin argues that this reductive attitude oversimplifies both the human psyche and the narrative possibilities of the novel form. Words like "fury," "love," and "contempt" are merely heuristic terms that can usefully indicate complexes of phenomena but are insufficient to fully account for mental processes or the motivations for human action, let alone form a satisfactory literary plot: "they cannot become the guiding thread of a plot that reproduces life."[5] In pretending to offer causal explanations for both affect and action, they serve as a simplistic narrative reduction that substitutes a deceptive linearity for much more complex processes, and they obscure the totality of life with an obsessive focus on private, individual fates.[6]

In place of the psychological novel's mystifying treatment of subjectivity, Döblin proposes two alternatives: either an unabashed lyricism that would embrace its immediacy and subjectivity, or a novel that would boldly forego the false promises of easy causality and legible motive: "actual novel prose according to this principle: the object of the novel is soulless reality [*die entseelte Realität*]."[7] His essay largely explores this second alternative, calling for "cinematic style" (*Kinostil*), "fantasy of fact" (*Tatsachenphantasie*), and an increased objectivity along the lines of psychiatry.⁸ Psychiatry, for Döblin, is thus both more invested than psychology in the living totality and at the same time more modest. Psychology pretends to offer an objective explanation, and yet it is necessarily reductive.⁹ "Fantasy of fact" must therefore be understood as an observational stance that respects the subject's complex entanglements in the object world, in nature. The essay ends by calling for the rebirth of the novel "as a work of art and a modern epic."¹⁰

In calling for a modern epic in response to a novel form that had become a historical problem, Döblin's short essay is thus part of a broader contemporary aesthetic discourse that grappled with various crises of representation and knowledge that dominated discourses of modernity and modernization in late nineteenth- and early twentieth-century Europe: the crisis of the novel, the crisis of narrative, and the crisis of historiography, among others.¹¹ Within this broader context, Döblin is often an overlooked interlocutor, despite his prominence at the time as both a theorist and practitioner of a new discourse of the novel. Critical attention has focused largely on *Berlin Alexanderplatz* (1929), his masterful contribution to the modernist city novel, yet I wish to suggest that the questions he posed and the provisional solutions he offered in essays and novels from the 1910s and 1920s are an essential way into the discourse of crisis that attended theorizations of the novel and of representation during the Weimar era. If the crisis of the novel largely consisted of a rejection of the nineteenth-century psychological novel and a reconceptualization of the novel as an open form in the face of sweeping social and technological changes, particularly changes in the reading public and new aesthetic media, then it is clear why questions of aesthetic and narrative closure would become especially vexing.¹² The relationship between *Leben* (life) and *Form* is perhaps *the* central question informing German-language theories of the novel, and indeed, it shaped much of the crisis of historiography against the backdrop of *Lebensphilosophie*. Within this context, Döblin's interdisciplinary critique deserves special scrutiny for the strategies by which it reoriented *Leben* in biological, organicist, and bodily terms.

Like Georg Lukács's *Theory of the Novel* (*Die Theorie des Romans*), which appeared three years later in 1916, and like Mikhail Bakhtin's "Epic and Novel," Döblin's essay "To Novelists and Their Critics" asks about the relationships between history and experience, subjectivity and genre, life and form, viewing the novel not merely as one literary option among others, but as the index of a historical problem. Yet, in contrast to Lukács's argument that the closure of the novel is a formal necessity dictated by history—the novel must offer a form of closure linked to the individual life and subjectivity because the modern relationship between self and world, unlike the closed cosmos of the Greek epic, has become arbitrary¹³—Döblin's essay rejects the contemporary novel's obsessive focus on the private and the individual and calls instead for a rebirth of the novel as a new epic, though the spatial tropes of his opening paragraph make it clear that he has a very different epic in mind than did Lukács. If for Lukács the Greek epic could be open because the symbolic order of Greek society and its cosmos, by contrast, were closed and harmonious, Döblin seeks to align literary form, social world, and individuality, rather than to contrast them. The author's closed *Stube*, his "personal side," and the literary form all need to be opened in parallel. As he would write in 1917, "If a novel can't be cut up into ten pieces like an earthworm, with each part still moving on its own, then it's no good."[14] Whereas Lukács identified the novel with closure, Döblin explicitly rejects this opposition, taking issue with the reductive understanding of individual psychology this implies, and with the tidy development of plot as a linear, causal narrative concatenation following the actions of a few individual characters: "poetically written psychology is nonsense."[15] And Döblin's integration of montage into his conception of the epic suggests that, in opposition to Bakhtin, he saw the epic rather than the novel as the site of heteroglossia.

Döblin's formulation of the epic presents a distinctly modern vision that transposes the question of aesthetic closure to other domains—domains such as a theory of subjectivity, debates on poetics, and, increasingly over the course of the 1920s, organic bodies—where the question of closure can then be subverted, reoriented, interrogated, and exploded, in short, reopened. Döblin's novels and essays from the 1910s and 1920s thus articulate a multifaceted critique of bourgeois subjectivity and its corresponding literary forms. A poetics that rejected the tidy closure of the novel accompanied his sustained criticism of the notion of discrete, autonomous subjectivities; a revision of the literary category of character went hand-in-hand with depictions in his novels of bodies being spatially explored, exploded, and reconfigured, and this exploration of both literary possibilities and the contours of human subjectivity was developed alongside philosophical speculations about the distribution of selfhood through all matter and the ontological tentativeness of all individual bodies down to the smallest scale. If the problem of the novel is one of giving form to life, Döblin's contribution is to bring other discourses of life into the equation, particularly a monist philosophy of nature and a medical knowledge of the human body, discourses that help him destabilize formal closure in ways that have aesthetic consequences.

Döblin's answer to these crises of representation is thus as idiosyncratic as it was exemplary: idiosyncratic because of his distinctive voice, tempo, and an associative logic that leaps among polemical, satirical, reflective, and descriptive modes, blending medical, mystical, and critical registers; and exemplary in that the interdependency in Döblin's writing of a poetics, a theory of the subject, and a philosophy of nature can serve as a paradigm for biological modernism. Particularly because Döblin's call for a new kind of text and a new understanding of the human subject was explicitly modern, in that it articulated itself in conscious opposition to inherited narrative forms, the conception of psychological interiority, and the dualist understanding of nature that Döblin associated with the nineteenth century and the bourgeois era, a closer look at his work of the 1920s can illuminate how the desire for newness and modernity sometimes took on unexpected forms. Put differently: the specific ways in which Döblin perceived the shortcomings of inherited ideas of the subject and of the novel marked by an emphasis on the individual—adumbrated by his critique in "To Novelists" and developed in more detail below—suggest why he was able to link nature and the organic to technological modernity and innovation, rather than drawing the expected association between nature and an idyllic past, for example.

This chapter will explore this side of Döblin's interdisciplinary modernist poetics. As my brief sketch of "To Novelists" suggests, Döblin's modernist critique consisted of a critique of the novel, a theory of the subject, and a burgeoning philosophy of nature. Crucially, however, these three were not simply discrete ingredients that combined to make a whole, but they each drew on the others' terms in order to articulate their aesthetic, psychological, or philosophical vision. While critical attention continues to privilege *Berlin Alexanderplatz*, a fuller reading of Döblin's modernism would see the 1929 city novel as only one articulation among others of his developing literary practice. It is necessary to do justice to Döblin's other major works of the two decades prior to the publication of *Berlin Alexanderplatz* in order to properly situate him amidst contemporary debates on representation, narrative, and the epic—debates in which he was both a prominent participant and a frequent topic of discussion. Novels such as *Mountains Seas and Giants* and *Wallenstein*, philosophical texts such as *The I above Nature*, and various programmatic and critical essays represent a complex, interdisciplinary modernist vision, closer attention to which might contribute to a deeper understanding of the disciplinary and discursive contours of Weimar culture.

Through detailed readings of descriptive passages in Döblin's science fiction novel *Mountains Seas and Giants* (1924) and with recourse to key essays from the 1910s through 1930s, I will show how Döblin's vision of modernity, his theory of the epic and accompanying prose style, his critique of bourgeois subjectivity, and his developing philosophy of nature relied and built upon each other. I will begin with essays in which he called for a new epic form by critiquing both the available literary forms and the idea of the subject inherited from bourgeois humanism. Crucially, this critique of bourgeois humanism, the psychological novel, and the autonomous individual made recourse to the biological, scientific, and medical knowledge available through Döblin's professional background as a doctor, and emerged in dialogue with his emerging philosophical monism. One finds in essays such as "To Novelists and Their Critics," "The Spirit of the Naturalistic Era" ("Der Geist des naturalistischen Zeitalters," 1924), "The Construction of the Epic Work" ("Der Bau des epischen Werks," 1929), "Water" ("Das Wasser," 1922), and "Nature and Its Souls" ("Die Natur und ihre Seelen," 1922) a vision of subjectivity that is simultaneously dispersed through the material, object world and decentered by means of a perspective that views the human not primarily in individual terms but as a mass, collective being (*Massenwesen* and *Kollektivwesen*). My reading of these essays will foreground the ways in which Döblin challenges a subject/object dualism, as well as the extent to which his aesthetic program depended on his philosophy of nature. I will then turn to *Mountains Seas and Giants*, where Döblin's radical rejection of any fixed spatial contours of the individual ontological unit takes vivid shape. In this wide-ranging vision of future history, the violent disruption and reconfiguration of individual bodies, and the consequent obstruction of technological instrumentality, are preconditions for imagining the kind of society that might be adequate to Döblin's revision of human subjectivity.

"What Is That from a Biological Point of View?" The Human after Humanism in Döblin's Essays

In essays written and published over the course of the 1920s, Döblin articulated a vision of embodied, material subjectivity, a theory of the epic work, and a philosophy of nature, all of which are in dialogue with his understanding of modernity. While some essays, such as "Nature and Its Souls," concentrate on his monist philosophy of nature and others, such as "The Construction of the Epic Work," foreground his aesthetic deliberations about literature, I propose that these different aspects developed in dialogue with each other during this period, and cannot fully be disentangled in any of these essays. Döblin articulates a theory of subjectivity through a monist philosophy of nature that disallows any kind of mind/body dualism, and the vision of an ensouled nature that emerges also serves as a model of poetic production. The model of subjectivity at play here is formed in conscious opposition to the closure of the autonomous, isolated individual, just as Döblin's rehabilitation of epic literature is posed as an antidote to the narrative assumptions of a novel form that privileges the psychology of the individual character as a window onto the world. In my reading of these essays, I will draw out the themes that are central to Döblin's modernist poetics during the 1920s: an idea of modernity as an epoch that frustrates clear distinctions between the natural and the technological; an understanding of the self as a property that is distributed throughout material nature, rather than being concentrated within the individual subject; the topological skepticism of closed units that facilitates this dispersal of selfhood throughout nature; and an objective, factual epic style that models itself on the generative potential of nature. Taken together—and I suggest that they must be taken together in order to be understood at all—these themes constitute Döblin's biological modernism, and will allow us to better make sense of what is at play in the violent reconfigurations that unfold in *Mountains Seas and Giants*.

If the writer's private interiority in "To Novelists" is "two-thirds self-deception and nonsense" and is thus not a fitting subject for the modern epic, "The Spirit of the Naturalistic Era" further develops this critique of a kind of individuality by identifying the mass or collective as the meaningful, modern human unit. The context for the essay's turn from the individual to the collective is a reckoning with a humanist view of history. Döblin begins "The Spirit of the Naturalistic Era" by mocking a common valorization of culture (*Kultur*) at the expense of civilization (*Zivilisation*). In the contemporary context, culture was understood as something particularly German and local, while civilization was coded as French or cosmopolitan. Döblin rejects this dichotomy because such praise of culture necessarily lionizes the past in ahistorical ways. The purpose of this essay, then, is to give an account of the present—the "naturalistic era"—that does not depend on nostalgia, metaphysics, or anachronistic oppositions between nature and technology. "The Spirit of the Naturalistic Era" is a praise of the modern, technological era, but a praise that sees this era as the expression of a fundamental biological drive. The essay thus rejects the legacy of bourgeois humanism in two ways—by situating human culture within biology, and by embracing technological modernity in a way calculated to foil a nostalgia that cannot come to grips with the present.

The concept of the "collective being" (*Kollektivwesen*) is used to relativize the individualism and belief in transcendence that, for Döblin, characterize the era of bourgeois humanism. "The cities are the centers and seats of the class of the human being. They are the coral stock for the human collective being."[16] Comparing cities to a "coral stock" suggests the biological perspective at play here, and the concept of the "collective being" is in fact developed in the same essay in order to rethink the status of technological modernity from a longer perspective than that of a classical "scholastic-humanistic school education," which obstructs an accurate view of the present. In contrast to the transcendence that marked the earlier "metaphysical period," increasing observation of the physical world gradually leads to the technological character of the "naturalistic era."[17] In setting out to undo the sentimental dichotomies of culture and civilization, past and present, Döblin thereby also undermines the distinction between nature and technology. In describing the social drive (*Gesellschaftstrieb*) of human beings toward greater complexity and agglomerations, he asks: "What is that from a biological point of view?"[18] He answers this question in terms of the "animal species of the human" and the "collective being," which allows him both to position his discussion of technology as a phenomenon that is the expression of nature, on the one hand, and to sweep not just bourgeois humanism but modern European culture in general into a relatively marginal corner.[19] Peter Sprengel characterizes this perhaps surprising use of biology in the service of modernity thus: "Biologism, which we usually see as a vehicle of *völkisch* ideologies, is here connected with an affirmation of modern forms of socialization."[20]

The concept of the *Kollektivwesen* must therefore be seen as a key moment in Döblin's sustained criticism of the autonomous bourgeois subject.[21] In situating the *Kollektivwesen* in the metropolis as the expression of a biological drive, Döblin is able to attack the notion of the contained individual from both sides: in terms of an embrace of mass, urban, technological society, and in the rejection of a transcendent human privilege vis-à-vis nature.[22] Similarly to "To Novelists," in "The Spirit of the Naturalistic Era" this rejection of an inherited notion of subjectivity comes with a corresponding critique of culture and art: "It takes a certain kind of inner obscuration (that is, a stultification) to bring artworks into the world. Only thus can one understand the fact that Germany was already a heavily industrialized country by 1890 but artists, painters and writers were still tarrying with sunrises and gooseherds."[23]

The object of Döblin's critique is a bourgeois humanism that would maintain traditional approaches and topoi amidst processes of modernization that are, for Döblin, far more interesting than these fusty idylls. "Even today it is certainly nonsense to let a column of Phidias be idolized while calling the subway a mere means of transportation. Technology is not a higher form of metalworking, but is of the blood of this epoch."[24] The new type of human that embodies this epoch, the "metropolitan" (*Großstädter*), has solved the philosophical, aesthetic, and religious quandaries of the humanists in the simplest possible way: namely, by abandoning them.[25] The technological character of an age necessitates, and produces, a new type of human with its own particular *Geist*: "The Cologne Cathedral is undoubtedly the expression of a strong, resolute spirit. The electric dynamo is a match for the Cologne Cathedral."[26]

Döblin attributes the origin of the naturalistic era to the rejection of a transcendental beyond (*Jenseits*) and the concomitant rejection of humanism and a turn towards technology. The rejection of transcendence is also implicitly a rejection of anthropocentrism and leads directly to a renewed engagement, under the sign of *Beobachtung* (observation), with the world. If humanity's insignificance provokes a distinctly modern anxiety, once transcendence has been rejected and humanity has lost its central place in the cosmos, it is also a source of freedom, independence, and activity.

> Next to this stands the feeling of freedom and independence that comes from the certainty of not having to live for a beyond, not having to accomplish everything on one's own. Connected to and immediately growing out of this feeling of freedom is the impulse towards the most vigorous activity. Things don't come to despair at all after the disappearance of the belief in the beyond. It becomes like this: the starry sky above me and the rails beneath me.[27]

Rails symbolize the speed and dynamism of modern technology, and the newly won symmetry of stars above and rails below departs from the Kantian certainty of the moral law parodied by this sentence[28] in favor of a more vital engagement—in the context of Döblin's essay, the subversion of moral interiority in favor of spatial relation ("within me" becomes "beneath me"), the substitution of movement for constancy, and the modern human's freedom amidst a cosmos that is natural and technological at once go hand-in-hand.

Döblin's account of the naturalistic age—which has decentered the human subject, turned its back on transcendence, and requires an epic, mass poetics—rejects humanism both as a historical era and as an interpretive framework, and it does so by re-situating human history within natural history. This diagnosis is echoed in other essays. Where the *Kollektivwesen* shifted the focus from individual subjects to humanity seen as a group or species, other discussions of the subject also situate it in complex entanglements with nature and the object world. In other words, it is not just that human subjects are necessarily also always part of a collective that is both social and biological; more significantly, Döblin's monism challenges the subject-object distinction in various ways, with repercussions both for his idea of selfhood and for his theory of the epic writer. In "The Construction of the Epic Work" (1929), for example, Döblin recalls his earlier commitment to facticity, narrative objectivity, and reportage: "I admit that even today communications of facts, documents make me happy, but documents, facts, do you know why? Through them the great epic writer, nature, speaks to me, and I, the little one, stand before it and rejoice at what my big brother can do."[29] Nature becomes "the great epic writer" in the sense that creation is seen as a model for artistic creation. Just as nature becomes an epic writer, the writer must be seen as an objective part of reality: "*The real writer has always been a fact himself.* The writer has to show and to prove that he is a fact and a piece of reality and still just as good and factual as the good invention of the Triergon or as the Karolus cell."[30] Because the good writer can himself be a fact and thus has a place in his works, he can dispense with the "compulsory mask of the report," which for Döblin represents merely the formal pretense of objectivity rather than an epic facticity.[31] Furthermore, if the writer is himself a fact, then he occupies two positions at once: subject and object, writer and written. Here writerly subjectivity is not a privileged remove, but a phenomenon among others in the world that the epic writer must explore.

Döblin's examples of facticity also warrant mention. The "Triergon," or "Tri-Ergon," was an early sound-on-film system invented by Hans Vogt, Josef Engl, and Joseph Massolle, which premiered in Berlin on September 17, 1922, and was sold to Fox in 1927.[32] The "Karoluszelle" or "Karolus cell" was a light valve invented by August Karolus in the mid-1920s, and was a forerunner of television technology.[33] It is therefore significant, as Stefanie Harris has suggested, that Döblin refers to two cutting-edge media technologies at this point in his dual argument that the epic poet is an objective fact and that nature is an epic poet.[34] On the one hand, this further demonstrates the extent of his epic theory's commitment to intermediality, in the face of rapid changes in media technologies and the social place of art.[35] On the other hand, the literary appropriation of such media technologies, like his earlier call for a *Kinostil*, reinforces his multifaceted challenge to a stable subject/object dichotomy—as technologically novel ways of transmitting acoustic and visual data, the Tri-Ergon and the Karolus cell could stand in both for objective technological advancements and as refinements in the subjective possibilities of perception.

This blending of subjects and objects allows Döblin to argue for a social potential of the modern epic that would differ from the poetic isolation of the artist in his closed cell. Despite the fact that the modern epic writer no longer has access to an immediate, listening public, the incorporation of massive amounts of documentary and linguistic material means that a social collective becomes present in the work and in the author, who is divided into the I (*Ich*) and the "writing authority" (*dichtende Instanz*):

> To clearly say it right up front: *in this moment the author no longer sits alone in his parlor* and reflects or broods. Of course, he doesn't go among the people like the old goliard and storyteller either, singing about what they pass on to him and guided by their wishes. But from this moment on the author carries the people in him.
>
> In our time the observing I takes on the role and function the people had with those old goliards. *The I becomes the public, becomes the listener, and a collaborative listener at that.* [*Das Ich wird Publikum, wird Zuhörer, und zwar mitarbeitender Zuhörer.*] . . . From this moment on a cooperative, a collaboration occurs between the I and the writing authority.[36]

The *Ich* that had been accumulating, absorbing, and incubating epic material now takes on the role of observing the author at work. Thus, the epic poet does not just have a factual existence that needs to be accounted for, but also must incorporate and then represent the absent collective. Furthermore, the opening of individual subjectivity to the collective is mirrored by the way that the closed form of the book is opened into the form of the epic—for Döblin, the epic work is "constitutionally unlimited."[37]

The claims that the writing self is itself a fact and "a piece of reality" and that nature is "the great epic writer" are made possible by Döblin's developing philosophy of nature, which has variously been described as vitalist, monist, and panpsychic.[38] This philosophy of nature sees the human as an inextricable part of nature, and, indeed, sees selfhood as distributed throughout the material world. In Döblin's writings of the 1920s, he rejects the existence of stable ontological units in favor of a fluid, infinitely scalable and ensouled materiality. In an essay simply titled "Water," published in *Die neue Rundschau* in 1922, Döblin explores the idea of fluidity in order to deny the stability of individual bodies of any kind.

> What is that: sea? Who is that? It is not "the sea" at all. These waves are not individual beings. In the water I never encounter individual beings. It is so pliable, fused into each other, moving into each other. I come across no part that I can isolate. . . . In fluid, the basic components sink back into a deeper anonymity. The sharper more heated churning of bodies, their isolation and flight from each other, comes to an end.[39]

Water here functions as a model for the ontological relationship between particle and fluid, mass and individual. Note that the refusal of a stable individual unit as such, and the play of waves that merge and dissolve into one another, would already seem to preclude on a purely topological level the very notion of an interior that Döblin had critiqued at the beginning of "To Novelists and Their Critics," and which he would go on to graphically annul in *Mountains Seas and Giants*. This indivisible material extension of subjectivity, and the corresponding rejection of an interior space that would serve as the site of a discrete subjectivity, are themes that Döblin would develop in more detail over the course of the 1920s, most notably in his 1927 book-length treatise *The I above Nature* (*Das Ich über der Natur*), in which he repeats almost verbatim the above passage from "Water."[40] This confluence suggests how tightly intertwined his considerations of the individual human subject were with his monist philosophy of nature. A later passage in *The I above Nature* reprises Döblin's topological strategy, since an ironically literal search for the soul cannot but report what the medical gaze discovers. Döblin at first considers that the soul must lie somewhere within the body, since all the sense organs seem to lead from the outside in; yet once within the body, all he sees are

> nerve centers and connective fibers. . . . It is a closed system that runs completely into itself with nerve fibers, sensory organs, muscles, a system that is constructed very clearly and finely, but in itself. The nerve fibers don't actually lead to the inside at all, they lead into the brain, into the cortex for instance, there they spread apart, form connective fibers with other paths, and beyond that there's nothing. What did I expect, after all? A hole for the thinking soul?[41]

Topologically stymied by the absence in the human body not only of a soul but even of an interior, Döblin returns to the surface, concluding that the individual only has a soul "as a whole" and not in any one part of the body. Here as elsewhere, Döblin's critique of mind/body and I/nature dualisms proceeds by way of a spatial challenge to the boundary between inside/outside, and to the boundaries between bodies, challenges that themselves draw on medical, biological, and scientific registers.

Another essay from 1922, "Nature and Its Souls," published in *Der neue Merkur*, gives a sense of the social stakes of this materialist conception of subjectivity:

> With this salt, this water, this protein we widen [*verbreitern*] into the world. With the ocean, the deserts, the mountains, the cliffs, the winds. This is why we can feel through [*durchfühlen*] the world. This is why one isn't this half-comical bourgeois figure who is happy to wear his frock coat, but is rather more dispersed, more serious and also darker, more anonymous. Anonymous: the magic word. The guiding word. The person is of no importance . . . Life and truth are only in anonymity.[42]

The appearance of the "half-comical figure" of the bourgeois recalls the scornful dismissal in "To Novelists and Their Critics" of the self-delusions of the outmoded conceptions of self and literature alike, based upon the hegemony of the autonomous individual and the narrative fictions of individual psychological motivation. In all of these instances, Döblin's attack is on the idea of a contained individual on every level—ontological, psychological, literary—and the snide mention of the frock coat (*Rock*) suggests the perceived cultural, social context in which Döblin was intervening—the autumn years of a long-dominant and self-satisfied bourgeois humanism, which he will eagerly bury and summarily elegize in "The Spirit of the Naturalistic Era."

Crucially, the rejection of a historical form of subjectivity seen as too private, too insistent on identity, draws force from the claim that materiality and selfhood are inextricably connected. On the one hand, humans are composed of salt, water, protein, sand, stones, and so on.[43] This material integration of human selfhood into nature, marked by the unusual formulation "we widen into the world" (*wir verbreitern uns in die Welt*), will be recapitulated in graphic detail in a scene from *Mountains Seas and Giants*, which will also use the word *verbreitern* to indicate a body and a self spreading materially into its surroundings.[44] Yet this is not a materialism that would deny the existence of the soul, for, on the other hand, these materials themselves already exhibit features of souls and selves. A letter that Döblin wrote to Fritz Mauthner in September 1922 to inform the philosopher of the forthcoming publication of "Nature and Its Souls" says that the text will "only express a feeling (not systematically at all and probably also illogically) that I have in the face of the so-called dead and inorganic."[45] In the same short letter, Döblin points to their shared interest in Spinoza and, "to complete the intellectual affinity," tells Mauthner that two pictures of Buddha hang on his wall. Döblin's developing monism—which he signals in the letter to Mauthner by his invocation of Spinoza and Buddha—is frequently expressed in his essays over the course of the 1920s by an often microscopic view of the interactions and interconnections of human subjectivity and material nature, for it is the flows and exchanges of shared substances such as salt, water, and protein that allow humans to "widen" into the world.[46]

Döblin will develop this dual strategy—insisting on the infinite divisibility of individual units on the one hand, and investing all of nature with the quality of selfhood, on the other—at greater length in his philosophical treatise *The I above Nature* (1927), which at times incorporates material verbatim from the earlier essays "Water" and "Nature and Its Souls." This text describes the individual as a heuristic construction that necessarily elides the concrete material composition of the human body and its metabolic relationship to its environment. Since the body is made of "water, salts, sand, and stones," substances that influence and direct mood, soul, and mind, any clear ontological demarcation between the self and nature is in fact arbitrary.[47] Shared metabolic processes mean that humans "widen into the world," and can thus "feel through" it.[48] It is therefore worth noting that while Döblin's terminology shifts from the "anonymity" privileged in the early 1920s to the "Ur-I" (*Ur-Ich*), an all-pervasive principle of selfhood in nature that emerges over the course of *The I above Nature*, anonymity and the *Ur-Ich* should not be understood as the contraries they might at first glance appear to be.[49] The "anonymity" that describes humanity's metabolic, material connection with nature in the passage from "Nature and Its Souls" quoted above is an early attempt at a theory of subjectivity that is not well-represented by available discourses of the individual, which posit bounded, identifiable bodies, selves, and subjects without recognizing that these are necessarily fictions.[50] "Anonymity" and *Ur-Ich*, in other words, are both ways of describing a non-individual, materially distributed subjectivity.

In *The I above Nature* Döblin also foregrounds the visible, ordered form exhibited by the physical world down to the smallest scale. In this self-organization he sees the manifestation of a guiding principle of subjectivity that complicates the distinction between mind and matter, organic and inorganic, so that water, for example, "is not a dumb, inorganic thing, as one says."[51] By identifying concepts such as "mind" and "soul" with formative activity[52] or regular behaviors,[53] Döblin takes nature's regularities and forms as evidence of a pervasive, diffuse subjectivity behind all natural phenomena and forces.

This philosophy of nature, which is monist in its rejection of a firm distinction between body and soul, and panpsychic in its assignment of soul to all of nature, informed and was influenced by Döblin's developing ideas about literature and his conception of the human psyche. Indeed, when he writes in "Nature and Its Souls," "With this salt, this water, this protein we widen into the world,"[54] we can hear an echo of his earlier formulation in "To Novelists and Their Critics" that "I am not I, but rather the street, the lanterns, this and this occurrence, nothing beyond this."[55] In both cases, the self finds itself distributed into the world. This common pattern therefore makes the difference between the two contexts all the more striking. While the sentence from

"Nature and Its Souls" is attempting to account for the relationship among materiality, affect, subjectivity, and nature, the rejection of self-identity in "To Novelists and Their Critics" is proposed specifically as a literary strategy to break "the hegemony of the author," and in its context must therefore be read as an elaboration (and not merely a justification) of the various terms that Döblin uses in that essay to call for a new kind of novel—"cinematic style," "stone style," and "fantasy of fact."

In other words, the reformulation of subjectivity that Döblin developed in essays over the course of the 1920s uses shared strategies—a topological skepticism towards interiority or the individual unit as such, and a dispersal of subjectivity into material flows—for multiple ends. The vision of a distributed, material selfhood that finds its fullest elaboration in *The I above Nature* has consequences that are both literary and philosophical. On the one hand, Döblin sought a model of subjectivity that could account for modern experience while putting the human being's relation to nature on a non-dualist grounding, and the result of this is a distributed I that inheres in all materiality and is evidenced by all patterns and formative activity. On the other hand, one literary consequence of this revision of subjectivity is that an inherited notion of character that privileged psychological interiority, personality, and agency is decentered and undermined. In place of the "half-comical bourgeois figure," Döblin will offer masses, drives, and fragmented, recombined corporeal assemblages in *Mountains Seas and Giants*. This is a scaled strategy that dissolves the individual both upwards, into masses and collectives, and downwards, into organs, fragments, parts, drives, and endless material interconnections. If, in other words, Döblin's essays discussed above use various rhetorical strategies to critique and revise subjectivity, strategies including an insistence on the material processes underlying subjectivity, and the rejection of the individual unit and of an interiority where the soul would be located, the science fiction novel offers the possibility of literalizing these strategies and allowing their consequences to unfold on the level of its plot, and in the fine grain of its style.

"Now Comes Life"—Body as Critique in *Mountains Seas and Giants*

This dense interplay between a theory of the subject, an epic poetics, and a philosophy of nature thus takes on especially vivid form in *Mountains Seas and Giants* (1924), an epic history of the future that chronicles the fitful, cataclysmic evolution of humanity's relationship to nature. This early science fiction novel gives narrative form to many of the ideas and critical strategies voiced in Döblin's essays: the anti-individualistic rupturing of individual bodies, the permeation and dissolution of subjectivity throughout nature, and the critique of bourgeois humanism that articulates a vision of modernity as something that is both biological and technological. Moreover, the novel's formal and stylistic features advance Döblin's earlier critique of the psychological novel by troubling clearly discernible concatenations of character, motivation, and action, both on the scale of the whole text and on the level of the novel's sentences. In what follows, I will focus on the depiction of instrumental bodies in *Mountains Seas and Giants* in order to trace the implications of Döblin's modernism. This dense and confounding novel has—perhaps understandably—been relatively neglected by scholarship on Döblin and Weimar literature more generally, which has tended to privilege *Berlin Alexanderplatz*. Yet because *Mountains Seas and Giants* occupies such a pivotal point in Döblin's intertwined ideas about nature, subjectivity, and the novel as form, it should be central in discussions of Döblin's modernism. In my reading, *Mountains Seas and Giants* represents Döblin's attempt to give an imaginative, literary—and often literal—form, by way of its depictions of bodies vividly ruptured and recombined, to the critiques of aesthetic and psychological closure that he articulated in the essays discussed above.

Döblin's science fiction novel spans the twentieth to the twenty-seventh centuries with a correspondingly broad geographic scope, and depicts a future history of power struggles, war, technological innovation, and rebellion. Because of its epic breadth, the episodic narrative is not so much character-driven as it is anchored to other types of continuity, such as geographic or thematic ones. The novel thereby departs from typical, popular science fiction novels of the period, which centered on strong-willed, calculating heroes engaged in ultimately successful monumental technological projects, as do many works of the related genre of the engineering novel.[56] While *Mountains Seas and Giants* does feature engineers and scientists involved in Promethean ventures, they are decentered both by the sweeping temporal scope and the epic role played by mass processes and movements. Yet the novel goes even further by insistently rupturing the individual bodies inhabited by individual characters. In so doing, it shares a thematic focus of contemporary science fiction on technological advances and war, but it radically differs from other early texts of the genre in the way it undermines rather than reinforces the status of the autonomous individual. Both the decentering effects of the epic narrative and the insistent destruction of the human body rework the literary category of character and the bourgeois ideal of the individual with which Döblin associated it.

Scholars have accounted for the novel's conceptual and aesthetic peculiarities by reading it as a cautionary tale about the fateful struggle between nature and technology in industrial modernity. Roland Dollinger, for example, describes it as Döblin's "grandiose vision of the heroic struggle between the ratio-technological impulse of modern man and nature." Gabriele Sander, who edited the critically revised republication of the novel in 2006, has dubbed it an "epic about the conflict between nature and technology." Irmgard Hunt has written that "man and nature, or man against nature, is obviously Döblin's overall theme in all its possibilities," and Ritchie

Robertson has called the central theme of the work "man's urge to control nature," while Klaus Müller-Salget's focus is the shifting role of the "I" in the context of Döblin's "naturalism."[57] In "Observations on *Mountains Seas and Giants*" ("Bemerkungen zu *Berge Meere und Giganten*") Döblin describes how, although he originally set out to write the novel in order to settle accounts with his creeping "nature complexes," the process of writing it yielded the opposite effect, namely a deliberate paean to nature. My reading of *Mountains Seas and Giants* draws on this work while departing from the idea that the novel is primarily *about* the relationship between humans and nature, or technology and nature. Rather than seeing nature as a discrete theme that interacts antagonistically or sympathetically with humanity, progress, technology, or some similar unit, I am more interested in the ways in which Döblin's epic science fiction undermines and complicates the idea of nature—thoroughly enmeshing it with human bodies, technological systems, and the movement of history—in order to probe and reconfigure the human subject in a way that might meet the demands of the essays discussed above.

A few of the more notable events in the novel include a new migration of peoples; the invention of synthetic food production, known as *Mekispeise* (Meki-food), which is indefinitely capable of sustaining a thereby superfluous population; a world war between Europe and Asia that chars and floods much of Russia; the struggle between the urban, technocratic centers of power and several waves of a back-to-the-land movement; the cataclysmic harvesting of Iceland's lava to melt Greenland's ice; the torrent of hitherto icebound prehistoric monsters that are thereby revived; and in response to them, the cultivation of living defense turrets (the novel's titular giants) that are made from human, animal, vegetable, and mineral elements. This sequence of events ultimately yields the new egalitarian collectivities that arise in Europe at the end of the narrative, and I will show how Döblin lays the groundwork for these communities in his presentation of the intertwined challenges he poses to the individual body and to its instrumental use. In my analysis, I will focus on episodes distributed throughout the novel (in the dedication, and in books 2, 3, 7, and 8 out of nine) in order to reconstruct the development of the relationship among technology, instrumentality, and the human body.

> Every minute a change. Here where I am writing, on the paper, in the flowing ink, in the daylight that falls on the white rustling paper. How the paper bends, wrinkles under the pen. How the pen bends, stretches. My hand guiding it drifts from left to right, back to the left from the end of the line. I feel the grip at my finger: those are nerves, they are washed round by blood. The blood courses through the finger, through all fingers, through the hand, both hands, the arms, the chest, the whole body, its skin muscles intestines, into all surfaces corners recesses. So many changes in this thing here. And I am merely a single being, a tiny piece of space.[58]

This scene of writing occurs in the middle of the unusual dedication to *Mountains Seas and Giants* and follows a sustained encomium to the recipient of the dedication—an all-pervasive force of change and becoming that Döblin dubs "the Thousand-named" (*das Tausendnamige*). This description of what the authorial voice sees, hears, and feels in the moment of writing—the pen, the paper, the May sunlight, and later the flowers on the desk—at first recalls a familiar moment of writerly self-reflection. Yet while the indexical, declarative quality of the phrase "here where I am writing" may seem to foreground the writing self, the quick shifts from the paper to the pen to the hand to the anatomic close-ups soon dissolve any sense of centered subjectivity.[59] The metonymic chain that links sunlight, paper, pen, fingers, nerves, blood vessels, and all organs of the writing body establishes a relation that interweaves body, instrument, environment, writer, and writing, effacing the distinctions between them. The organs of the body themselves become media technologies through which knowledge is recorded and transmitted and thus are no different from the pen, since the integration of the body with its environment undermines any easy demarcation between subject and medium or perception and production, a move further reinforced by the invocation of metabolism that attends the mention of "intestines," recalling Döblin's material articulation of subjectivity in the earlier essays. This integration of the body, the human perceptual apparatus, and its environment thus recalls similar subversions of clear demarcations between body, technology, and environment in texts such as "To Novelists and Their Critics" and *The I above Nature*.

In the space between the initial "I am writing" and the "I am" at the end of the passage, the meaning of "I" undergoes a curious transformation. The active quality of "I am writing," once this action is situated within a chain of bodily and environmental processes, becomes something that happens to the body as much as it is something the body does. The apposition to "I feel"—"those are nerves"—dislocates the agency of the "I" in both perceiving and guiding the pen, a dislocation subtly reinforced by the image of the blood vessels weaving throughout the body. By the time we read "I am only a single being," it is clear that the "I am" is not the expression of a grounded, autonomous selfhood, but rather a statement of subjective implication in a relationship that transcends the limits of the individual body. Similarly, "single being" does not refer to a contained, monadic individual, but exists in a synecdochal and material relationship to the wider world. Furthermore, the "tiny part of space" that is the self both recapitulates and decenters the initial "here."

While this scene of writing fails to produce or stabilize a writing subject, it also conspicuously avoids partaking of the modernist discourse of a crisis of language made familiar by Hugo von Hofmannsthal's "A Letter," Rainer Maria Rilke's *The Notebooks of Malte Laurids Brigge*, or Robert Musil's *The Confusions of Young Törless*. The breakdown of a sovereign, writerly subjectivity does not correlate here to an inability to write or to convey meaning. Rather, it is precisely the act of writing, conceived as something that takes place within a dispersed network of corporeal and environmental media technologies, that constitutes a new model of decentered subjectivity.[60] A key feature of this model is the ambivalent role of the body as both the tool that generates the self in the act of writing and, on the other hand, the entity in which the self is most commonly located. It is this paradoxical, dual status of the body both as an instrument for producing the self in interaction with the environment and as the metonymic representative of the self that Döblin probes.

Helmuth Plessner's distinction between the body as *Körper* and as *Leib* can help make sense of the dual status of the body in Döblin's dedication. Plessner, we recall, described the *Körper* as the body in which the subject is located, while the *Leib* is the body through which the subject interacts with its environment.[61] For Plessner, the human is at once located inside and outside the body: the human *is* a body and, as a self-reflective subject, *has* a body that it deploys instrumentally.[62] Coming to a similar conclusion as Döblin's essays from a very different perspective, Plessner's positional phenomenology of the human body disallows any static dichotomy between nature and technology, because it is precisely a logic immanent to organic life that produces the human eccentricity that gives rise to culture and technology. The concept of eccentricity—the insight that the dual role of the body displaces the subject and complicates its relation to both its body and its environment—provided Plessner with a way to conceptualize the relationship between body and subject and to sidestep a body/mind dualism.[63] By deriving the unique human characteristic of eccentricity from an immanent development within things' relationships to their borders, Plessner is also able to offer a definition of the human being as qualitatively and relatively—but not absolutely—distinct from other living things. The prominence of reflections on the figure of the border in Döblin's writings from the 1920s, and especially in *Mountains Seas and Giants* and *The I above Nature*, places his work in a similar intellectual constellation.[64] By unfolding the relationship between the self, the body, and instrumentality, he mobilizes a logic of organic growth that collapses the bounds of the autonomous body. Yet Döblin arguably pushes the tension between being and having a body further than Plessner by staging the clash between being and using a body in the ruptured and reconstituted interfaces between organs and organisms, body and environment. In Döblin's novel from 1924, instrumentality is not only a decentering or eccentric feature, as it is for Plessner, but also one which ruptures the very boundaries that eccentricity still presupposes.[65]

In this sense, the scene of writing from the dedication can be understood as a condensation of the novel as a whole. Where the former traces a movement from the body that writes to the self which is inscribed across a media relationship consisting of corporeal, technological, and environmental elements, ending in an image of dispersed subjectivity,[66] the fate of instrumentalized bodies in *Mountains Seas and Giants* results from a similar dialectic and culminates at the end of the novel in a de-individualized collective freed from the instrumentality that was originally tied to the contours of the individual body. The dedication constructs a technological relationship of perception and signification that is inseparable from the relationship between body and environment. Döblin's topological strategy of rupturing the bounds of the individual body also produces the dissolution of any conceptual boundary between nature and technology as separate spheres. More precisely, the extended de- and reincorporations that take place demonstrate that nature and technology cannot coherently be conceived as separate spheres in the first place. Thus, rather than reproducing the violent fantasy of the armored body, in *Mountains Seas and Giants* Döblin unfolds the immanent implications of the trope of the body-as-tool to show the inseparability of nature and technology and to explore the body's ambivalent instrumentality.

An early scene in the novel renders this convergence of nature and technology graphic by depicting the wiring-together of organic and technological elements. Meki's laboratory, in the vicinity of twenty-sixth-century Edinburgh, is the leading center of global research in synthetic food production, and this section of the novel sets the tone for much of what follows. The production of synthetic food eliminates agriculture's dependence on unpredictable natural cycles, thereby creating the material surplus and attendant bodily and spiritual torpor that results in the global "Ural War" and subsequent bloody chaos. Moreover, the entire project of synthesizing food requires the total instrumentalization of organic bodies. Yet as later episodes will show, this undertaking marks the beginning of a relationship between bodies, growth, and instrumentality that ultimately results in the defeat of instrumentality, since the disruption of the distinction between individual bodies undoes the distance necessary for these bodies to be controlled in the service of a rational end.

Meki's researchers, called "Greens" after the uniforms they wear, conduct experiments on the at first unwitting human test subjects, the "Guests" or "Violets." In their experiments, the body itself is not a privileged site— "The physicists and chemists emancipated themselves from animal and plant bodies"—but the organs are, as the Guests are habitually vivisected and incorporated into various apparatuses.[67]

> Around [the Guests], in glass closets, in boxes waterbeds, at temperatures varying from subterranean coolness to high degrees of warmth, white and red organs and parts of organs lay on cotton wool, floated in containers wrapped and bare. From upright vessels the nourishing circulation fluids flowed into them in thin tubes. . . . The observing apparatuses were pushed up against all of them, living organisms, living organs, pulsated organ parts. . . . The immensely tall glass cylinders, in which white red-veined intestines moved slowly

vermicularly [*wurmartig*] on their mesentery, separated or connected to the organism. Substances were poured sprayed spread onto them, the metamorphosis they underwent on the oozing mucosa, on the thin intestinal wall was observed. The skulls of some of the people were opened, the hairy capsule lay next to them. The swelling pulsing brain was laid down backwards in a warm liquid bed. The full blue veins ran thickly over the furrowed whitish mass; it was taken apart, wires and tubes ran into its interior. Wires and tubes led also to the intestines, into the blood, into the liver.[68]

This total, capillary interpenetration of organic elements and scientific apparatuses is characteristic of the technology depicted in Döblin's novel. It is not just the image of tubes and wires leading into human organs that gives this scene its particular quality, but the repetitive insistence with which laboratory equipment is interlayered with living organs. The enumeration of body parts and components—livers, muscles, cells, intestines, mesentery, mucous membrane, skull, brain, scalp—gives an impression of completeness, which paradoxically reinforces the sense of fragmentation. The body parts are spread out separately from one another and interspersed with apparatuses, observing scientists, and purposive bustle. The end effect is an image of an entity or system that is as technological as it is biological; or, better, the microscopic integration with living matter is sign and symbol of this fictional advanced technology. Döblin depicts a circulation and a metabolism, but these can only be described as biological processes mediated by technological apparatuses, or technological processes mediated by organs.

The "confusion" (*Wirrsal*)[69] of tubes and wires running through the "glass coffins" in Meki's laboratory is connected to a greenhouse, in which plants and trees are similarly wired through their leaves, trunks, and roots: "They too were surrounded by a confusion of wires and pipes. They were split, tapped into; wires led into the treetops trunks roots."[70] Here again an enumeration of parts creates a sense of fragmentary accumulation rather than organic wholeness. To the extent that Meki's violent dismembering and coupling of organs and plants represents a Promethean quest for knowledge, it could certainly be seen as the domination of nature by technology. Yet the textual emphasis on interpenetration and interwiring challenges the very distinction on which this hierarchical antagonism would need to be based. Seen in this way, the gruesomely literal interpenetration of technology and nature in the *Mekiwerke* serves as a model for the way that nature and technology are increasingly interwoven in the instrumental body throughout the novel. Furthermore, it seems as though technology can only be technology in this novel to the degree that it *becomes* nature. The awed popular reaction to the rumors, and then the products, of the *Mekiwerke* suggests as much: "People dreamt, were in Cockaigne. 'They have artificial animals. They can make trees.' "[71] It is not simply the domination of nature that is at stake in this passage, but its production. What the dissection and reconstruction of life in Meki's laboratory shows is emblematic of *Mountains Seas and Giants* as a whole. The literal fusion of nature and technology mirrors the conceptual breakdown of the distinction between the two, and these radical mergers yield and are yielded by the rupture of individual bodies.

Seen in this light, the dismemberments depicted in Meki's laboratory, where the emphasis is placed on organs over organisms, become ambivalent. On the one hand, the violent integration of organs and apparatuses is in the service of a rational procedure with a clearly defined instrumental end. While the "guests" are forcibly de-individuated, this rationalistic procedure solidifies the technocratic selfhood of Meki, whose name will be associated with the synthetic food for the remainder of the novel. As if parodying the Cartesian division of the world into *cogito* and *extensa*, a later passage about the Meki works will distort human bodies into fat and growth, and reduce mind (*Geist*) to ghosts (*Geister*).[72] On the other hand, the rupture of human bodies and their integration into technological, biological assemblages, in keeping with Döblin's programmatic critique of the sovereign individual, will generate its own logic, which will come to undermine individuation, instrumentality, and dualism.

This ambivalence is magnified in a subsequent scene, where it is no longer the body that is instrumentalized, but the principle of organic growth itself. Marduk, the second Consul of Berlin and one of the most prominent characters in *Mountains Seas and Giants*, ascends to power through a gruesome stratagem. After the death of Marke, the first Consul, Marduk seizes power with a decisive action—he takes forty-two leading researchers by surprise, imprisoning them in an enclosed forest of beech trees near his Brandenburg laboratory. The hostages, not expecting further hostilities (since Marduk is a researcher like them), nevertheless begin to notice strange features of the surrounding trees.[73] The trunks are split in places, and the fissures are leaking a strange yellow slime. They dimly recall Marduk's experiments with plants: "In the Meki laboratories he had supposedly produced peculiar changes in the growth of animal organ parts, especially of parts of plants."[74] As they speculate what preventive measures might have led Marduk to confine them there and when he might arrive, they notice that the trees are warm in places, and seem to be making noise: "When they laid their heads on the bark, it hummed whirred buzzed inside. That was the sap; it was spring. It was just strange, how shrilly it moved in the pith and in the wood."[75] The steam that erupts from a broken branch renders one of the party unconscious. Overnight, the trees grow at an alarming rate, cutting off what had recently been open space: "They looked for the open spots between the thick, ever thicker trees, as if they did not know that each space had still been open hours ago."[76] One woman's arm is pinioned and crushed between two trees; in desperation, two men kill her to silence her cries before strangling themselves with their belts. The trees continue to grow, accompanied by fluid and splintering sounds, as they sporadically eject fatal juices. Birds wandering into the canopy fall into the trees and are consumed by the wood. The section ends with this passage:

> The mammoth trickling cracking growth pressed squeezed crushed mashed the people, cracked their ribcages, broke their vertebrae, shoved the bones of the skull together, poured the white brains over the roots. The trunks touched. Root trunk treetop a mass, one fused heaving burrowing steaming block. Up top it burst, sizzled. Down below it sprouted swallowed pushed it up, pushed sideways all the way to the wall.
>
> Das mammutische triefende krachende Wachsen zerpreßte klemmte malmte manschte die Menschen, knackte die Brustkörbe, brach die Wirbel, schob die Schädelknochen zusammen, goß die weißen Gehirne über die Wurzeln. Die Stämme berührten sich. Wurzel Stamm Krone eine Masse, ein verschmolzener wogender wühlender dampfender Klotz. Oben barst er, zischte. Unten trieb schluckte drang es auf, drang seitwärts bis an die Mauer.[77]

The disturbing character of this passage results from the way that the destructive fusion between individual organisms stems from a tendency innate to these organisms. The technological upper hand that allows Marduk to carry out his coup is the principle of organic growth itself: "A terrible inner life stretched the rutting agitated plant beings."[78] Just as in Meki's laboratory, the progress of technology depends upon a violent rupturing of individual forms. The same components of a tree that were enumerated in Meki's laboratory—"root trunk treetop"—recur here, and again the result is the disruption of an integral form. If, in Meki's laboratory, the end effect was a ghastly fragmentation, the agglomeration that occurs here is no less monstrous.

Shortly before his death, Marduk, now a penitent renegade, returns to the theme of bodily integrity. He has taken up with Elina, the former lover of Marduk's now dead companion Jonathan. Marduk's actions as Consul had led to Elina's capture and torture, including the laming of one arm, but they have reached a reconciliation of sorts. At the edge of a wood, Marduk expresses a hitherto uncharacteristic aesthetic sensibility. "'Beautiful life,' he whispered, 'beautiful trees, beautiful fog . . . beautiful fog, beautiful tree,' he held her to himself, 'beautiful human. Beautiful human. Human hair. Human fingers. Human ears. Human neck. . . . Human hair. Human hand. Wounded shoulder. What have I sinned.'"[79] Is Marduk naming the body parts as parts, reinforcing a disintegration in language that he has already made in practice, or is he attempting to atone by delineating the contours of a healed whole? His mention of a wounded shoulder might refer either to Elina's shoulder or to the shoulder of the woman pinioned between the trees. In either case, it is an injury to be reckoned against Marduk, which would support the reading that his enumeration is an attempt to think broken bodies back together again. Similarly, the appreciation of natural beauty is strikingly uncharacteristic for the aging Consul and scientist. Yet the things he mentions—life, trees, fog—in addition to being what he sees, all have another meaning that undermines a restorative interpretation. Fog is a dissolver of forms, trees are the weapon of his first battle, and life, as the principle of growth, is what elsewhere causes the dissolution of individual forms.

Even the way Marduk names these items and organs bears upon the relationship between integrity and dissolution. His paratactic listing echoes the most striking aspect of Döblin's prose in the novel, namely, the way it stacks parallel syntactic units, whether nouns, verbs, or adjectives, without connectors, commas, or other markers that would help a reader navigate the confounding semantic multiplicity. In his manuscripts, the visible deletions of commas and conjunctions such as "and" and "but" show that he adopted this style relatively late while writing the novel. Such deliberate omissions suggest that the style of the text must be considered in its own right, in relation to other aesthetic and thematic aspects of the novel, as much as to Döblin's earlier connections to Expressionism.[80] The expected boundaries of the sentence unit are sundered by the repetitive introduction of multiple semantic possibilities, which require not a decision between them, but an acceptance of all of them. In the absence of a hierarchical sorting mechanism to help process the multitudes of actions, actors, subjects, objects, and modifiers, which often lack even the scaffolding of commas that might generate the sequentiality of a list, series, or an unfolding in time, the hapless reader tends to be compelled to accept all of the meanings at once. It is evident even on a first reading that this contorted style has some expressive connection to the violent contortions described, and indeed, a "fused heaving burrowing steaming block" may well be how we wish to describe the very sentence in which we read these words, and Döblin's prose in the novel in general.

What is striking is the way that the parataxis here and elsewhere, by undoing the expected syntactic joints in a given sentence, manages to formally reproduce the dense description of bodies being broken and rejoined that occurs in various contexts throughout the novel: in a laboratory researching synthetic food production by wiring together human and animal organs and plant parts, in the monsters described at great length, in the description of how giants are constructed to combat the monsters, and in depictions of masses breaking and submitting to machines. This is a kind of mass poetics, and to understand it we need to look beyond the Expressionist cry of the subject in revolt or a Futurist mimicry of technological dynamism.

So what are the effects of this stylistic tendency? For one thing, when adjectives, nouns, and especially verbs are stacked together without subordination or overview, this creates the impression of a simultaneous multiplicity of agents and processes so that the basic narrative potential of an active, transitive sentence in the form of "X did Y to Z" is suspended and ultimately dispersed into a depiction of masses and mass processes. But this effect goes beyond a simple pluralization. The suspension of a syntactical order caused by the accumulation of parallel words also frustrates their expected completions, to the point where verbs sound like things, nouns interact with each other and weave together in quasi-verbal ways ("root trunk treetop"), and adjectives or participles gain a density that allows them to do more than merely modify. In so doing, it is almost as if, at moments in the text, the parataxis is able to frustrate the opposition between subjects and objects by stretching their syntactical ligaments to a breaking point. In the sentence "Root trunk treetop one mass, one fused heaving burrowing steaming block," for example, the missing copula "were" (*waren*) re-creates the fusion of the trees on the linguistic level, and the stacked participles "fused heaving burrowing steaming" agglomerate the action of the sentence into an amorphous mass of attributes of the resulting "block."

To put it differently, if the parsed sentence tells us that the parts of a tree became one mass which then did these things, the sentence's peculiar structure confounds doing and being, parts and wholes, acting and being acted upon, in ways that recall the organicist themes of the passage. The parataxis and deemphasis of the individual subject have their fitting analogue in an unconstrained principle of growth associated with *Leben* (life), which ruptures both the boundaries of individual bodies and the defined contours of a linear narrative syntax. The dense and often bewildering style of *Mountains Seas and Giants* must therefore be understood as the product of Döblin's early critique of the psychological novel, his linguistic skepticism, and his monistic vitalism; indeed, it shows just how strongly key terms of Döblin's aesthetic program, such as the "cinematic style" or the "fantasy of fact," reflect an organicist vitalism with roots in Döblin's philosophical monism. Thus, while Döblin's later turn to mysticism is often seen as a repudiation of his earlier avant-garde leanings, *Mountains Seas and Giants* demonstrates, with its de-individuated bodies and the prose that both echoes and produces their de-individuation, that the vitalist seeds of this mysticism informed Döblin's avant-garde critique of language, subjectivity, and the psychological novel from the beginning.

For another thing, this parataxis dislocates the narrator's voice by frustrating a stable vantage point in time or space. If this is a "cinematic style" (*Kinostil*), in other words, then the connotation is not that of a distanced vision, let alone a perspective guided by a single camera, but would be more akin to a kind of discontinuity editing that heaps images, moments, things, and movements upon the screen without the illusion of spatial continuity or narrative sequence. As in "To Novelists," the purpose of this style is to undermine a linear narrative that would reinforce the stability of the individual subject.[81] Döblin's *Kinostil* is thus *both* a literary borrowing of the possibilities and connotations of a modern media technology *and* an expression of his monism. If we recall Döblin's dismissal, in "To Novelists and Their Critics," of terms like "anger" and "love" as deceptive poetic fictions, then this disruption of a straightforwardly causal narrative thread by piling words on top of words can suggest what he means when he calls in the same essay for observing and noting (*Beobachtung* and *Notierung*): not in the first instance what we might think of as a documentary style (for the parataxis frustrates the stable framework that such would imply), but rather as a way to convey an attitude of observation as a negative, corrective stance contrasted to the linear, causal narrative concatenation that Döblin criticizes in the early essay and disrupts in the novel. In other words, observation would be at play in this kind of parataxis not primarily because it lists objects and actions (though this is important), but because it disallows the construction of a facile narrative thread that works by simplifying the myriad, multidimensional connections that Döblin views as essential to the body, the psyche, and the narrative text.

We can see, in this sentence-level parataxis, a style that reflects and indeed enacts Döblin's critique of the individual, autonomous subject, a critique that has an aesthetic, a psychological, and a philosophical dimension. More specifically, by decentering, rupturing, and pluralizing the syntactical thread that would tie the sentence's meaning together in one individual strand, Döblin's prose compels the reader to work with simultaneous processes in list form, a kind of reading that reflects the aspiration for an epic, mass poetics. Thus, in this seemingly niche question of the development of sentence-level stylistic choices, larger questions are at play, questions that reflect the particularly interdisciplinary nature of Weimar modernism. Specifically, Döblin's conceptual rejection of the individual unit and his critique of bourgeois subjectivity alike find linguistic expression in a paratactic style that sunders the conventional joints between parts of sentences that themselves so often depict bodies being burst open, dissolved, and fused with other bodies.

The play of bodies and technology quickens as the novel's plot continues. If the dissections and capillary penetration of body and apparatus in Meki's laboratory represent an instrumental dismemberment of the human body that ruptures the physical contours of the individual, and if Marduk's manipulation of runaway organic growth is still an instrumental use of a biological phenomenon that completely destroys the corporeal substrate of selfhood, then the giants demonstrate a paradoxical culmination of technological development that undermines the very conditions of its own instrumentalization. While the giants are marked as the most advanced and powerful technology in the novel, the very principle of unconstrained growth that was needed to produce them ultimately dissolves their individual subjectivities into that of a collective organism. As their autonomous selves fade into the collective biological assemblages that compose them, their ability to function instrumentally melts away as well.

Enormous defensive towers constructed out of humans, animals, and plants, the giants are intended as a desperate response to the onslaught of the monsters (*Untiere*) unleashed by the rapid melting of Greenland's ice cap. The lengthy scenes that describe the birth of the monsters advance the now-familiar logic of dissolution and rampant growth. Stirred into new life by the "tourmaline veils" (*Turmalinschleier*), devices used to store the tremendous energy harvested from the volcanoes of Iceland, the prehistoric remnants of bones and seeds begin to grow towards one another, forming, breaking apart, and re-forming into instinctively driven biological assemblages. It will be useful to cite a longer passage here:

> The worn debris of the Cretaceous, bones plant splinters found life again. This raging light baked whatever it could find into bodies. The vertebrae, the shattered skeletons drank the glacial dampness in the clay, drew themselves to each other. From the clay flowed substances they incorporated into their bodies, which they laid around each other; soil, welling water, salts. In them and on them it was already transforming into the substance of their own bodies.
>
> Around all the remnants and debris the earth clenched into something alive, swelled up. So wild was the urge to find bodies, to flow to each other and to move, that the bare land burst in whole rows everywhere on the island, here it rolled itself into a teeming mass, there it grew rampantly under arboreal shapes as if hit by rain. These were no beings that the earth had borne before. Around bare limbs, heads bones teeth parts of tails vertebrae, around fern leaves parts of pistils root stumps the waters the salts soils gathered; it often grew into creatures that resembled the ancient ones of this era, often strange beings turned, sucked at the earth, danced. It was heads skulls whose jaws had become legs, the pharynx an intestine, the eye sockets mouths. Ribs rolled as worms. The living earth streamed together around a spinal column, stabilized itself. It was as though a tangle of veins shot out to all sides from the remnants of bones, as if they were crystals, seed crystals in the oversaturated solution. And whatever lay around the vortex of whirling beings, whatever was touched by the veins, was seized, drawn in whether it wanted to become a body or not. The whirling creature pulled the worms that had formed around the ribs to its mouth if they didn't flee, planted them next to its lips; they swallowed predigested for it.
>
> Die zermürbten Trümmer der Kreidezeit, Knochen Pflanzensplitter fanden wieder Leben. Dies wütende Licht backte zu Leibern zusammen, was es fand. Die Knochenwirbel, die zertrümmerten Skelette tranken in dem Lehm die Gletschernässe, zogen sich aneinander. Aus dem Lehm strömten ihnen Stoffe zu, die sie zu ihren Leibern machten, die sie um sich legten; Erde, quellendes Wasser, Salze. Es wandelte sich in ihnen und an ihnen schon um zur Art ihrer Körper.

Um alle Reste und Trümmer ballte sich die Erde zu Lebendigem, quoll auf. So wild war der Drang zu Leibern zu finden, zueinander zu fließen und sich zu bewegen, daß überall auf den Inseln das bloßliegende Land in ganzen Strichen barst, sich hier zusammenrollte zu einer wimmelnden Masse, dort wie vom Regen getroffen aufwucherte unter baumartigen Gebilden. Es waren keine Wesen, wie sie die Erde früher getragen hatte. Um bloßliegende Glieder, Köpfe Knochen Zähne Schwanzstücke Wirbel, um Farnblätter Stempelteile Wurzelstümpfe sammelten sich die Wasser die Salze Erden; oft wuchs es sich zu Geschöpfen aus, die den alten dieser Erdzeit ähnelten, oft drehten sich sonderbare Wesen, sogen an der Erde, tanzten. Das waren Köpfe Schädel, deren Kiefer Beine geworden waren, der Rachen ein Darm, die Augenlöcher Münder. Rippen rollten sich als Würmer. Um eine Wirbelsäule strömte zusammen die lebendige Erde, befestigte sich. Es war als wenn ein Adergeflecht nach allen Seiten ausschoß von den Knochenresten, als wären sie Kristalle, Keimpunkte in der übersättigten Lösung. Und was um die Wirbelwesen lag, von den Adern berührt wurde, faßte es an, zog es zu sich her, ob es selbst Leib gewinnen wollte oder nicht. Die Würmer, die sich um die Rippen gebildet hatten, zog, wenn sie nicht flohen, das Wirbelwesen an seinen Mund, pflanzte sie sich neben seine Lippen ein; sie schluckten vorverdauten für ihn.[82]

If, in earlier sections, the rupturing of bodily integrity had been a spectacular, violent event, here it is the medium of life itself. In representing the principle of indiscriminate, blind growth, this passage imbues parts, bones, seeds, and organs with motive force, as the paleontological dregs glom to one another, incorporate each other, break, dissolve, and re-form. As Döblin writes in *The I above Nature*: "Thus within nature nothing becomes form, what is formed is merely re-formed."[83] Even rock and stone burst into dissolution in this orgiastic miasma of a protoplasmic nightmare. Verbs indicating fluidity abound (*trinken, strömen, aufquellen, fließen, bersten, schlucken, träufeln*), lubricating the image of a riot of forms in manic flux.

Between the novel's manuscript and the published version of the above passage, an important word went missing. The sentence that reads, "It was as though a tangle of veins shot out to all sides from the remnants of bones, as if they were crystals, seed crystals in the oversaturated solution" originally ended with the words "of the mother liquor" (*der Mutterlauge*), which are crossed out in Döblin's manuscript: "It was as though a tangle of veins shot out to all sides from the remnants of bones, as if they were crystals, seed crystals in the oversaturated solution of the mother liquor" (figure 12).[84]

Mutterlauge, in English "mother liquor" or "mother lye," is defined by *Duden* as a "fluid that remains after a compound has crystallized out of a solution."[85] It happens to be a trope that appears at a few key points in

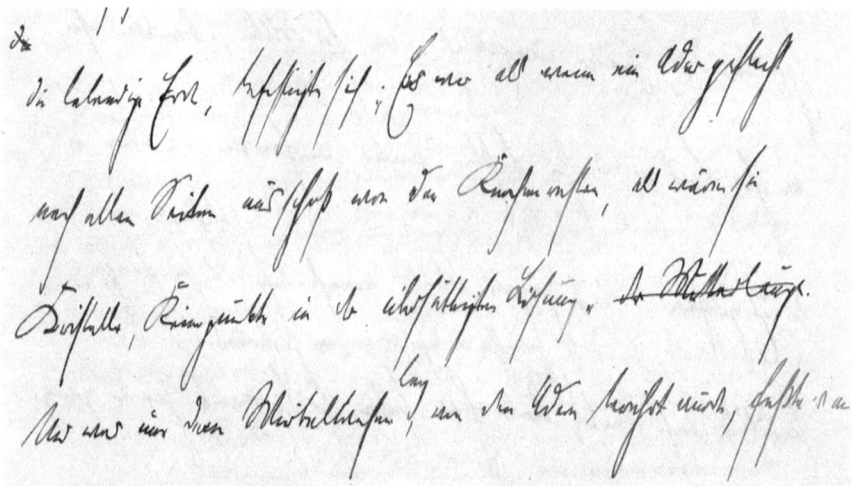

Figure 12. Alfred Döblin, *Berge Meere und Giganten*, manuscript. "Es war als wenn ein Adergeflecht nach allen Seiten ausschoß von den Knochenresten, als wären sie Kristalle, Keimpunkte in der übersättigten Lösung der Mutterlauge."

Döblin's writings from the late 1910s to the late 1940s to variously mean an individual's capacity for change, the process of poetic creation, and the form-rupturing tendency of life itself. In other words, the *Mutterlauge* stands at the juncture of those three fields that are so closely caught up in each other in Döblin's work of the 1920s: his theory of subjectivity, his epic poetics, and his philosophy of nature.

Döblin's various uses of the trope illuminate this juncture and further demonstrate the extent to which the descriptive scenes of violence in *Mountains Seas and Giants* can also be read in dialogue with his vision of subjectivity and his epic poetics. Furthermore, the longevity of the trope of the *Mutterlauge* in Döblin's work, which he used from the 1910s to the late 1940s, points to a persistent continuity in Döblin's thought that is often obscured by shifting political, artistic, and spiritual commitments, which have often given rise to strict scholarly periodizations and to the view of the ever-shifting, non-self-identical "Proteus Döblin."[86] In his autobiographical account of exile, *Destiny's Journey* (*Schicksalsreise*, 1949), Döblin uses the trope to discuss his wartime conversion to Catholicism. Specifically, the *Mutterlauge* allows him to describe his experience of change and continuity in the period immediately after his 1943 conversion:

> One has become more defined, but one is never completely defined through, defined out [*durchbestimmt, ausbestimmt*], in the same way a saline solution crystallizes out. Through all circumstances, all ages, one keeps a portion of mother liquor. That is a floating, nebulous,

seed-bearing mass.... This mass does not need to fear time, it never flees time. Time gives it ever new determinations and forms.[87]

In describing how an individual changes and ages, Döblin writes that a person becomes more definite without, however, moving towards an essential self or ever becoming fully defined: one keeps a portion of "mother liquor" that remains constant precisely in order to allow for change. This "seed-bearing mass" would therefore be a constant that—only apparently paradoxically—offers an individual the possibility of radically different forms of self-expression. The *Mutterlauge* is thus a complex metaphor that ties continuity to change, time to timelessness, possibility to actuality. It is not "afraid" of time but rather gives time the passing, perishing forms with which it can become visible at all. Necessary for this trope is therefore an imagined relationship between the ceaseless fluidity of *Leben* and the forms that give it temporary expression, a nexus that Martin Lindner has argued is central to German thought and literature of the early twentieth century, and particularly to what he calls a "life-ideology" (*Lebensideologie*).[88] In the context of *Destiny's Journey*, the *Mutterlauge* allows Döblin to both explore and relativize his conversion to Catholicism. Around the same time that Döblin was writing about his conversion in *Destiny's Journey*, he was also reflecting on his earlier poetic process. In his essay "Epilog," written in 1948, he describes the moment of poetic inspiration: "Then at some time or another a piece of news, a report would grip me. It would have had to be a special news report and account, for when it caught my attention and had an effect and I got hold of it, then it proved to be like the seed in a mother liquor, an oversaturated solution [*als Keim in einer Mutterlauge, einer übersättigten Lösung*]: now the crystals rushed together."[89] Here the *Mutterlauge* offers an image of the emergence of a work out of the mass of epic potentiality. In this respect, this passage recalls the much earlier description of the creative process in "The Construction of the Epic Work," according to which the epic emerges after a lengthy period of reading, assimilation, and inner fermentation. As discussed above, Döblin describes how this process interweaves the epic poet and the factual world of nature, "the great epic writer," blurring the boundaries between subject and object. So it is fitting that his depiction of poetic inspiration in "Epilog" deploys a trope that can also express the shifting configurations of self and world. Here the individual work crystallizes out of epic potentiality, which however persists and gives rise to new forms. This idea of a forming formlessness also bears on the essential unboundedness of the epic work as described in "The Construction of the Epic Work," which Döblin contrasts to the closed form of the book.[90] And finally, in an early instance, the *Mutterlauge* is used to characterize the relationship between society and culture, particularly the background conditions for the emergence of a new cultural movement such as Expressionism. In the essay "Of the Freedom of a Writerperson" ("Von der Freiheit eines Dichtermenschen") from 1918,

Döblin writes that Expressionism "has the well-known effect of the kernel of salt in the mother liquor [*Mutterlauge*], around which crystallization takes place, but the crystallization of the mother liquor."[91] In the interactions between Expressionism and the individuals who constitute it, Döblin sees the capacity for a cultural movement to crystallize processes and tendencies that are already latent in the historical moment and in individual people alike. Döblin also uses a geological comparison to describe this latency: individuals are already complexly "shifted" (*verschoben*) and "intricate" (*verschachtelt*) more so even than the earth itself,[92] such that a new movement can activate hidden connections within the potentiality and polyvalence that Döblin locates in both individuals and historical moments alike.

In all of these examples, the metaphor of the *Mutterlauge* has both a positive and a negative significance. Positively it expresses the presence of countless tendencies, drives, and possibilities for the formation of a work of art, an individual, or a historical phenomenon. Negatively, it implies that the emergence of a definite possibility does not restrict the generative potential of time: the crystals emerge but the mother liquor remains. These examples also suggest that the relationships between form and fluidity, emergence and latency inform Döblin's thought on a deep level, allowing him to analogically link an individual life, a historical collective, and an epic poetics as layered instances of a single relation.

One can only speculate why Döblin deleted the mention of the *Mutterlauge* from *Mountains Seas and Giants*. Perhaps he thought it superfluous. Perhaps he thought it too obscure for the context. Perhaps this deletion was only a local example of the stylistic revisions in a novel marked throughout by deletions in favor of more elliptical formulations. Yet the *Mutterlauge* remains in the book's logic in vestigial form despite its deletion in the manuscript. For one thing, the words that remain in the passage in *Mountains Seas and Giants*—"oversaturated solution" (*übersättigte Lösung*)—are also used as an apposition to *Mutterlauge* in "Epilog": "then it proved to be like the seed in a mother liquor, an oversaturated solution: now the crystals rushed together."[93] For another thing, recovering the linkages between this passage in *Mountains Seas and Giants* and Döblin's other uses of *Mutterlauge* can help explain what precisely might be at stake in the novel's protracted scenes of primordial body horror. Far more than a graphic reverence for the awesome power of nature, the corporeal fusions of the *Untiere* in Greenland—and the *Giganten* to come—must also be read as a vivid rendering of a trope of becoming and change, a trope Döblin also used to represent change and constancy in an individual life, the conditions of emergence of a cultural movement, and the crystallization of an epic out of the mass of historical material. The writhing coalescence of bones and other organic material into new life is also, in other words, a self-reflexive statement of a poetics and a model of subjectivity. And if the constellation of these instances of the *Mutterlauge* shows that Döblin was invested in rethinking nature, literature, and subjectivity in shared terms and analogically, then there can be no question of *Mountains Seas and Giants* offering a straightforward parable about nature's humbling response to humanity's hubris. Such a reading would also help explain why this organic violence is a stage in the reworking of human subjectivity that is necessary for the post-apocalyptic communities to appear by the end of the novel. The trope of the *Mutterlauge*, borrowed from chemistry and applied to several distinct yet overlapping discourses, exemplifies a pervasively interdisciplinary modernism that may have shifted its terms and focus over the decades while continuing to work from some of the same impulses and with some of the same guiding tropes.[94]

These connections among various discourses and registers can help illuminate how the violent dissolution of individual bodies in *Mountains Seas and Giants* can possibly come to have a positive function. As the monsters—now enormous bricolages of various components—float or fly from Greenland to Europe, their destructive effects are homologous to their own genesis. Whatever they come into contact with is submitted to the same somatoclastic growth that produced the monsters in the first place. Those unlucky enough to be caught in the vicinity of other species fuse with them, spectacularly and agonizingly: "the bird's talons grew through the arms of the screaming piercing hitting soon unconscious woman. The animal lay on the woman, grew on her, bigger than a person."[95] In response, researchers begin constructing the giants of the novel's title by fusing humans, animals, plants, and inorganic material together. More than any previous technological endeavor portrayed in the novel, the giants embody nothing so much as the force of a rampant growth that destroys the barriers between individuals, bodies, and species: "The terribly destructive nature of this power became clear in the experiments: it burst every connection, forced parts out of the body, to the destruction of the organism."[96] Here the instrumentalization of the human body is pushed to an immanent consequence, namely, the total disintegration of that body.

Yet in contrast to earlier scenes of terror, in the formation of the giants, disintegration here serves a positive function. The instrumentalization of human bodies proves to be self-defeating, since the principle of dissolution ultimately renders a sustained instrumentality impossible. The man chosen by the scientist and technocrat Delvil to be among the first implanted into a giant addresses the latter defiantly: "'When I see your tower, Delvil, I praise the power of the Earth. You will not conquer it. I praise the great power. I feel myself in it. There is no border between it and me. I am not afraid. You are going to dissolve me. Okay. I want to go there.'"[97] All elements of the giants tend towards fusion, but they are still at least partly recognizable as elements, and the scientists strive to keep the human essence (*Menschenwesen*) of the growing giants awake so that they can fulfill their instrumental deployment against the monsters. "They were often on the verge of giving up their mind and their human essence and dozing off into mere rampant growth."[98] Like the monsters, the parts of the giants grow towards each other in omnivorous need, once the principle of growth has been provided by the tourmaline veils. Animal, vegetable, and mineral elements merge as the giants grow into creatures, scenes of struggle, and even landscapes:

> Their eyeballs were bigger than a living man; their breath blew like a storm from their mouth, which they kept open as if they were screaming.... Only rarely were small amounts of food brought into their mouth, brought over the hanging jaws and dumped out; the giant beings, laboriously gurgling and swallowing, rooted in the animal and plant ground. Their legs were bulbous stiffened from the hips, the pelvis down; the legs stood broadly, widened [*verbreiterten*] massively towards the bottom, merged with the mass of the ground, dissolved into strands, losing their fleshy character. From the ground fluids and masses of nourishment flowed into their body. Tree and animal trunks grew rampantly into them, through their abdominal wall, into their flanks, spread out in the mesentery, broke into the intestines, melted together with them. They poured animal blood, plant saps into the intestines, which slowly rose and fell, contracted and stretched out like worms. This was the motion that one observed halfway up the human towers: the slow back and forth of the intestines, which stiffened heaved and unclenching descended again. Each time, they pulled the swaying loose slope to themselves, the climbing forest, the extended animal bodies sprouting out of the forest: the enormous horses standing upright, their front legs buried in the body of the animal people, writhing with their necks out of its body and chewing unconsciously on the leaves, the soft wood. The cattle that seemed to leap from the abdominal cavity of the human giant, rooting in the grass of the forest floor down below, as if lusty in their urge to eat; but they bent their bodies upwards to the rear; what they were eating they were not eating for themselves; one would not see their hips and rear legs; they had disappeared in the stomach of the tower people and baked together with it. They were cattle chewing and a mouth that the giant opened above them, a tube from which he sucked. The testicles of the men fused with treetops and blossoms; they poured their juice into the round objects that they bore like berries. One would often see the giants bend under the excess of juices, moan and spill their semen.

> Ihre Augäpfel waren größer als ein lebender Mann; sturmartig blies der Atem aus ihrem Mund, den sie offen hielten, als wenn sie schrien.... Wenig und selten wurde Nahrung in ihren Mund, über die hängenden Kiefer gefahren und gestürzt; die Riesenwesen, mühselig gurgelnd und schluckend, wurzelten in dem Tier- und Pflanzenboden.

> Ihre Beine waren von den Hüftgelenken, dem Becken an knollig versteift; breit standen die Beine, verbreiterten sich massig nach abwärts, gingen in Stränge aufgelöst, ihren Fleischcharakter verlierend, in die Bodenmasse über. Von da strömten Säfte und Nährmassen in ihren Leib. Durch ihre Bauchdecken, in die Weichen wucherten Baumstämme und Tierrümpfe in sie, breiteten sich in dem Gekröse aus, brachen in die Därme ein, verlöteten mit ihnen. Tierblut, Pflanzensäfte ergossen sie in die Därme, die sich langsam hoben senkten, wurmartig zusammenzogen und streckten. Dies war die Bewegung, die man in halber Höhe der Menschentürme sah: das langsame Hin und Her der Därme, die sich versteiften hoben und ihren Krampf lösend wieder heruntersteigen. Mit sich zogen sie jedesmal den schwankenden lockeren Abhang an sich, den aufklimmenden Wald, die hingedehnten, aus dem Wald sprießenden Tierleiber: die übergroßen Pferde, die aufrecht standen, die Vorderbeine in den Leib des Tiermenschen vergraben, mit ihren Hälsen sich aus seinem Leib windend und bewußtlos an den Blättern, dem weichen Baumholz kauend. Die Rinder, die aus der Bauchhöhle des Menschenriesen zu springen schienen, ganz wie wollüstig im Freßdrang in die Gräser des Waldbodens unten gewühlt; aber ihre Körper bogen sie nach hinten hoch auf; was sie fraßen, fraßen sie nicht für sich; ihre Hüften und Hinterschenkel sah man nicht mehr; sie waren im Bauch der Turmmenschen verschwunden und mit ihm verbacken. Sie waren mahlende Rinder und ein Mund, den der Riese über ihnen öffnete, eine Röhre aus der er sog. Die Hoden der Männer verschmolzen mit Baumwipfeln und Blüten; sie strömten ihren Saft in die runden Körper, die sie wie Beeren trugen. Oft sah man die Riesen unter der Überfülle der Säfte sich biegen, stöhnen und ihren Samen vergießen.[99]

This passage is, in a sense, the culmination of the novel's dedication. Where the hand holding the writing instrument evoked an image of the human body as a nexus of sensory and physiological flows, the giants push this immanent logic of the instrumental body to a point where distinctions between bodies, organs, organism, and environment are no longer tenable. The self is not something that is distinct from the body or located within the body, but is rather dispersed throughout the body and its environment. The word "widen" (*verbreitern*), used in 1922 to describe how the self is integrated into the world, here describes the grotesque fusion of the giant bodies into the earth.

Two points deserve emphasis here: one concerns a precursor image to this scene of corporeal agglomeration and distributed selfhood, and the other concerns the status of interiority in Döblin's work in the 1920s. In a very literal sense, the depiction of the giants presents the reader with a "collective being" (*Kollektivwesen*) made up of human, animal, and vegetable components. In this respect, the passage is redolent of the depiction of General Tilly in Döblin's historical novel *Wallenstein* (1920).¹⁰⁰ The significant difference between the two passages—that the fusion of animals, plants, and humans in *Mountains Seas and Giants* is meant to be taken literally, as a representation of a futuristic technological undertaking, while the depiction of the seventeenth-century Catholic general is a vivid metaphoric rendering of the presence of his past violence—makes the convergences all the more noteworthy. Both Tilly and the giants are vast bodies that incorporate other plants and animals in ways that are both violent (the creatures are locked into a tableau of rending, fending, and consuming) and metabolic, even symbiotic, in the sense that the animals and plants both feed on and constitute the gigantic human bodies. The two passages further share the visceral, digestive register that enables this simultaneous violence and symbiosis, with words such as *Darm* (intestine), *wurmartig* (vermicular or worm-like), *Gekröse* (mesentery), *geädert* (veined), and *Röhre/Röhrchen* (pipe, or tube), as well as the combination of red and white, occurring in this passage in *Wallenstein* and in various passages throughout *Mountains Seas and Giants*, particularly in the passages discussed in this chapter. The depiction of Tilly in *Wallenstein*, as an instance of the *Kollektivwesen* that blends Döblin's epic poetics with his philosophy of nature, is thus a precursor to the titular giants from *Mountains Seas and Giants*.¹⁰¹ This suggests not only that this violent bodily fusion was an image that gripped Döblin over half a decade, but also that the science fiction novel was a privileged vehicle for Döblin to test and push ideas, tropes, and concepts because its futuristic conceit allowed him to literalize configurations that were otherwise metaphorical.

This literalization bears on the second point. If Döblin's critique of bourgeois subjectivity as early as "To Novelists and Their Critics" had worked topologically—that is, by probing the boundaries between supposedly autonomous bodies and, correlatively, by undermining the distinction between inside and outside—then the endless entwinement of the bodies that make up the giants echoes the complete rejection of interiority as a bodily category in *The I above Nature*. In that text, recall, Döblin disputes not only the presence of the soul inside the body, but even the category of interiority itself. This insistence on material embodiment is also seen when Döblin characterizes thought not as an immaterial cognitive affair but rather as something situated in the body—or, more precisely, in the body's integration with the surrounding environment. Accordingly, Döblin refers to sense organs and the central nervous system as "extestines" (*Ausgeweide*): like digestive organs, sense organs are used to break down, incorporate, and interact with the environment.¹⁰² In a similar vein, "thought" is understood as the active, material integration of the body with its surroundings; not just the capacity of the individual to perceive, recognize, or cogitate the outside world, but to act upon it. "Thought" is thus a nodal point between the competing tendencies of individuation and de-individuation: "The world-being thinks with our muscles and bones just as with the darkness and the light and the elements and our souls. And what is this: we have organs? That is: we radiate. We flow into the world. We participate in the construction, in the existence, in the reality and the realization of the spiritual world-being."[103]

Likewise, with the giants there is neither an interior nor interiority, only an endless entwinement. By attending to the material flows and physiological processes of living bodies, Döblin is able to literalize and thereby to subvert a language of psychological interiority and the spatial sense of containment and closure implicated in that trope. And it is not just corporeality or contained subjectivity that these bodies undermine, but instrumentality as well. While the giants do battle and ultimately defeat the monsters, the de-individuation required for their production results in their gradual drift away from all matrices of instrumental control. Shortly before the conclusion of the novel, the now only vaguely humanoid giants dissolve into the earth, forming a new mountain range in Cornwall.

In a curious twist, the organic agglomeration of the giants and the monsters provides a model for the human communities that arise in their wake. These communities should not be seen as evidence for Döblin's promotion of a naively primitivist stasis (let alone a reactionary organicism), but as a gesture towards the kind of collectivity that would incorporate the critiques of individual subjectivity raised in Döblin's programmatic essays and enacted in the rupture of individual bodies in *Mountains Seas and Giants*.[104] The organic dissolution of individual bodies throughout *Mountains Seas and Giants*, at first portrayed in scenes of terror, thereby comes to provide a utopian model of collectivity and de-individuated subjectivity. The logic of corporeal dissolution and reintegration that culminates in the creation of the giants serves to effect a deliberate movement away from the authoritarian centralism that has been the dominant political form up to this point. The alternative forms of subjectivity prefigured by the giants' monstrous bodies are carried forward by the societies that arise in the giants' wake. Not only do the survivors develop ways of living that are explicitly tied to the catastrophic lessons of the expedition that had melted Greenland's ice and unleashed the monsters on Europe, but the decentered subjectivity that allows for these social forms is itself produced by the ecological integration announced in the novel's dedication and taken to an extreme in the depictions of the giants.

This utopian vision of ecological integration is ultimately embraced by the populations that have abandoned the fortified, underground cities of Europe, populations constituted by a mixture of the remnants of the Iceland expedition and various settlers and sects:[105]

> The chest rose and fell as if on a spinning wheel, sucked air in, let it out. The people clung tightly to the air, saturated themselves with invisible forces. They let the saps and fluids of many plants and animals flow into their intestines, took them into themselves and let the powers that had descended to the earth blaze through them.[106]

The language Döblin uses here is strikingly similar to that of earlier passages on the giants' monstrous bodies, yet here, the metabolic processes of the body provide a model for ecological integration that will shape the novel's later descriptions of their society. Similarly, the way that various organisms strive towards each other and combine is echoed in the portrayal of sexuality after the time of the giants:

> Man and woman to each other. For this one had feet and knees, could walk, approach each another. Gazes to each other, hands to each other, mouths to each other. And not only mouths. One had a body; the only burrowing. What one felt embraced: that one wasn't water, in order to melt away with it. That one abided, this reassurance calming: this staring and fading in the fire's glow.[107]

Given the importance in the novel of the relationship between technocracy, violence, and reproduction (in multiple senses of the word), it should not come as a surprise that the new societies and subjectivities arise in tandem with a sexual revolution. An early counterpoint to the increasingly centralized power located in the cities of Europe is provided by the "Snakes," wandering groups of people characterized explicitly by a liberated sexuality. The key figure of the final book is the eponymous Venaska, "a slender woman with sallow brown skin and thick black hair," who embodies the force of sexuality associated with her namesake.[108] Yet what is interesting here is not so much the relationship, somewhere between cause and analogy, of sexual and political liberation, but rather the way that this sexuality is conveyed in terms that both recall the scenes of corporeal dissolution from the rest of the novel and announce a conception of dispersed, ecological subjectivity that will find its fullest expression in *The I above Nature*. In that treatise, Döblin describes the tendency of things to grow towards each other, a fundamental "clinging to each other of things" (*Aneinanderhaften der Dinge*), as a property so innate to physical matter as such that he is compelled to ask whether there are even distinct beings at all, or whether matter is "merely a dense, indivisible net."[109]

In demonstrating the tendency of all matter to grow towards and integrate other matter, this principle of *Aneinanderhaften* recalls the scene of writing from the dedication. The rampant growth that destroys any distinction between individual bodies in *Mountains Seas and Giants* and the suspicion Döblin expresses about the very existence of individual units in *The I above Nature* ultimately issue in the vision of a collective, dispersed selfhood prefigured in the dedication, where writing and selfhood are distributed over a chain of body and environment: ink, sunlight, paper, pen, hand, nerves, blood, muscles, intestines. This is not a blind organicism in which the individual disappears entirely into the mass, but rather an attempt to imagine what the relationship between individual and collective could look like beyond the psychological primacy of the autonomous individual that Döblin criticizes as anachronistic in his programmatic essays. By the time we reach the final passage of the novel, the depiction of the societies that have come after the giants echoes the environmental integration and the dispersed subjectivity that had developed in the giants:

> The multitudes of humans in rest and death, in courting and fighting for mates, through volcanic eruptions and drownings. . . . And always yearning, the gases of the air into the alveoli of the lungs, and the little cells, the nuclei, the soft protoplasm, always absorbed and passed on. And when their hearts stopped, the cells divided and dissolved, they were new souls, disintegrating protein ammonia amino acids carbonic acid and water, water that turned into steam. Eager for suffering and eager for pleasure, yearning for the long way, groups of souls in snow-covered landscapes, in the broad swinging sea, in blowing storms, in the stone peoples pushed up by the ground into mountains.
> Black the ether above them, with little balls of sun, glittering slagging heaps of stars. The blackness was cheek to cheek with the people; light glowed from within them.
>
> Die Scharen der Menschen in Ruhe und Tod, in Werben und Brautkämpfen, unter Vulkanausbrüchen und Ertränkungen. . . . Und immer sehnsüchtig die Gase der Luft in die Lungenbläschen hinein, und die kleinen Zellen, die Kerne, das weiche Protoplasma, immer angezogen und weiter gegeben. Und wenn die Herzen stillstanden, die Zellen sich trennten und auflösten, waren sie neue Seelen, zerfallendes Eiweiß Ammoniak Aminosäuren Kohlensäure und Wasser, Wasser das sich in Dampf verwandelte. Leid- und lustbegierig, wanderungssüchtig, Seelenvereine in Schneelandschaften, in dem pendelnden weiten Meer, in den blasenden Stürmen, den Steinvölkern, die der Boden zu Bergen hochtrieb.
> Schwarz der Äther über ihnen, mit kleinen Sonnenbällen, funkelnden verschlackenden Sternhaufen. Brust an Brust lag die Schwärze mit den Menschen; Licht glomm aus ihnen.[110]

As in the dedication, selfhood is located along a material chain that links organism and environment. The language of this passage, like that of similar passages from "Nature and Its Souls" and *The I above Nature*, evokes a collection of elements in relation and flux in order to situate subjectivity in material processes of embodiment that weave the individual into the landscape. The implicitly long, open-ended duration of this ecological metabolism complements the shifting scale from the level of the group to the cellular, molecular level, as agency and attributes subtly shift from the humans to material processes and flows. If it is human breathing that "yearningly" pulls the different gases of the air into the alveoli, the passive participles "absorbed" and "passed on" refocus from the human subject to the process as an exchange, a change of focus facilitated by the prose's microscopic zoom from a yearning breather to the protoplasm within the cells. The next sentence—about death and decomposition—pivots on a series of finite verbs that have as their subjects "hearts," "cells," and finally "they," referring to the humans, but now as components in a dispersed material flow. The metabolic exchange conveyed through the passage's syntax has dislocated agency from human subjects into a broader material flow, so that the "groups of souls" is ambiguous, referring both to the "multitudes" of people and to the "new souls" composed of the freed chemical components, an ambiguity compounded by the way that "yearning for the long way" (*wanderungssüchtig*) echoes the "yearning" (*sehnsüchtig*) for breath—by the end of the passage, by the end of the novel, the material dispersal of disintegrated human bodies is bestowed with an agency, a desire that echoes the desire to draw the breath that started the whole process.

In *The I above Nature* Döblin writes: "Here I am protein, protoplasm, cell mass—I am water, calcium, carbon, salt, phosphorus, iron, magnesium, silicon, which move everywhere out there. . . . I am all this, and it has come from afar, prairie, mountain and valley, deluge, open nature."[111] Note the similarities to the closing passage of *Mountains Seas and Giants*: not only do both provide a material listing of biological processes, but the sense of a dispersion of the ecologically embedded individual is underscored in both passages by the connection to distance and travel ("yearning for the long way" and "it has come from afar"). This confluence suggests the extent to which the depiction of the communities at the end of the novel was informed by Döblin's philosophy of nature. The same kinds of connections between individual body and environment—an underlying dynamic of animated matter growing, ceasing, dividing, and recombining—here extend into the projected future with which the novel ends, a cyclical, pulsing, social time of "multitudes of humans in rest and death, in courting and fighting for mates, through volcanic eruptions and drownings."[112] Moreover, the location of this passage at the end of a long development, in which bodies have been broken, joined, and reconstituted, suggests that this development and its attendant violence were prerequisites to the creation of the egalitarian communities at the end of the novel. Reconfiguring the self within the individual body—so that "souls" are located within the metabolic play of matter—enables this shift in the relationship between individual and collective.

Identifying souls with the metabolic play of matter also effectively eliminates death, and this absence perhaps best illuminates the contours of Döblin's organicism during this period. Whereas a common association would hold that all organic beings are defined by the inevitability of death as much as by the vitality of life, death here is underplayed, as it must be if the emphasis of organicism is shifted from the individual organism to the vital, recombinatory potential of living matter itself. The idea of protoplasm is key. While it no longer has currency in biology, protoplasm was held in the nineteenth century to be "the physical basis of life," and was believed even at the subcellular level to exhibit traits of agency, movement, and response that characterized life.[113] It thus offered a conceptual substrate to an organicism like Döblin's, which located life, agency, and selfhood in the metabolic play of matter itself. Döblin mentions protoplasm by name in these passages from *The I Above Nature* and *Mountains Seas and Giants*. Furthermore, carbonic acid—mentioned in the novel in a list of the "new souls" that disperse after the death of an individual—was held to be one of the components of protoplasm.[114] Döblin would almost certainly have been familiar with protoplasm from his medical studies, but, as Gabriele Sander has shown, he also borrowed heavily from Mathias Jacob Schleiden's *The Sea* (*Das Meer*, 1888) when researching and writing *Mountains Seas and Giants*.[115] In Schleiden's book we can find, for example, the claim that "the carrier of life is protoplasm, which is the name given to the living substance."[116] And Robert Brain has shown how nineteenth-century physiologists were looking for the rudiments of consciousness in "cellular protoplasm and the movements of unicellular organisms."[117] The appeal of the concept to scientists (and to Döblin, one suspects) "was its capacity to explain biological *plasticity*."[118] In short, protoplasm offered Döblin yet one more way to decouple life from the individual body and the individual organism, deploying organic imagery to represent malleability, change, and becoming. While death figures throughout the scenes of violent dismemberment in *Mountains Seas and Giants*, the idea that matter itself is alive and ensouled allows for a continuity that preserves and privileges life over death, without having to rely on a religious or metaphysical option that would dematerialize the human soul.[119]

Conclusion

I have argued in this chapter that Döblin articulated his modernist vision in terms of *Leben*, drawing on tropes, registers, discourses, and disciplines related to the idea of life in order to develop his parallel projects of an epic poetics, a theory of the subject, and a philosophy of nature. Döblin's philosophy of nature can be called panpsychic in its attribution of soul to all matter, vitalist in its emphasis on organic growth and change and on *Leben* in flux, and monist in the way it troubles distinctions between subject and object, I and world, mind and matter. But the fact of this confluence between modernity and *Leben* should hardly be surprising in its broader strokes, since the thought of the era was practically drenched in *Leben*. Theoretical, experimental biology was making strides as a cutting-edge, modern science in the public eye, with prominent debates such as that between Köhler's mechanism and Driesch's vitalism making waves that would resonate in unexpected ways well outside the field of biology. Furthermore, monism and panpsychism were popular currents of thought for the generation that came of age around the turn of the century, not least because of the popularizing influence of Ernst Haeckel's translation of Darwinism into the German context.[120]

Thus there is nothing particularly unusual about the fact of Döblin's participation in any of these contemporary discourses. But the specific contours of his biological modernism do stand out. As we have seen in his essays and in *Mountains Seas and Giants*, Döblin mobilized a collection of tropes, ideas from the natural sciences, metaphorical registers and scientific knowledge from his medical background, and eclectic, wide-ranging engagements with contemporary thought to articulate a distinctly modern vision for what he called the "naturalistic era." His philosophy of nature worked through conceptual and metaphorical questions raised by his literary program, while novels like *Mountains Seas and Giants*, *Wallenstein*, and *Berlin Alexanderplatz* offered an imaginative space for literalizing and testing out ideas and configurations—such as the self that cannot be physically contained by the individual body—which are articulated in his more speculative texts. Notions of the subject and collectivities necessitated by his view of the modern era were enunciated in the terms of his philosophy of nature. Monism, vitalism, and organicism, far from representing a retreat from an increasingly technological modernity, were mobilized by Döblin to challenge what he saw as the inadequate strictures of a bygone bourgeois, humanist age, especially its form of subjectivity and its conception of art as the expression of private, interior, individual truths.

There are many different ways of mobilizing a metaphoric of nature. One can emphasize the course of an individual life, derive from it a rhythm of birth, growth, aging, and death, and transpose this rhythm from the individual to the group, in the form of a national collective or civilization, as did Oswald Spengler in his widely influential *Decline of the West*.[121] Döblin too derived a basic narrative structure—the *Mutterlauge*'s constant potential for change—from a biological trope, but to very different effect. One can also derive an aesthetic category from an organic one, as the idea of the unity of an artwork has drawn since Aristotle on the organic unity of the living body. Another venerable tradition relates the unity of the artwork not to the wholeness of the organic body, but rather to the narrative unity of the individual life, where the individual biography bestows narrative form on the chaotic multiplicity of experience. Yet, if we recall Döblin's essay "To Novelists and Their Critics" from the beginning of this chapter, this analogy between individual subjectivity and narrative form had become a problem for Döblin,[122] because the ideological fiction of the "closed" individual subject and the narrative closure expected of the novel had come to justify and explain each other in a tautological way, ultimately limiting both the individual subject and the novel as form. Thus, within the range of possibilities for linking form and *Leben*, Döblin mobilized *Leben* not as biography but as biology, and the valence of this biology is not the organic unity of the body, but the principle of the ceaseless creative destruction of organic growth that makes such a unity impossible. *Leben* gives form only by rupturing it, and the bodies that populate *Mountains Seas and Giants*, like the waves in *The I above Nature*,[123] are not stable entities but momentary configurations of parts of bodies and selves within the vaster flux of an animated materiality. In this way Döblin was able to transfer the question of closure across disciplinary boundaries, too, bringing the disruption of bodily contours, rooted in his philosophy of nature and his medical training, to bear on aesthetic questions of closure—the closures of character, narrative, and style—in the context of his theory of the epic.

Such interdisciplinary transfers as Döblin's corporeal reworking of subjectivity in the service of an epic poetics might also challenge our notion of the political stakes of various cultural narratives of technology within German modernism. Indeed, the novel's utopian vision of egalitarian collectives predicated on a complexly distributed subjectivity bears implications for our understanding of Weimar culture, but not because Döblin thereby asserts a final reconciliation between nature and culture. Rather, in drawing out the immanent consequences of the instrumental body, *Mountains Seas and Giants* complicates Helmut Lethen's logic of "disarticulation" (*Entmischung*), which hinges on the strict separation between the armored body of the cold persona and the passive organicism of the "Kreatur."[124] Döblin's science fiction novel of 1924 poses a challenge to Lethen's characterization of Weimar culture because it subverts the very categories with which Lethen draws his distinction. The violence in Döblin's novel does not ultimately protect the armored subject from internal and external threats. On the contrary, it effects the dissolution of the isolated, autonomous subject in order to enable the new collectives at the end of the narrative. In this reading, *Mountains Seas and Giants* stands as an implicit critique of the discourse of *Entmischung* by staging the coalescence of the organic and the technological and demonstrating that they cannot coherently be thought separately in the first place.

The contours and borders of organic bodies are anything but clear in the face of the corporeal ruptures and reconstitutions that run throughout the novel, and yet they are not merely dissolved into a "warm" fusion either. Instead of the polar stasis that Lethen identifies in the literature of the 1920s, *Mountains Seas and Giants* presents us with a restless movement between contour and dissolution, subject and object, organs and machines, as Döblin refuses both the pole of "exposing" (*Entblößung*) and that of "armoring" (*Panzerung*).[125] Whereas Lethen's cold persona ruthlessly instrumentalizes its own body, the bodies in *Mountains Seas and Giants* are ruptured and reconstituted in order to confound the corporeal mastery necessary for their instrumental use. Because Lethen's teleological characterization of the Weimar political landscape depends on the polarization between the "separation experts" of the Left and the "proponents of fusion" of the Right,[126] Döblin's novel is a crucial document for thinking about the political and technological imaginary of the period as well, precisely because he explores in it logics of separation and dissolution on the literal, topological level. While the violence involved in this exploration has led critics to assess *Mountains Seas and Giants* as a cautionary tale about the dangers of the technological desire to dominate nature, the function of the violent destruction of individual bodies is, in fact, to advance the logic of corporeal rupture and reconstitution that ultimately issues in the complex utopian vision of the novel. Thus there is fusion, and fusion aplenty, in Döblin's novel, but it is inadequate to attribute this fusion to a reactionary politics. The dissolution of the individual in the novel does not serve a vision of power or nation, but must be understood within a complexly interdisciplinary context that sought to surmount an inherited bourgeois conception of the individual and the various dualisms on which this conception was understood to rest. Indeed, other writers of the time such as Paul Scheerbart and Gustav Landauer also advanced the ideas of an animate cosmos and material selfhood—like Döblin, their utopian visions and anarchist, pacifist leanings lend credence to Carolyn Merchant's claim that "as a philosophy of nature, vitalism in its monistic form was inherently antiexploitative."[127]

Rather than simply exemplifying the avant-garde trope of the armored, instrumental body, in *Mountains Seas and Giants*, Döblin concretizes the figure in order to allow its implications to play themselves out on the narrative level. In so doing, his novel is thereby able to imagine the concrete, real bodies that could fulfill the avant-garde demand for de-psychologization and de-individuation. Yet these bodies are radically different from the type of the cold persona detailed in Lethen's study, precisely because of the way that the relationship among bodies, technology, and subjectivity is allowed to unfold over the course of Döblin's novel. By pushing the avant-garde trope of the technological or armored body to its necessary conclusion, Döblin critiques a notion of autonomous subjectivity predicated on psychological interiority and the aesthetic forms that privilege this notion, without, however, falling prey either to a reactionary organicism or to a facile technological fetishism.[128]

The bodies ruptured, dissolved, and reconstituted in this science fiction novel, for all their instability and frailty, thus also serve as missing links among the various discourses and disciplines that Döblin drew on over the course of the 1910s and 1920s: his critique of the psychological novel and its version of interiority, his epochal considerations of technological modernity, and his burgeoning philosophical monism. The dense interpenetration of body, apparatus, and environment that we find throughout *Mountains Seas and Giants* signals the way that Döblin was rethinking issues of identity, subjectivity, technology, nature, politics, and media in tandem. In this sense, the significance of the novel rests on the extent to which it shows that these questions must be thought in relation to one another.

The novel is thus exemplary of the way that discourses central to the culture of the Weimar Republic—discourses of the organic and the mechanical, technology and nature, progress, catastrophe, and society—could not but articulate themselves in shared terms. Far from assuming conceptual dichotomies, it is Döblin's project to explore and collapse them in his novel. Those seeming incongruities in Döblin's work that have made him consistently difficult to situate among a host of disparate disciplines, movements, styles, and commitments in fact demonstrate his importance for understanding German modernism, and not only because he was an interdisciplinary thinker for all seasons whose texts are "paradigms and repositories of modernism," though this is also important.[129] Above all, the interlocking multitude of his positions and approaches compels us to question their relationship to one another and the ways in which they are necessarily articulated through each other.

In allowing for a utopian vision that is not assimilable to the desire for organic fusion often attributed to the political Right, the relationship between violence and instrumentality in *Mountains Seas and Giants* is more nuanced than an instrumental kind of violence that would serve primarily to repress, discipline, and protect the vulnerable self. Rather than standing in the service of the armored personality, the violence in Döblin's novel, by collapsing the dichotomies between organic and technological, body and environment, subject and object, interrupts the cycle of instrumental exploitation on which the construct of the armored personality is necessarily based. Precisely for this reason, Döblin's vision is symptomatic of a broader contemporary imaginary, the conceptual and political contours of which are perhaps better characterized as a dense *Aneinanderhaften* than as the sharp borders of the armored body.

Closer attention to the contours of this contemporary imaginary, here represented by Döblin's interdisciplinary explorations of selfhood, aesthetic representation, and narrative form, might also help us to rethink how we periodize German modernism. If Döblin's turn from the avant-garde experimentation of the 1910s and the 1920s to an inwardly focused humanism, Catholicism, and even conservatism in the 1940s and 1950s seems emblematic of a more general cultural trajectory from the ferment of the prewar and Weimar eras to the isolation of exile and the reaction of the postwar years, then perhaps the continuities in Döblin's thought from the 1910s to the 1940s can offer a useful corrective. If the engagement with biology and vitalism that allowed Döblin to rethink the novel and the subject alike during the 1920s had roots that stretched back into the late nineteenth century, and if his consideration of change and becoming—seen in his long use of the *Mutterlauge* trope, to recall one specific example—drew on these roots well into the postwar period, then this suggests a broad and coherent intellectual development that was not entirely determined by the historical and political ruptures associated with the years 1914, 1918, 1933, and 1945. Thus, rather than a symbolic biography of daring cultural experimentation that was buffeted and ultimately defeated by overwhelming epochal shifts, this narrative might offer the more nuanced account of a sustained, shifting, yet continuously biological articulation of modernity that was inflected—but not overturned—by the vicissitudes of history. From this perspective, *Mountains Seas and Giants*, and Döblin's writings of the 1920s more generally, would represent a momentary intensification of a longer development from the Wilhelminian era to the postwar period, rather than something fragile and singular.

Chapter 4

Organic Modernization

Wholeness and Development in Ernst Jünger's *The Worker*

At first glance, the face that looks back at us from the pages of Ernst Jünger's *The Worker* (*Der Arbeiter*, 1932) is a metallic one. This treatise, which marks the culmination of Jünger's early work,[1] diagnoses a frantic and bellicose modernity that comes as a radical break with the past. Under the organizing concept of work, *The Worker* presents a sweeping panorama of a totally mobilized society that has cast off the vestiges of a bourgeois era characterized by individuality, subjective interiority, and abstract rights and freedoms; unmoored from the past, it careens toward a future marked by its global realization. The symbol and agent of this violent modernization is the eponymous worker; no mere member of the masses, Jünger's worker is coruscant, organized, galvanized. His face "has become more metallic, galvanized on its surface, so to speak; the bone structure is prominent, the features sparse and taut. The gaze is quiet and fixed, trained in the observation of objects apprehended under conditions of high speed."[2] This avatar of speed, violence, and control is no longer a person or an individual, but a Type.[3] The combination of hardness, speed, invulnerability, and anonymity might tempt the reader to see in *The Worker* the depiction of a thoroughly technological society, polemically refined into an emphatic negation of the organic softness and creaturely vulnerability that characterize the bourgeois era and Enlightenment values which Jünger's text seeks to jettison. Or, on the contrary, the text's pervasive invocation of the organic might incline one to situate it within an older framework of organicism—the insistence on wholeness modeled on the living body, seen as a defensive, conservative reaction to the complexity and differentiation of modern society.[4] Yet both of these possibilities would rely on a dichotomy of organic and mechanical that *The Worker* strives to transcend; in so striving, it inflects the meanings of both terms, to the extent that the metallic face of the worker should be read, counterintuitively, as the very marker of the text's organicism. The organic asserts itself throughout *The Worker*. It is there in the treatise's particular vein of teleological thinking, in the way it organizes parts and wholes, in its concept of work, and in its rhetorical strategies. *The Worker* represents a technophilic vision of modernity as an organicist project.

This chapter explores the seeming paradox of a vision of modernity that was both technophilic and organicist. *The Worker*, even aside from this apparent paradox, is a strange text. It is not a work of fiction but a diagnosis and prognosis of what Jünger saw as an epochal shift from the bourgeois era to a coming age of the worker. It is considered an "essay," though the first edition ran to 300 pages. Within Jünger's oeuvre it is thought to mark a turning point, as the culmination of his attempts over the course of the 1920s to determine the deeper historical and philosophical significance of the First World War, which Jünger experienced firsthand as a soldier on the Western Front,[5] an experience that provided the basis for Jünger's 1920 war memoir, *Storms of Steel* (*In Stahlgewittern*). Jünger's text combines a diagnosis of modern forms of social and technological change with the search for a kind of vision and writing that would be able to identify fundamental, underlying forms that give expressive shape to historical changes and anchor a given moment in a deeper meaning. The various modes of this text are tightly linked, as *The Worker* teaches its reader to move from the aesthetic congruence of surface phenomena to the underlying rhythms that portend these phenomena's full realization in a future age. Jürgen Brokoff has identified six distinct aspects of *The Worker*: (1) a diagnosis of the decline of bourgeois society and the rise of a new age, (2) a metaphysics that claims to be able to recognize the Gestalt of the worker, (3) a politics proposing an authoritarian, totalitarian state model, (4) a social theory elaborating on an original concept of total mobilization that should be seen in the context of the discourse on technology from the Hitler-Stalin era, (5) an aesthetic theory that seeks to subsume "nearly all phenomena of modern social life" under a "standardizing, totalizing optics," and (6) the literary and artistic character of the text itself, the way it works through metaphor, analogy, depiction, thought experiment, and the like, rather than with any kind of recognizable scholarly or philosophical apparatus.[6] As a diagnosis of technological modernity, *The Worker* is similar to other texts from the period in enthusiastically welcoming the deeper social and even metaphysical changes associated with technology.[7]

Politically, it may be hard at first glance not to read *The Worker* as a protofascist, or simply a fascist text. Moments in Jünger's text seem to augur, or even welcome, the fascist order that would rise to power less than a year after the publication of *The Worker*. The text starts with a diagnosis of the German national character as "not a good bourgeois," and its illiberalism is flaunted in pronouncements such as the claim that the worker "knows no dictatorship because, for him, freedom and obedience are one and the same."[8] So why should we not read *The Worker* as either representing an iteration of a fascist organicism, or on the contrary as the technophilic repression of organic, creaturely vulnerability? The tension between these irreconcilable options suggests that Jünger's text is doing something more complex than either of them. Jünger's contribution to a discourse of biological modernism seems less paradoxical when one considers what it opposed and how it did so. Modernity, as portrayed in *The Worker*, erupted into the placid world of bourgeois security and values in the form of the First World War. Jünger sees the "total mobilization" that accompanied the war, completely transforming the social, political, economic, and even the ontological landscape, as a necessary rupture that inaugurated a new era and a new kind of human being, symbolized by the worker. In opposing such seismic changes to the bourgeois era, and even in welcoming danger as a respite from historical ennui, Jünger was swimming well within the current of his time.[9] Yet by reading the signs of social, technological, and cultural change everywhere visible in the Weimar Republic as the symptoms of a coming global work-state (*Arbeitsstaat*), Jünger's text goes well beyond the antibourgeois revolt common to his generation. As an explicit rejection of the bourgeois era, *The Worker* takes particular issue with the conceptual abstraction, subjective interiority, rights-based politics, and ontological dualism it identifies with that era and its form of individuality. The political, subjective, epistemological, and ontological aspects of *The Worker*'s critique are closely intertwined. In order to articulate this critique of the bourgeois era and advance his vision of the new human, Jünger adopts strategies from biological discourses: an organic model of the relationship between part and whole, a notion of development based on entelechy, and a pervasive anti-dualism. If Jünger's rejection of the Wilhelminian bourgeois era was broadly shared by contemporaries, the specific contours of his biological borrowings had consequences that make *The Worker* a unique text. In what follows, I will describe these borrowings and their implications for the text's rhetoric, epistemology, and its concepts of work and history. As we will see, *The Worker* differs from older organicisms predicated upon a *restorative* wholeness, yet even in its reconciliation of organicism and technological modernity, it continues to rely on *teleological* notions of wholeness and closure that distinguish Jünger's biological modernism from Döblin's. The differences between Jünger and Döblin, which lie in the details rather than in the fact of their uses of organicism, help illuminate the common ground upon which these writers drew on nature to theorize and construct modernity while also showing how biological modernism was an internally differentiated site of contestation.

The nature of the relationship between organicism and technology in Jünger's text is a vexing question, yet posing it is essential to grasping *The Worker*'s modernism. Rather than opposing these two terms, *The Worker* complexly articulates them through each other. Commentators on the text have often read it under the guiding trope of armor, a trope that suggests an instrumental and protective relationship between technology and organism, as well as attributing a psychological motivation to this armoring. This image of the armored body also entails a series of dichotomies: metal/flesh, hard/soft, invulnerable/vulnerable. While one might be tempted to extend this series to include an opposition between machine and organism, or even between technology and nature, *The Worker* cannot support such dichotomies; indeed, the rejection of precisely these dichotomies is central to the text's project. The trope of armor is at best incomplete, and at worst misleading, for understanding the relationship between the organic and technological dimensions of Jünger's text. Drawing on the work especially of Harro Segeberg, Thomas Löffler, Thomas Pekar, and Benjamin Bühler, this chapter reads key aspects of the organicism of *The Worker*—the way that the organic whole is more than the sum of its parts, the teleological development associated with this wholeness, the fusion of bodies and technology that waits at the end of this teleology, and the anti-dualism this fusion represents—in order to consider the picture that emerges from their interplay. Writing against the presumption of an opposition between the organic and the mechanical, Segeberg reads the fusion of technology and organic body in *The Worker*—the "organic construction"—as an emblem of modernity. Pekar also analyzes the concept of the organic construction, but in terms of *The Worker*'s heterogeneity as a text, in order to account for the various motivations and strategies involved in Jünger's global application of the concept, while Löffler recovers the influence that Hans Driesch, Jünger's former professor of biology, had on the theory of development propounded by *The Worker*. Bühler's work shows how the modern idea of the organic wholeness of the self-regulating living body that emerged in the biology of the early twentieth century influenced Jünger's text. Such complex organicism allows *The Worker* to raise questions that are of broader and deeper interest than its militaristic overtones might suggest, questions concerning the status of the de-psychologizied individual and the possibilities for thinking about the vast time scales of human and natural history once a vision of steady, incremental progress has become problematic. As an instance of biological modernism, *The Worker* mobilizes nature in the service of a radical newness, and weaponizes organicism in the fight against the bourgeois subject.

A Type, but Not Therefore an Armored Body

For Jünger as for many other writers of the Weimar Republic, this bourgeois subject—who was characterized by individuality, psychological interiority, intellectuality, and crucially, dualism—could not meet the demands of a catastrophic modernity that was forcefully realized in the First World War.[10] "After the armistice, which appears to end the conflict but in truth fences in and undermines all the borders of Europe with whole systems of new conflicts, what remains is a situation in which catastrophe appears to be the a priori of a transformed thinking."[11] In such conditions, the individual must be replaced by the Type, whose galvanized visage we have already seen looking at us.

Organic Modernization 151

> The face staring back at its observer from under the steel helmet or the pilot's cap has also changed. The range of its expressions has diminished in its multiplicity and thus in its individuality, as can be seen in a gathering or in group photographs, while it has gained in the precision and specificity of its singular features. It has become more metallic, galvanized on its surface, so to speak; the bone structure is prominent, the features sparse and taut. The gaze is quiet and fixed, trained in the observation of objects apprehended under conditions of high speed. This is the face of a race which has begun to develop in response to the particular challenges of a new landscape and which the individual represents not as a person or as individual, but as typus.[12]

The depiction of the worker's face as sharp, defined, metallic, bony, and attentive evokes a sense of uniformity, even as the description of the fixed gaze suggests the importance of individual experience. The shift between subject positions in this passage demonstrates the ambivalent project of the book as a whole. Just as *The Worker* frequently shifts between a motivated depiction of its contemporary moment and predictive or exhortatory prognostications, thereby altering its mode of address and the reader's implied position from actual, contemporary subject to ideal, future subject, here too the gaze becomes a chiasmus. Where the passage begins by describing the face of the worker from the outside, drawing its associative force from the various connotations of the hardened physiognomy, the portrayal of the gaze puts the reader into the position of the worker. If the outward manifestation of the worker's calm mastery is the steady gaze, schooled in the observation of rapid movement, part of the project of *The Worker* is to school the reader's gaze in the rapid movements of workers themselves. In other words, the line of sight suggested here is a mirrored and autogenerative one: the worker's face looks the way it does because of the way it has learned to look. The multiple, intersecting gazes of this passage suggest the rhetorical structure of the book as a whole, in which observation and description generate prediction and transformation.

Yet, to return to the worker's body, it is true that *The Worker* juxtaposes corporeal solidity and instrumentality to the bourgeois individual and its plural form, the masses, which are seen as problematically uncontrollable and diffuse. The Type of the worker, for Jünger, is able to instrumentalize its body as a precise machine:

> Here images of the highest cultivation [*Zucht*] of hearts and nerves have become history, ones which can sit alongside and match the best traditions—examples [*Proben*] of an extreme, most sober, metallic coldness, as it were, from which a heroic consciousness can handle the body [*Leib*] as a pure instrument, and extract from it, beyond the bounds of the instinct for self-preservation, a range of complex achievements.[13]

By describing the worker's subjectivity as a "heroic consciousness" that has the calculated distance from its own body needed to use that body as a powerful modern technology, Jünger is able to construct the Type of the worker in opposition both to a bourgeois subjectivity predicated on psychological interiority and to the unstructured human masses of liberal democracy. It is worth noting an important difference between Jünger's concept of the masses and Döblin's. Where the latter uses the mass in opposition to the individual, as a preferred form of subjectivity and collectivity in his epic poetics and philosophy of nature, Jünger views the mass negatively, as the corollary of the individual. In *The Worker*, the mass is simply the plural form of the bourgeois individual, unorganized and marred by the same additive logic that constitutes the bourgeois era.[14] The mass and the individual, that is, are simply "two sides of the same coin."[15] In describing how the Worker differs from the creative individual (*Schöpfer*), the text categorizes the features of bourgeois subjectivity that the worker opposes: a finely differentiated soul, uniqueness of character, individual achievement, and a less than robust physical health.[16] "Kultur" is even invoked in opposition to the "Zivilisation" represented by the worker to broadly indicate the intellectual and spiritual virtues of the cultivated interiority of the individual in a specifically German context.[17]

The Type thus serves the strategic function in Jünger's polemic of allowing him to attack what he saw as correlated forms of subjectivity and collectivity. Put positively, the Type was a way of advancing an idea of individual control and sovereignty within the framework of a particular kind of collective. In this sense, the Type is a strategy of aestheticization: just as the gaze of the worker linked the clear contours of the face to the clear vision that allowed for action, the Type is an aesthetic form capacious enough to accommodate sovereign individual action within a reworked vision of mass society. *The Worker* is not holding onto an antiquated form of subjectivity in the face of processes of modernization that have rendered the former obsolete (or even obscene), so much as it is advancing forms of individual subjectivity and collectivity that embody the modern era. The individual and the group fit together because they both demonstrate a "crystalline" structure:

> The mass is essentially formless, which is why the purely theoretical equality of the individuals that are its building blocks is sufficient. By contrast, the organic construction of the twentieth century is a crystalline structure [*Gebilde*], hence it requires from the typus, arising within it, a structure of an entirely different measure. This entails that the life of the individual gains in a clarity achieved through mathematics. It is therefore not surprising that numbers, in fact, precise figures, begin to play an increasing role in life; this relates to the mask-like character of the typus, of which we have already spoken.[18]

Organic Modernization

This passage concisely thematizes the vision of society that *The Worker* opposes. The purely theoretical equality of liberal democracy, the shades of bourgeois interior life, the expressive (rather than "mask-like") character of bourgeois individuality, and the formlessness of masses of individuals are connected. Jünger's text deploys metaphors of liquidity to characterize the uncertainty and weakness associated with liberal, bourgeois culture.[19] Where the worker is hard, the bourgeois individual is soft; where the bourgeois individual is expressive and ambiguous, the worker is functional and determined; and where the work-state exhibits a determining order from the micro- to the macrocosm on the model of crystal formations, the masses of individuals are shapeless and blurred.

At several moments throughout *The Worker*, we read that the body of the masses is vulnerable or unable to defend itself:

> Wherever they have come up against a resolute position, the movements of the mass have lost their irresistible magic—in the same way as two or three old warriors behind a functioning machine gun were not troubled by the message that a whole battalion was advancing on them. The mass of today is no longer able to attack; indeed, it cannot even defend itself anymore.[20]

Beyond the fantasies of power and the evident misanthropy of such claims, Jünger's argument is working on a metaphoric level that contrasts the tightness of order to the looseness of an amorphous mass. This is an underlying pattern that unifies the various areas discussed in the text, from the control of individual perception, to the hardness of the body of the worker, to the epistemological clarity of the Type, to the crystalline integration of the work-state. Where one of the strengths of the worker is the total integration of organism and machine, the body of the masses is marked by a messier, more vulnerable integration of technological and social infrastructures: "The traffic system, the supply of elementary needs like fire, water, and light, a developed credit system and many other things . . . resemble thin strings, exposed veins, by which the amorphous body of the mass is bound up with death and life."[21] The difference would seem to be topological. Where the positive integration with technology represented by the "organic construction" of the worker involves an incorporation of technology into the working body, here it seems to be the outed interior, in the form of exposed veins, that creates the sense of vulnerability. The extended body-machine integration that inverted the individual body in Döblin's *Mountains Seas and Giants*, serving there to explode the isolated autonomy of the bourgeois individual, is here seen as the characteristic vulnerability of that body. Concretely, then, one can, at least at first glance, make a much stronger case for the presence of the armored body in Jünger than in Döblin; the worker is invulnerable precisely because the apparatus has been contained within the closed contours of the typical body. The problem with the bourgeois masses, in this reading, is precisely the amorphousness of that body. Yet the difference between the bodies in Döblin and Jünger hinges not so much on the question of armoring, but on the relationship between organicism and wholeness. As discussed in the previous chapter, Döblin's organicism seeks to subvert wholeness and even the possibility of an individual entity at any scale; Jünger's organicism, by contrast, is deeply committed to an idea of wholeness.

This depiction of the mass explains why Jünger insists that the mass is the "mirror image" of the individual[22]—it also signals a paradoxical historical reversal in the individuality of the individual, who has grown anonymous and indeterminate. Where Döblin deploys the type and the mass more or less synonymously against the bourgeois individual, Jünger articulates his definition of the Type in contradistinction to the mass of individuals. The looseness of the mass—Jünger refers to the "mob" (*Pöbel*) as drawing its strength from the swamp (*Sumpf*)[23]—corresponds to the unique, ambiguous, sensitive bourgeois individual that Jünger identifies with the nineteenth century. "Therefore we will not find the individual [*den Einzelnen*] within this mass. Here we only encounter the individual [*Individuum*] in decline, whose suffering is engraved on tens of thousands of faces and whose sight fills the onlooker with a feeling of senselessness, of enfeeblement."[24] The Type, by contrast, appears in social formations that are seen to be much more discrete and more organized, and which are local expressions of an overriding and teleological Gestalt. This change in social organization can be seen in the new names used for collective forms:

> "Marching parade" instead of "convention," "followers" instead of "party," "camp" instead of "congress"—in these expressions we see that the free decision of a number of individuals is no longer the unspoken premise for any gathering. Such a presupposition already sounds trivial and ridiculous—just as it clearly does in words like "association," "assembly," and others.[25]

By depicting the individual as a serial component of the masses rather than as the center of subjective agency, the text undermines the individual's claim to individuality, bestowing the powers of agency, action, and decision on the Type instead. In a similar vein, a feature of the bourgeois individual comes to be its featurelessness—as suggested by the contrast between the image of "a row of individuals" and the depiction of the worker's face discussed earlier,[26] it is now somewhat paradoxically the Type that is recognizable because of its accentuated, if mask-like character, while the uniqueness of the individual, reproduced in an endless series, merely lends a sense of fatality to its dissolution. To anticipate an important feature of Jünger's text, this diagnosis of the de-individuation of the individual helps explain why this individual seems to be faulted both for its claims to uniqueness and its reliance on a

Organic Modernization   155

logic of fungibility and abstraction. Put simply, the demands of modernity have rendered the individual obsolete; the Type, by contrast, regains agency and control by embracing the loss of bourgeois individuality. This reversal is important for Helmut Lethen's reading of *The Worker*—read as a code of conduct for a radically unsettled era, Jünger's worker armors and sharpens its perception, epistemology, and possibilities for action.

And indeed, thus far I have followed the basic contours of Lethen's reading of Jünger. In stark contrast to the blurriness of the nineteenth-century mass of individuals, "the outlines of the worker-soldier type . . . never blur," as Lethen argues.[27] The armored body and the clear gaze seem inextricable in *The Worker*, and the repeated insistence on the metallic appearance of this new Type suggests that we can, with Lethen, extend the parallel contraries of individual/Type, mass/work-state, expression/mask, and vulnerable/armored to add organic/mechanical. To be sure, such a move is crucial to Lethen's argument, which needs to see the mechanical, cold persona repressing its organic, creaturely side in order to be able to identify a code of conduct that would help navigate the fraught and uncertain landscape of Weimar culture. And yet to see in Jünger's text a strong dichotomy between the organic and the mechanical is to fundamentally misread *The Worker* by ignoring how it was working within existing discourses of the relationship between the body and mechanicity; doing so also risks conflating the Gestalt with the Type and thereby missing the epistemological specificity of the former, which was not merely about making distinctions or armoring perception. When Lethen writes,

> A modern human being, the type realizes the dream of synchronization between organism and technical apparatus. Its being is integrated into technology. Enclosed within an "armored cell," it is the intelligence of a bullet; an electric machine replaces the functions of a central nervous system. Jünger presents the type in centaurlike images, in the concentric encasement of body and machine, as an "organic construction." . . . *Radio signals inform us that an organism yet lurks inside the metal shell. Or is it just the radio simulating its presence?*[28]

one must object that it is not Jünger who is repressing the organic, but Lethen. To suggest, as Lethen does here, that the presence of the organism within the machine might be illusory is certainly seductive and provocative. It is necessary to his argument that the armored technological body represses its organic side, yet it is also completely untenable. For Jünger, there can be no question about the presence of the organism within the machine, because his attack on the autonomous bourgeois individual, like Döblin's, does not necessitate an organic/mechanical dichotomy but rather explicitly rejects such a dichotomy.

The Gestalt and Organic Wholeness

Crucial to Jünger's distinction of the Type from both the individual and the mass is a unifying excess that must be characterized as organic. Jünger describes the difference between a body and a corpse in the following way:

> It is very important that we recover a full awareness that the corpse is not some kind of soulless body [*Körper*]. Between the body at the very instant of death and the corpse at the next, there is not the slightest relationship; this we learn *because the body contains more than the sum of its parts, while the corpse is equal to the sum of its anatomical parts*. It is a mistake to think that the soul, like a flame, leaves dust and ash behind it.[29]

This passage signals an important difference between the living and the dead body, with ramifications that may not be immediately apparent. Where the living body is more than the sum of its parts, the corpse is "equal to the sum of its anatomical parts." The seeming redundancy of the phrase "anatomical parts" signals the valence taken on by anatomy in *The Worker* and echoes the characterization of the bourgeois era as an "anatomical age."[30] Crucially, "anatomical" is here not simply a modifier of the noun "parts"—since the passage is about a body, what other kind of parts would they be?—but rather functions in a precisely reduplicative sense. "Anatomical" does not mean anything like "bodily," but rather expresses a logic of partialness. Thus, in a rather surprising turn, "anatomical" does not correspond to organic—as one might reasonably expect—but rather to "mechanical," which indicates not merely that which is related to machines or technology more generally, but rather that which is modular, and functions without reference to an organizing whole.

For an organizing whole is precisely what is at stake in the claim that a living body is more than the sum of its parts. And while one might see a metaphysical vitality in this passage, a living principle that marks the difference between corpse and body, this is not right either, since the final sentence rejects the image of a departing soul. Furthermore, the problem of accounting for the organic excess implied by living beings was in fact one of the most prominent questions being posed by biology in the late nineteenth and early twentieth centuries. Crucially, the problem involved both the relationship between part and whole and the question of individual development. Donna Haraway has traced the shift from the mechanist/vitalist divide to the new paradigm of organicism. Where mechanists believed that living beings could be understood in terms of mechanical laws, and were ultimately reducible to the picture of the behavior of matter offered by physics and chemistry, vitalists argued that life represented a distinct principle in need of a distinct explanation. Yet, as Haraway suggests, by locating life's uniqueness in a metaphysical claim, vitalists thereby shared the mechanists' presumption that the distinct principle of life was not accessible to empirical observation.[31] Organicism, by contrast, held both that the living being could not be explained solely by recourse to physics and chemistry (and, by extension, that biology was not a subfield of either of these disciplines), and that the principle for life's distinction was to be located immanently, in the ways in which living bodies are organized and formed, rather than metaphysically.

In differentiating the body from the corpse, I suggest that Jünger reprises in miniature this paradigm shift. Distinguished from both the mechanist ("anatomic") and the vitalist views, the surplus that marks the living body is a distinctly organic one. While Haraway's account looks at organicism as it emerged in England and the United States, Jünger's own education was steeped in these debates as they transpired in Germany. As Thomas Löffler and Thomas Pekar have shown, both Wolfgang Köhler's use of the concept of Gestalt and Driesch's neovitalist concept of entelechy influenced Jünger's thought. Other scholarship has situated Jünger's deployment of the concept of Gestalt in its rich and polyvalent contexts, which included the biology of Wolfgang Köhler, the Gestalt psychology of Christian von Ehrenfels, and its broader applicability as a reaction to social differentiation.[32] Jünger's mobilization of these contemporary scientific discourses was not free of contradiction. But then again, Jünger was not working as a biologist but as an essayist. In transposing the idea of organic wholeness from one discipline to another, he freed the terms from the obligations of systemic coherence and empirical validity so that they might resonate more freely with ideas of the individual, society and history.[33]

It is significant in this regard that even the scientific representatives of the new organicism that Haraway describes saw the question in terms of a Cartesian legacy, with the mechanism/vitalism split being the logical outgrowth of a body/mind dualism.[34] Jünger for his part explicitly ties a nature/technology dichotomy to precisely this dualism. As we recall, Plessner made a similar move at the beginning of his book. Clearly, the legacy of Cartesian dualism was seen as an obstacle to any account of the human being that sought to provide a minimum coherence, could account for the experimental and theoretical knowledge of modern biology, and did not rely on a metaphysical exceptionalism.

Beyond anti-dualism, *The Worker* is rife with rejections of any kind of merely agglomerative organizing principle; as the abstract subject of abstract rights and freedoms, the bourgeois individual for Jünger is an entity that cannot coalesce into any collective other than the loose mass. Describing the shift away from an older model of individuality and collectivity, Jünger writes:

> The totality of individuals, insofar as they appear as a mass, cannot escape the process of dissolution to which the single individual is

subject. The old mass . . . belongs just as much to the past as those who claim it as a decisive factor do. . . . Here individuals are piled up like sand into a heap that, as sand is wont, just trickles away.[35]

In his play on the sorites paradox, Jünger's text implies that no amount of sand can ever amount to a unity at a higher scale—a mass of individuals remains a mass of individuals. In the same vein, any model of history that sees it in terms of successive ages, and any theory of society predicated on the abstractions of class, are similarly rejected, because they lack a vision capable of seeing the Gestalt, the whole that organizes and goes beyond a collection of parts.

> For the Gestalt is the whole containing more than the sum of its parts. A man is more than the sum of atoms, limbs, organs, and fluids of which he consists; a marriage is more than man and wife, a family more than man, woman, and child. A friendship is more than two people and a nation is more than can be expressed through the result of a national census or through an aggregation of political polls.
>
> In the nineteenth century, one was accustomed to relegating any spirit [Geist] who sought to invoke this more, this totality, to a kingdom of dreams more at home in a beautiful world than in reality.[36]

The nineteenth century is characterized in terms of a positivist materialism that rejects an organic surplus and organizing totality. Materialist, mechanical, anatomical, abstract—the predicates that accrue to "The Age of the Third Estate" (as Jünger dubs the bourgeois era in the heading of the book's first section) amount to a picture of an age that can talk about parts but not about wholes. Its historiographical correlate is the idea of an endless progress, which Jünger explicitly links to the unique individual. "The flow of a limitless development, the boundless movement of a reason imposed on nature—this is what gives the individual the sense that his experience is unique and so lends him his perspectives."[37] While this connection between the infinite and the particular may at first seem paradoxical, what links them is a partial logic that functions without reference to a closed totality.

By contrast, *The Worker* depends on the category of totality, both in its vision of the relationship between part and whole and in its picture of history. The idea of the Gestalt offers an organizing principle that is formally motivated by the idea of the whole, always understood as more than the sum of its parts. And this logic of wholeness is also what guarantees *The Worker*'s concept of history as a development towards an immanent fulfillment. There is a strong connection, in other words, between the organizing logic that *The Worker* locates throughout modern, totally mobilized society and the teleological development the text claims for history. To see history in progressive terms, as a succession of different classes in power, is itself the sign of mechanistic vision. If the bourgeois individual that Jünger rejects is the correlate of an abstract notion of progress, then the worker, its tightly organized society, and history seen as fulfillment rather than as mere succession constitute the terms of the Gestalt.

In this respect, it is important to understand the Gestalt's paradoxical relationship to time, for it is both eternal and teleological; as we will see, this paradoxical temporality also bears upon Jünger's conception of modernity. A kind of transhistorical, symbolic unity that lends meaning and shape to transience, Gestalt for Jünger manages to be both the expression and ground of temporal change. "A Gestalt *is*, and no development increases or diminishes it. . . . History does not bring forth forms; rather, it changes itself with the form."[38] What is significant amidst these sometimes hieratic pronouncements about the Gestalt is the way that the term's elucidation allows Jünger to distinguish among different ways of standing outside of history. The Gestalt is not to be confused with infinity, but is emphatically a closed totality. "The Gestalt cannot be captured through the universal and intellectual [*geistig*] concept of infinity, but the particular and *organic concept* of totality."[39] Note the contraries: infinity/totality, general/specific, intellectual (*geistig*)/organic. In each case, Jünger contrasts an abstract and linear model of time to a specific, rounded one, and does so in a way that links a relationship between part and whole to a model of history and temporality. The end effect is that the ideas of development and progress are subsumed under a model of organization—the Gestalt—that is spatial and temporal, teleological and meaningful alike.[40]

While the concept of the Gestalt allows Jünger to talk about a kind of wholeness that pertained both to spatial organization and to temporal development, a notion of entelechy, adapted by Hans Driesch from Aristotle and revised for modern, experimental biology, deepened this connection between organization and development. Driesch, with whom Jünger studied in Leipzig,[41] introduced the concept of a "causality of wholeness" (*Ganzheitskausalität*) in 1919 to express the kind of causality, unique to living nature, that stems not from individual factors but from the functioning of a whole system. After conducting experiments on the embryos of sea urchins, Driesch postulated this causality in order to describe the capacity of biological development to form a whole organism from part of an embryo.[42] According to Driesch, entelechy could explain, in a way that mechanist models of development could not, how an organism develops into a whole. The specificity of living nature over inorganic nature thus lay in its innate relationship to totality, exemplified by a unique kind of causality found only in living matter. Thomas Löffler has shown how Driesch's concept of entelechy offered Jünger a model for thinking about the relationship between wholeness and development. Entelechy, which Driesch postulated as a challenge to Wilhelm Roux's mechanistic, "mosaic" theory of development, was an explicit challenge to the idea that an organism could be understood as the sum of its parts. In asking how cellular material organized itself into the discrete, functional parts of an organism, embryology posed at a basic level the question of the relationship among form, totality, and time, and was thus ripe for transdisciplinary borrowings of the sort I am locating in *The Worker*. In early twentieth-century biology, Gestalt and entelechy in fact offered competing approaches for explaining the specificity of organic life, yet Jünger's borrowing of them, by removing them from their disciplinary contexts, was able to mobilize the suggestive ways in which they related wholeness and development.[43]

As Löffler shows, both Driesch's entelechy and the teleology of *The Worker* involve a necessary connection between the organic whole that is more than the sum of its parts and the guiding drive that propels it toward self-fulfillment:

> Driesch and Jünger proceed from the assumption of a teleologically operative formative power, which determines and harmoniously coordinates, so to speak, inner and outer reality. This power brings about the wholeness and unity of everything alive, or rather, everything real. It is so to speak immanent and has a metaphysically transcendent reality. "Entelechy" or the "Gestalt" work "in relation to the final unity" [*endganzheitsbezogen*], the "whole" cannot be derived from the sum of its discrete units, but rather has a teleological surplus.[44]

To be sure, Jünger's idea of the Gestalt differed from Driesch's entelechy or *Ganzheitskausalität* in a couple of key ways. For one, Jünger's application of the concept pertained not to the individual organism but to society and history on a large scale. For another, Driesch's teleology was analytical, whereas Jünger's use of it was prognosticative.[45] In this conceptual borrowing, Jünger was thus not merely adopting Driesch's neovitalism, but was modifying the concept as well. Driesch's solution of entelechy was ultimately rejected by biologists working in the 1920s and 1930s because, like vitalism, it posited a metaphysical force that is inaccessible to observation. In Haraway's account, Driesch's neovitalism left the fundamental problem of the mechanistic view untouched—that is, dualism, or how to account for the behavior of life without assuming two distinct kinds of substances.[46] In his use of teleology in *The Worker*, by contrast, Jünger's project can be said to be a properly organicist one, inasmuch as he seems to reject both the mechanist *and* the vitalist accounts of the relationship between part and whole (in his distinction between body and corpse, for example). His borrowings can be seen therefore not merely as a casual slippage, or as a careless extension of neovitalism into the social realm, but as the attempt to mobilize terms and ideas that could help him account for (and accelerate) the antibourgeois tendencies he saw in modern society, symbolized (as we will see) by a prevailing dualism. In associating a model of totality with a historical teleology, Jünger was drawing on a biological problem to argue against the kinds of dualism that plagued both mechanism and vitalism. Though their visions otherwise differed greatly, the critique of dualism as a trait of an obsolete bourgeois order was something that Jünger shared with Döblin. In *The Worker*, the kind of organic wholeness that guarantees historical development as a teleological fulfillment also marks the state of humanity at the end of this development. Crucially, Jünger frames this state—which he calls the "organic construction"—as the index of dualism overcome.

"Organic Construction" contra Dualism: Life as Order

The Worker uses the figure of "organische Konstruktion" to describe a state where technology has been perfected to the point where it is indistinguishable from nature.[47]

> We already mentioned in passing the concept of organic construction, manifesting itself, in relation to the typus, as the intimate and noncontradictory fusion of man with the tools at his disposal. With respect to these tools themselves, we can speak of organic construction when technology reaches that highest degree of self-evidence inhering in the limbs of animals or plants. . . . We experience how the course of this process generates not only a higher satisfaction of the intellect, but also of the eye—and indeed does so with that same absence of intentionality that also characterizes organic growth.[48]

The telos of technology is the attainment of a state that negates its categorical distinction as technology. The Type is characterized by the complete fusion (*Verschmelzung*) of the human with its tools. Furthermore, with "organic construction" technology becomes as self-evidently a part of the body as plant or animal limbs—in a literal sense, one must speak of an incorporation of technology. The "self-evidence" of technology needs to be understood in a strong sense, as opposed to an arbitrary, abstract, or purely instrumental appendage. What is *selbstverständlich* organically belongs to the body; it *is* organic, and this in a way that pleases the requirements of visual form.

So what is at stake in this idea of incorporated technology? One way of looking at it is as *The Worker*'s redefinition of the mechanical. If elsewhere in the text the mechanical is aligned with the anatomical, as representing a logic of parts, fungibility, transmission, and modularity, here technology has been incorporated, fused into the organic, meaningful whole.[49] So this section of the text can be understood as subsuming the mechanical under the organic—the concept of the organic construction, in other words, expands the meaning both of the organic and of the mechanical.[50] And underlying this shift in the valences of "mechanical" is an even larger dynamic. For Jünger, the concept of technology expressed by *organische Konstruktion* also represents the attempt to transcend the alienating dualisms of nature and civilization, body and soul.

A strong nature/technology dichotomy is experienced as a rift and a form of alienation to be overcome. Just as the armored Type needs the broader context of the diffuse Gestalt to be properly understood, the programmatic thrust of *The Worker* only really makes sense in light of the trajectory towards a state where technology is not experienced as exogenous to the body but rather as a natural part of it.

> Organic construction is therefore only possible if man appears in a closer unity with his means, and only after rectifying the *painful rift* which, for reasons we have already examined, causes him to experience these means today as revolutionary. Only then will the tension between nature and civilization, between the organic and the mechanical world, be resolved, and only then will it be possible to speak of an ultimate formation [*Gestaltung*], at once original, as equal to any historical standard.[51]

To see either an antinomy or a value distinction between the organic and the mechanical is in fact a sign of the "weakened" bourgeois existence, the transcending of which is the project of *The Worker*.[52] That technology cannot, and must not be seen as merely an abstract instrument detached from considerations of purpose is already implicit in the text's criticism of partial, anatomical logic—the claim that it must belong organically to a human whole makes sense, given *The Worker*'s ongoing and tendentious refusal of abstraction. Furthermore, the criticized opposition of organic and mechanical echoes the classical, structuring dualism of body and soul—"the sentiment of a decisive opposition between the mechanical and the organic world, in which we see a final flattening of the old opposition between body and soul."[53] To understand how broad the point was that Jünger wanted to make, and how entrenched was his target, it must be clear from this identification of these two dichotomies—mechanical and organic worlds, body and soul—that the stakes were high. It was not just a historical epoch or form of social organization that *The Worker* was written against, but a long-standing dualist worldview. This much he shared with Plessner and Döblin: all three writers were explicitly aiming for a non-dualist model of the subject. This is also why, despite *The Worker*'s obsession with technological control and its rejection of the diffuse, disorganized contours of the bourgeois era, Jünger's text cannot be read merely as the technological suppression of the organic body, for such a reading depends on the dichotomy which *The Worker* associates with a bourgeois worldview and explicitly repudiates. Far from representing the assemblage with at best ambiguous signs of life within,[54] the "organic construction" fulfills the principle of organic wholeness that Jünger locates

Organic Modernization

in the living body, in contradistinction to the corpse. To see technology as *merely* mechanical is itself the sign of a mechanical, partial vision. Thus, far from the technological repression of organic, creaturely vulnerability, what we find instead is the claim that a dichotomy that pits technology against nature or the organic is itself the symptom of an era it is the text's project to overcome: "Technology and nature are not opposites—if they are felt as such, this is a sign that life is not in order."[55]

Jünger's phrasing here is worth dwelling on. One way of parsing "this is a sign that life is not in order" would be this: if technology and nature are seen as contraries, this is the sign of a deep discord in a given social arrangement or historical moment. Yet given the nature of the organicism of Jünger's text, both "life" and "order" demand closer attention. Life is central to the image of totality that *The Worker* has advanced in the figure of the Gestalt; it is an organizing surplus that differentiates the whole from a collection of parts, while guaranteeing the entelechical unfolding of the whole. Order, on the other hand, is not just an indication that things are right, "in order," but rather signifies the particular kind of organization provided by life. In the bigger picture of the developments described by Jünger's text, this order is a posthistorical, teleological fulfillment. Order is the resolution of the dynamic chaos of the essay's present in the fixed, reconciled, crystalline structure of its invoked future.

To the extent that life and order determine each other, one might usefully identify a parallelism rather than a predication in their relationship. That is, rather than being two terms that merely happen to accord when a nature/technology dichotomy has been resolved—life could either be in or out of order—here each term inflects the other to the extent that they function as synonyms. *Leben* is an ordering principle, *the* ordering principle in *The Worker*, that both gives form to its concept of wholeness and guarantees a teleological development for history. Life is order in *The Worker*, and this foundational copula shapes the contours of the vision for a work-state beyond imbalance and alienation, a final stasis.

In its global realization, the work-state with which *The Worker* ends is both the fulfillment and the negation of the contemporary moment that Jünger diagnoses. It is a fulfillment because work, in the form of the total mobilization that had become increasingly dominant, for Jünger, in the wars, revolutions, and cultural forms of the 1910s–1930s, has now become the total organizing principle of all human activity. And the work-state is a negation because the totalization of work as principle, in *The Worker*, amounts to a new historical equilibrium that would put an end to the strife, chaos, and turbulent developments that Jünger identifies in his present. This conclusion makes perfect sense if one considers that the development towards this stasis—"life in order"—is consistently portrayed in terms of dualisms surmounted.

The "fusion of organic and mechanical forces"[56] is absolutized, and comes to be identified with other oppositions associated with the era *The Worker* seeks to overcome, such as the difference between city and country.[57] Thus, while the period of transition to a world where every human activity falls under the sign of work is necessarily experienced as one of upheaval and rapid change, one problem with reading *The Worker* as Lethen does, where the total mobilization of the present is projected onto a future of permanent war, as it were, is that such a reading does not account for the repeated insistence on the stasis to come. In other words, the value of "codes of conduct" is not clear if the text's vision is a world where these wouldn't really be necessary.

> There is no valid reason to contradict the assumption that one day a constancy of means will ensue. Such a stability is generally the rule over long periods of time, while the feverish pace of change in which we find ourselves is without historical precedent. The duration of this kind of impermanence is limited because the will underlying it either breaks down or attains its goals. Since we believe we can see such goals, for us to consider the former possibility is meaningless. ... We mean by this that the fulfillment [*Abschluß*] of the mobilization of the world through the Gestalt of the worker will enable a life lived according to this Gestalt.[58]

The "totale Mobilmachung" envisioned by *The Worker* is supposed to come to an end in a state of constancy (*Beständigkeit*).[59] In accordance with the biological logic of this entelechical unfolding, the economic and social instability of capitalism and a liberal democracy in transition will be replaced by an economic, social, and political order that has more in common with more proportionate, "natural competition":

> We have entered into a process of mobilization with destructive qualities that consumes men and means—and this will not change as long as the process is unfolding. Only when it achieves its end [*Abschluß*] will it be possible to speak of any kind of order, hence of an ordered economy: that is, of a calculable relationship between expenditure and income. Only the unconditional constancy of means, of whatever nature, is capable of returning excessive and incalculable competition to a state of natural competition, as we observe in the natural world or social situations of the past.
>
> Here again the unity of the organic and the mechanical world is revealed; technology is becoming an organ and goes back to being an independent power only when it achieves perfection and thus becomes self-evident.[60]

Accompanying this stasis is a spatialization of historical processes, as a dynamic turmoil is replaced by an orderly spatial distribution: the perfection of technology "indicates the substitution of a dynamic and revolutionary space by a static and highly ordered space. Thus what is taking place here is a transition from transformation to constancy—a transition that will, of course, have very significant consequences."[61] Life as order: in the repeated insistence on the constancy to come, in the invocations of a natural organization, in the multiple mentions of the "perfection of technology," where "perfection" must be heard in its etymological sense of "completion," Jünger's text heralds a coming state where inherited dualisms—technology and nature, city and country, soul and body—have been overcome, and where the turbulent dynamism of history is replaced by a rigidly ordered, static space.[62]

Arguably, this vision of life in order, far from being just an imposition of an incongruous and rigid vision onto the messy contingencies of history (though it is also certainly that), is already implied by Jünger's very concept of work. So capacious as to be almost meaningless, the semantic vagueness of "work" nevertheless has a functional precision. The dominance in *The Worker* of a belligerent register—the total mobilization, the hardened veterans at the machine gun, and so on—has led commentators on the text to interpret Jünger's concept of work as the apotheosis of a highly technological means-ends instrumentality, an absolutization of human purposive (and frantic) endeavor that subsumes everything under its logic. Yet in this metaphysical magnification of work, it seems to be human activity that is itself subsumed, as the local embodiment of cosmic processes. After reading a description of work such as, "Work is the rhythm of the fist, of thoughts, of the heart; it is life by day and night, science, love, art, faith, religion, war; work is the oscillation of the atom and the force that moves stars and solar systems,"[63] one could justifiably add the dualisms of subject and object to the growing list of dualisms *The Worker* seeks to transcend. If *Arbeit* can cover phenomena like gravity and the vibration of atoms, work is not so much something that is done as something that happens. A "life in order" in this reading would also involve the absolutization of a logic of nature, since the realization of the work-state would not merely entail the global extension of instrumental rationality, but would rather mean that human activity would completely conform (whatever that might look like in practice) to the humming of the cosmos—neither active nor passive, but simply there.

Fusion (*Verschmelzung*), then, takes on an added significance. While Jünger uses it to describe the fusion of humans and technology, and, more generally, of organic and mechanical spheres, the idea of fusion may be identified at a deeper level in this conception of work—as the fusion of work and existence, actor and action, life and order. This fusion at the heart of *The Worker*'s conception of work has its corollary in the relationship between individual and society, where the individually willed act of affiliation is replaced by a logic of belonging, of integration. Jünger refers to the "fusion" (*Einschmelzung*) of the Type with its modernized, mobilized world,[64] the "inclusion" or "integration" (*Einbeziehung*) of the individual (*Einzelne*) within the total mobilization,[65] or a "real interconnection" (*tatsächliche Verflechtung*) of people and the organic construction,[66] at one point using the analogy of an electric grid to represent the kind of belonging he has in mind; one belongs to an "organic construction" not by a voluntary act of affiliation, as one belongs to a party, but rather due to a "real integration," as one is wired into an electrical grid "as a consumer of electricity."[67] More significant than the connotations of electricity (modernity, technology; global scope coupled with an immediacy of signal and response; danger) is the kind of relation implied by this logic of integration. To be wired into an electrical grid, in this comparison, amounts to a kind of participation that involves the subject without being dependent on it. If, in other words, the form of social participation appropriate to the bourgeois individual is that of the act of affiliation, then this implies the possibility of a critical distance or "bipolarity" between the world and the individual, a distance which is no longer available to the Type.[68] What links the particular conception of work and the vision of social integration on display here, beyond the echo of *Verschmelzung* and *Einschmelzung*, would also seem to result from the same underlying rejection of dualisms—here, the distance between individual and world is jettisoned alongside that between subject and object, actor and action, doing and being. Neither active nor passive, the logic of Jünger's text collapses the distance between subjects, objects, and actions. This concept of work, suspended between activity and passivity, is far removed from the Type of the worker who, by dint of sheer will, masters and instrumentalizes his own body. The coexistence of both these models—the heroic Type that is able to treat his own body as a "pure instrument"[69] and work understood as the background humming of the cosmos[70]—is one of the important paradoxes of *The Worker*, since it indicates the ambiguous, changing status of the individual.[71]

And just as work is more like existence than action in *The Worker*, the removal of agency has obvious political implications for the text, as well as important structural implications. While the total, involuntary nature of social participation in *The Worker*, which is akin to an electricity grid or a modern battlefield, admits of no exceptions and means that the distinction between combatants and noncombatants is entirely effaced,[72] Jünger's conceptions of work and of action more generally bear upon the text's discussion of freedom. Clearly, if the distance and polarity between subject and object, individual and world, actor and action, is refused, then freedom cannot mean the freedom of an individual to choose among various possibilities, but rather becomes identical to what a bourgeois age would presumably consider freedom's opposite. "The typus knows no dictatorship because, for him, freedom and obedience are one and the same."[73] It is hard to escape the conclusion that such pronouncements constitute a fatuously self-serving fetishization of militaristic obedience. But it is also important to place such a dictum into its larger context. Early in the text, Jünger opposes the abstract, bourgeois concept of freedom to a different notion of freedom: "A trait considered above all others as the hallmark of the German, namely order, will always be undervalued if we cannot recognize in it the steely reflection of freedom."[74] Given that order signifies not merely hierarchy or obedience but, modeled on life, indicates a particular kind of relationship between parts and wholes, the concept of freedom that is rejected is rejected because it is abstract and lacks a necessary connection to its ends. And if work is not a free choice to attain an instrumental end but is rather a form of existence that links the individual's integration into modern society to the vibrations of atoms, then freedom and obedience both must signify that attitude which corresponds to an innate telos. It would make as little sense to speak of a plant's growth as an expression of either freedom (agency) or obedience (in the sense of heteronomous passivity).

The Worker's Rejection of Abstraction

This refusal of dualisms and collapsing of distance—seen in the fusion of bodies and technology, the "organic and mechanical world"; in the assimilation of subject and object; in the indistinction between doing and being in the conception of work; in the complete integration of the individual into society—also bears on the ways in which *The Worker* argues and signifies. This slippage between the content and the form of the text—or better, between its themes and its mode—is no accident. The "bourgeois era" is criticized both because it organized society and the individual abstractly and mechanically, and because it saw the world in those terms; it was an "anatomische[s] Zeitalter" ("anatomical age") both in terms of its social forms and in terms of its vision. *How* an era perceives is linked to *what* it sees; thus the total fusions of the work-state and the organic construction facilitate and necessitate a totalizing vision, and the text's rejection of abstraction, causality, and conceptuality is closely tied to its reliance on analogy and symbolism.

On the one hand, this slippage between epistemology and ontology serves as a methodological short-circuit that allowed Jünger to magnify a usefully heuristic conception of wholeness into an absolute ideology.[75] Yet, on the other hand, a closer look is necessary, because it shows that the organic dimension of Jünger's idea of history, in *The Worker*, goes deeper than a borrowing of the idea of entelechy. It also suggests a paradox at the heart of the way the text argues, a peculiar vacillation between example and symbol that informs both the text's modernity and its conservatism. To reconstruct this paradox, it is necessary to consider the text's rejection of abstraction more closely, for its rejection of abstract freedom and abstract work corresponds to its historical vision—a wholesale refutation of the optimism of a boundless progress. By tying fungibility to an abstract, mathematical conception of infinity, *The Worker* is able to link its critique of the bourgeois era to a kind of anagogical hermeneutics that would be able to hasten that era's demise by asserting everywhere the signs of the Gestalt that would replace it.

The Worker rejects abstraction early and often: abstract power, abstract freedom, abstract technology, abstract work, and even abstract reason. In part, this is surely the expression of a kind of cultural pessimism that is constantly ruffled by the various dislocations and unmoorings associated with modernity. The criticism is not of abstraction per se, as opposed to concreteness, but rather of fungibility, of the possibility of detaching an attribute from a specific purpose. As we read, "There is no more an abstract power than there is an abstract freedom. Power is a sign of existence, and correspondingly there exist no means of power as such; rather, the means acquire their meaning through the being that avails itself of them";[76] or: "Power, however, like freedom, is not a matter that can be seized anywhere in empty space, or to which any nonentity can relate himself at will. It stands, on the contrary, in an indissoluble bond with a fixed and determined unity of life, an unambiguous existence";[77] and "Technology, like reason, does not exist in itself; every life has the technology commensurate and innate to it."[78] Technology, power, freedom—these cannot be seen, argues Jünger, as entities that are indifferent to the question of who might use them, and for what. Rather, they belong in a specific way to the particular being (*Sein*) or organic unity (*Lebenseinheit*) that uses them; they are not transferable. We have already seen the idea of organic technology; the claim that "every life has the technology commensurate and *innate* [*angeboren*] to it"[79] joins this organic logic of fusion to a more general rejection of abstraction as such. What holds true on the thematic level and the level of images in *The Worker* is also true on a linguistic level, since all of these rejections of abstraction take the form of a rejection of predication. In other words, these passages refuse the possibility of sentences that take the structure "*A* has power," or "*B* is free," since such sentences tell us nothing about an innate, motivated connection between subject and predicate that, according to Jünger, such ideas as power and freedom must have. What connects this refusal of abstraction, fungibility, and predication to the text's critique of the ideas of infinity and progress is the suspicion of a quality-destroying quantity, a kind of arbitrariness that would sunder ideas such as freedom or technology from cause and consequence. The tacit insistence is that phenomena must *mean* something.

This refusal of fungibility, of abstraction, of substitution also plays a role in *The Worker*'s picture of history. A notable characteristic of Jünger's criticism of the bourgeois era is his rejection of the notion of progress. The idea that history develops as a potentially infinite progression, or as a succession of classes and modes of production, is criticized because it entails, according to Jünger, a merely abstract, formal understanding of both technology and history. To view history in terms of a limitless progression, rather than as a closed totality, is necessarily to accept an abstract, detached notion of technology.

> Once we have recognized [the fact that technology has a necessary, innate order and goal], we no longer overestimate *development* as

characterizing the relationship between progress and technology. . . .
Here too we find the concept of infinity intoxicating the spirit and
yet already no longer attainable for us. . . . This is precisely why
this aspect of infinity belongs to the age of progress; it did not exist
before, and it will not be intelligible to future generations.[80]

The modern, secular era had replaced, Jünger claims, religion with knowledge (*Erkenntnis*), to which it granted the saving role. Yet despite the eschatological overtones of such a replacement, progress in the "era of progress" is understood in terms of a limitless growth. Technology, in this picture, must be seen as abstract because its connection to infinite progress detaches it from any purpose other than the vague one of freeing humans from toil. By contrast, Jünger continues, the "development of technology is not limitless; it completes itself at the moment when, as tool, it corresponds to the specific requirements to which the form [*Gestalt*] of the worker subjects it."[81] Without making the specific content of technology's uses any less vague, Jünger is nevertheless able to establish a set of contrasts that suggest the particular concreteness of technology when subordinated to the supratemporal Gestalt of the *Arbeiter*: the limitless progress of the understanding and a merely ameliorative technology on the one hand, and the bounded totality of a tool subordinated to appropriate demands on the other; on the one side the empty time of a future that, in constantly arriving, never comes, and on the other side the decisive moment (*Augenblick*) when a tool fits its uses. What is curious is the way the text seeks to embrace the instrument while pushing away the idea of instrumentality.

At pains to distance his worker from liberal or Marxist theories of historical change, Jünger frequently rejects a model of historical succession of classes or castes, at one point identifying this model with a mechanical way of seeing. "Only an intelligence [*Geist*] habituated to thinking in mechanical images can picture the procession of successive dominions such that, just as the hand of the clock casts its shadow over the hours, one estate after the other passes through the frame of power, while below a new class is already awakening to consciousness."[82] The mechanical image of a clock suggests through contrast the organic fulfillment that should guide the reader's understanding of the rise of the worker—precisely *not* as the next class whose time has come, because as such it would be equivalent to a mere placeholder. This image thus symbolizes the deeper logic of abstraction, substitution, and replaceability that *The Worker* must reject. The worker, by contrast, does not represent a new class, society, or economy, but rather, a distinct and characteristic (*eigentümlich*) Gestalt with its own laws, its own vocation, and its particular kind of freedom.[83]

The paradox at the heart of *The Worker* is that the worker is the historical event that will abolish history, the phenomenon whose signs must be scrutinized for the meaning that it alone can guarantee. This paradox goes beyond the slippage between epistemology and ontology in *The Worker*—indeed, for Jünger, the identity of ontology and epistemology is precisely the point. The worker, as Gestalt, is both a way of seeing and the thing that needs to be seen. This identity, which exasperates paraphrase, stems from the organic wholeness that characterizes the worker and the Gestalt. Only something fragmentary or modular—mechanical, in the terms of *The Worker*—is susceptible to analysis. Organic unities must be intuited, perceived in a unified fashion.

This is a position that Jünger will maintain long after the publication of *The Worker*. In another lengthy essay, *Typus Name Gestalt* (1963), he distinguishes between simple and complex phenomena, urging that the simple things are hardest to understand. Characterizing the difficulty of understanding the Type and the Gestalt, he writes:

> The topic is simple [*einfach*], and therein lies its difficulty. Simple things are more difficult to describe than complex things because they are closer to the Nameless, and because whoever is describing them has to reach back to the bottom of language. A complicated machine with its individual parts and their combinations can be represented in a set of instructions with absolute exactitude. Far simpler things that are formative everywhere, such as Types and Gestalts, are much more difficult to access.[84]

The example of the machine is of course no accident, for it is precisely its articulated, modular, open structure that admits a perfect correspondence between description and function. Simple, self-identical forms, such as Types, Gestalts, and the worker, do not offer such ready access points for language to latch onto. This contrast between simple and complicated forms gains additional traction in the juxtaposition of the German words for "simple"— *einfach*, literally "onefold"—and "individual parts"—*Einzelteilen*. The semantic connection between simplicity and unity throws the complex multiplicity of the machine into stark relief, while the individual parts of the machine recall the merely agglomerative model of society, as an agglomeration of individuals, that *The Worker* seeks to transcend. Unity, simplicity, wholeness—such qualities pertain to both vision and viewed, and they are opposed to a logic of the fragmentary, the analytical, the modular, the additive. Describing the kind of vision necessary to perceive the new era, Jünger writes in *The Worker*:

> No perspective freed by cosmic distance from the play and counterplay of movements can miss that a *unity* has fashioned here its spatial reflection. This manner of observation differs from efforts to understand the unity of life in its most superficial possibility—that is, as mere addition. It differs because it grasps the creative structure, the finished work, occurring despite, or even with the help of, all contradictions.[85]

The organic unity represented by the worker and by the Gestalt, by contrast, signifies and must be perceived in a different way. Jünger dubs this the law of "stamping and imprinting" (*Stempel und Prägung*)[86]—an image of signification that is opposed to the law of cause and effect, and which is neither arbitrary nor conventional, but necessary, expressive, and perfectly congruent. The thing leaves a perfect, matching imprint; at the moment of imprinting, there is no distance between thing and sign.

One begins to see how these notions of perception and signification, themselves implied by the deep structure of organic unity that *The Worker* insists upon, consequently affect the rhetorical shape of Jünger's text. We might characterize this as a vacillation between the particular and the general, the specific and the abstract, or better, between the example and the symbol. We see this early on in the text, in a nagging tension between the global scope of the worker, on the one hand, and the unique suitability of Germany to inaugurate the new era of the worker, on the other.[87] More pervasively, this tension appears in the text's simultaneous reliance upon and disavowal of epochal succession as a model for historical change—the worker emphatically heralds a new age, but not just one new age in a sequence of others that are functionally equivalent. Such a vacillation makes sense if we recall the refusal of abstraction, fungibility, and predication that characterizes *The Worker*. The very form of the example implies substitution. By definition, an example is one of multiple possibilities, yet the structuring logic of organic unity, and the signifying model of stamping and imprinting, cannot admit multiple possibilities. The consequence of this is easily one of the most disorienting features of Jünger's text, since it frequently results in a jarring movement between the subordination of the example and the self-evidence of the symbol.

In *Typus Name Gestalt*, Jünger situates the Type between the multiplicity of individual phenomena and the indeterminacy of the Gestalt, a structure that Jünger illustrates with a botanical analogy: the lily is to the Type as the plant is to the Gestalt, with all individual lilies subordinated to the clear comprehensibility of the Type. Yet lest we confuse Jünger's scheme with a taxonomic structure, where individual, Type, and Gestalt would represent nesting categories of various sizes, we must note that Type and Gestalt function differently. Type is not a subset of Gestalt but is rather an intermediate stage on a spectrum that leads from the concrete object to the "undifferentiated" (*Ungesonderte*); the lily as Type is not taxonomically contained within the Gestalt of plant, but is a specific, more differentiated manifestation of the tendency towards growth represented by the Gestalt.[88] Furthermore, Jünger's invocation of Goethe's concept of the *Urpflanze* ("archetypal plant"),[89] and his comparison of the Gestalt of the worker to the *Urpflanze*, cast doubt on the possibility that the analogy of the lily/plant relationship is merely a helpful illustration. Indeed, in "The Tree" ("Der Baum"), a 1962 essay written to accompany a book of photographs by Albert Renger-Patzsch, Jünger describes the tree as a symbol of time and as an "archetype" (*Urbild*) that offers a master pattern for nature and time itself.[90] If, in other words, there is something fundamentally plantlike about the Gestalt, as a nameless vegetative force, then the relationship between Gestalt and plant is not a convenient example but a necessary, expressive connection.

So where does this leave Jünger's reader? Anyone approaching the Gestalt as a category that can be applied to other material is soon likely to be stymied. All of the examples Jünger gives of the Gestalt (such as the plant, the worker, and the ocean) have a necessary, intrinsic relationship to the very idea of Gestalt. Their various properties define the category they are supposed to exemplify, in a circular way. The worker is the Gestalt because the concept of work implied in *The Worker* is that mixture of activity and existence, that same blurring of categories that the Gestalt implies. The plant is a Gestalt because its mysterious, unfixable power of growth symbolizes generative nature. The ocean is a Gestalt because its ceaseless flux represents the principles of change, emergence, and indivisibility per se.[91] Yet, again, these three examples are not merely examples, linked solely by virtue of their Gestalt-quality, but synonymize and inflect each other. Just as work describes the movements of the stars, the generative qualities of the plant and the changing nature of the ocean bleed over into the concept of work.

Organicism and Modernity in *The Worker*

Organicism suffuses *The Worker*, structuring it on every level. Against the fragmentary, anatomical, fungible, additive abstraction associated with the "era of the third estate," organic wholeness—always more than the sum of its parts—characterizes the worker and the Gestalt. The text's concepts of order and work, which efface the distinctions between doing and being, subject and object, also rely upon a logic of life, and it is a specifically organic kind of development that delineates the teleological trajectory towards the static end point of *The Worker*, that "organic construction" marked by a fusion between bodies and technology, and between tools and their appropriate ends. And these various, related appearances of the organic in *The Worker* on the thematic level recur in the text's representational commitments and signifying strategies. The refusal of abstraction complicates the workings of subsumption, causality, and exemplarity; in their place we find expressivity, congruence, symbolism, and intuition. The modernism of this organicism is essentially twofold: it consists of the kind of subjectivity it was mobilized to reconfigure, and of the particular transdisciplinary borrowings that made it possible. One cannot understand organicism in *The Worker* without accounting for its context, and what it defined itself against. Bourgeois individuality, rather than the complexities and differentiations of the modern era, is the primary target of the text's organicism. Jünger identifies this individual with the bourgeois era in general and the nineteenth century in particular; it is depicted as the container of psychological interiority, the subject of abstract rights and freedoms, and the bearer of a history understood as incremental and potentially unlimited progress. The categories that link and underpin Jünger's depiction of individuality include fungibility, abstraction, conceptual subsumption, and mathematical infinitude. Against a mechanical, additive vision that sees the world as mechanical and additive, the text inveighs for an organic whole that must be intuited organically, holistically. In place of a bourgeois individual, then, the de-individuated Type; in place of a boundless historical progression or the formal succession of eras, a strong teleology; in place of dualisms, fusion.

The contours of this revision of subjectivity are made possible by ideas, tropes, and questions that were made available by contemporary biology. Jünger was not simply returning to older discourses of wholeness, harmony, or natural history to evade the challenges of modernity, but was drawing on new disciplinary possibilities in order to meet these challenges. Like Döblin and Plessner, Jünger's project in *The Worker* is to reimagine the human being without dualism or metaphysical exceptionalism, without the private interiority of the bourgeois subject. The organicism that facilitates this reimagining is of necessity totalizing and cosmic. Not just a vision of society, the work-state becomes a fulfillment of history writ large, and even of Being as such. Once the conceptual framework of structuring oppositions between nature and culture, subject and object, human and nonhuman, soul and body, and organ and machine has been rejected as the inheritance of an obsolete era, these terms are free to fully invade and occupy each other, to the extent that the modern era can herald the self-realization of nature, and work can be defined as the vibrations of atoms and the force that moves stars. Thus, while the contours of Jünger's biological modernism differed from those of Döblin's—most notably in the differing values assigned to wholeness and closure, and in Jünger's militaristic chords—their commonalities point to the availability, in the Weimar Republic, of organicism as a potent and subversive counter-discourse to the perceived obsoleteness of the autonomous individual. Perhaps even more notably, this shared field indicates the degree to which different discourses and disciplines were able to speak each other's terms and productively borrow from one another. By mobilizing logics, tropes, ideas, and relations from biology and organic nature, Jünger was able, in *The Worker*, to offer a summative vision in response to the ruptures and demands of a modernity experienced as a cataclysmic liberation, a vision that offered new models of epistemology, subjectivity, and history.

For Jünger, modernity is an acceleration that realizes timelessness; a quickening of elemental, transhistorical rhythms. This is how the Gestalt seemingly manages to be both historical and timeless, to partake of both technological acceleration and elemental rhythms. The vision capable of seeing the Gestalt must consequently be able to see both wholeness and speed, both the deep shapes and their surface indicators.[92] This is a distanced vision—the guiding Jüngerian concept of *désinvolture*, signifying a cheerful detachment, is relevant here[93]—though it is not necessarily an armored one, at least if the concept of armor relies on the familiar dichotomies. Helmut Lethen, in constructing the edifice of the cold persona on the foundation of *The Worker*, links Jünger's amoral perception to de-psychologization; in Lethen's reading, this cold vision turns the objects of its gaze into physical bodies without any ethical or psychological claim on the viewer. The "*de*moralization of perception goes hand in hand with the *de*psychologization of the observed object, which then behaves in the manner of a physical body. The latter not only slips out of sight from an ethical perspective but in doing so loses its organic quality."[94] It is the way Lethen links the organic to morality and opposes it to physicality that causes problems for his analysis, for doing so overlooks the way that physical bodies are often emphatically organic in *The Worker*. Lethen is correct to assign de-psychologization an important role here—Jünger was, after all, attacking a notion of subjectivity predicated on abstract individuality and psychological interiority. So was Döblin; the search for forms of subjectivity and collectivity characterized by traits other than individual psychology was common to many writers of the time. Yet what Lethen's linkage of psychology to the organic occludes is the possibility that Jünger, like Döblin, pursued strategies of de-psychologization precisely through organicism, rather than by repressing the organic. This should not come as a surprise—after all, to represent subjects as biological organisms distances them from psychological interiority as surely as does encasing them in armored hauteur. A problem for Lethen's analysis at this point is that it depends on a dichotomy of the organic and the mechanical which Jünger's text, as we have seen, depends on rejecting. And in rejecting this dichotomy, *The Worker* does not simply assimilate the two terms but also changes the meaning of each. In the concept of the "organic construction," the organic incorporates the mechanical, in its broader sense of "technological" or "instrumental," and is thereby able to signify both organic wholeness *and* technological acceleration. By contrast, those connotations of the mechanical that are not thus absorbed by the organic construction—partiality, fungibility, abstraction, modularity—are developed into its contraries. So there is in fact, on some level, a kind of binary definition at play between the organic and the mechanical, but the terms are so altered that they cannot support the kind of dichotomy that Lethen presupposes. *The Worker* is quite distanced from the inherited associations of the mechanical with materiality, physicality, soullessness.[95] In the final analysis, as a binary, "organic" and "mechanical" do not refer to kinds of objects in the world—certainly not to "nature" and "technology"—but rather to purely formal possibilities for thinking about the relationship between parts and wholes. Paradoxical in its newness, turbulently rushing towards a placid resolution, technologically accelerating to an organic fusion, revolutionary and elemental at once, *The Worker*'s picture of history maps out one of the possible shapes that the idea of modernity could take in the Weimar Republic.

CONCLUSION

In this book I have tried to recover an important and neglected side of the interdisciplinary culture and thought of the Weimar Republic. What I have called "biological modernism" involved various metaphorical and conceptual borrowings in order to theorize modernity, technology, art, and the human being *through* organic life, rather than against it. The figures of this study were modern precisely in their various attempts to overcome the kind of static dualism that would pit the organic against the mechanical, or the modern age against a state of nature. Indeed, such dualisms were seen as an antiquated legacy of bourgeois humanism; by historicizing them in this way, Weimar writers sought to transcend them. Their engagement with the idea of modernity, by contrast, relied upon tropes, concepts, and discourses associated with living nature. Biology, as an emergent set of knowledge practices that engaged with questions concerning form, development, and history, offered contemporaries a way to rethink the human beyond the dualisms of mind and body, machine and organism, redefining it in ways that might be more adequate to the social, technological, cultural, and epistemological upheavals of the early twentieth century. Moreover, biological modernism was extraordinarily self-reflexive, as contemporaries not only grappled with what they saw as outmoded paradigms, but frequently also brought epistemological and disciplinary considerations to the forefront of their investigations, indicting the inherited divisions of labor between the humanities and the natural sciences that divided the human being into incommensurable domains.

Helmuth Plessner developed a logic of positionality he identified as central to living things as such in order to derive the "eccentric positionality" that is characteristic of the human being, that animal which is "artificial by nature." The photographic practice and theory of August Sander, Karl Blossfeldt, Alfred Döblin, and Siegfried Kracauer complicated the identification of photography with objectivity, indexicality, and speed by constellating photography with other media, representational forms, and fields such as literature, history, natural history, and film. Döblin's 1924 novel *Mountains Seas and Giants* graphically joins an epic poetics, a theory of the self, and a monist philosophy of nature—three projects he articulated in essays and books over the course of the 1910s and 1920s—precisely by repurposing the organic as the site of endless material interconnection and recombination, rather than seeing it as a symbol of wholeness. And Ernst Jünger's *The Worker* offers a global, organicist vision of work, society, and the future writ large, transforming familiar terms by casting history as entelechy, and the behavior of matter as such as the expression of a vitalist, cosmic notion of work.

Several shared themes and preoccupations emerge as an important part of the context within which biological modernism took shape. Most notably, the legacy of Cartesian dualism becomes visible as something that Weimar writers wished to shake off, often by name, in order to rethink subjectivity, nature, art, and the relationships between the disciplines. Their rejection of dualism entailed, for instance, the recurring idea that technological modernity is an outgrowth of nature. The critique of dualism also yielded a multifaceted attempt to imagine the new human. No longer defined as an individual characterized by psychological or rational interiority, no longer parceled into immaterial, thinking mind and physical body or irreconcilably split between the sciences and the humanities, poetry and engineering, the new human was understood in terms of embodied cognition and perception, located within masses and types rather than single individuals, and defined as a nexus of nature and technology. Yet we have also seen that the new human was not the same, in these texts, as other, adjacent figures that have been used to theorize the period, such as the armored body or the deficient being. Moreover, the question of form, especially as it relates to narrative, development, life, and history, is a guiding idea for all the figures of this study: when we listen for the resonances with contemporary biology and organicism, the recurrence of formal questions in these texts offers a way to link otherwise apparently unconnected topics, such as Alfred Döblin's rejection of the unity of the artwork, the typifying, comparative photographic representation of August Sander and Karl Blossfeldt, Helmuth Plessner's concept of "eccentric positionality," and the shape of history in Ernst Jünger's *The Worker*. Certain questions and strategies connected to this attempt to reimagine the human being and modernity—such as the rejection of the individual in favor of the type or mass as the privileged level of analysis, the prominence of organic imagery and tropes, and the complication of temporalities of acceleration, speed, or progress—can only be properly understood within the fuller intellectual and cultural context of the time, especially these vibrant, prolific, and transdisciplinary confrontations with the idea of life.

Understanding biological modernism in these terms can also help make sense of some of the important differences between these various figures, since it was by no means a homogenous field. Yet even the differences suggest that this was largely a shared project—for instance, even a reinvestment in organic wholeness does not necessarily signal a retreat from modernity so much as the attempt to theorize it. The difference between Jünger and Döblin when they compare modern, urban space to an organism is instructive because it shows their opposing approaches to the question of wholeness. One final look at the texts will allow us to map out some of the internal differentiation within biological modernism, in order to then pose a few last questions about the implications of this paradigm and its relevance for the present.

At one point, *The Worker* reflects on the tension between epistemology and ontology, indicating an awareness that wholeness can be an attribute both of a thing and of the organizing vision brought to bear on that thing. In an early passage, Jünger's text takes the reader to the moon, telescope in hand, to identify the distinguishing marks of the age of the worker in the modern metropolis. From such a vantage point, all internal differentiations that constitute the complexity of modern urban society disappear, leaving only the impression of a meaningful whole attesting to a new kind of vital force.[1] To focus on the differences of the individuals constituting this picture would be absurd and arbitrary, suggests the text: "The thought of its differentiations lies as far from here as if an individual were to see himself with a microscope: that is, as a heap of cells."[2] The tension between organizing perspective and organized phenomenon is palpable: the individual is a collection of cells, after all, just as the city is a collection of individuals. Yet the point of Jünger's comparison is to remind the reader that individuals do not generally think of themselves as aggregates. Likewise, to view a modern city in any way other than the distanced, macroscopic view that discerns the Gestalt of the worker would be to miss the point. Jünger's image slyly has it both ways, undermining the significance of the individual human being by subordinating individuals to the whole city and the Gestalt of the worker, while also upholding the individual body as the relevant organizing principle. The cells are invoked not to undermine the solidity of the individual organism but to reinforce it. Thus, while the comparison reminds us of the teeming aggregations that always constitute wholes, it paradoxically brings this fact to our attention only to suggest its irrelevance.

Here the difference from Döblin is striking. Döblin, in "The Spirit of the Naturalistic Age," *The I above Nature*, and *Mountains Seas and Giants*, also decomposes the body into its constituent parts and depicts modern society or the modern metropolis as a kind of conglomerate superorganism, a *Massenwesen*, or a "coral stock," undermining the solidity of the individual body—and the autonomous individual typically located within it—both microscopically and macroscopically.[3] But where Döblin is interested in pointing out and thereby destabilizing the levels of organization, leaving the reader with an endless scalability, Jünger insists on an organic wholeness. For Döblin, in other words, to indicate the aggregate nature of individual units at every level—their fundamental "dividuality"—is an end in itself. As he puts it in "Faces, Images, and Their Truth," "The distinction between the individual and the collective (or the universal), then . . . becomes a matter of varying degrees of distance."[4] The fact that we can shift our attention to different organizational levels of living matter and thereby arrive at different understandings of life and selfhood is precisely the point, for such epistemological flexibility suggests a deeper understanding of materiality and nature in general. For Döblin wholeness, if it exists at all, exists only in the entire play of matter and selfhood. Jünger, on the other hand, invokes aggregation and fragmentation to reinforce organic wholeness as a normative category; it exists in some places but not in others, and its presence or absence means something. The bourgeois era is characterized by its lack of a relationship to wholeness and totality, while the worker's state must be total and it must be whole. Thus, although both writers use organicism and even some of the same imagery to undermine the stable, bourgeois individual, Döblin and Jünger's works from this period nevertheless embody contrary views of fragmentation and totality.[5] Fragmentation, aggregation, and disaggregation are the patterns in which Döblin dissolves the body and the autonomous individual, in the service of a transcendental, collective notion of selfhood that can only be located at every level if it is to be found at any one level. Jünger, by contrast, associates fragmentation, abstraction, subsumption, fungibility, and infinity with each other and with the bourgeois era; the organic whole is his answer to these. This difference can also be seen in their relationships to the mechanical: where Jünger spurned the modularity, endless articulation, and partiality of the machine as the emblem of the bourgeois era, Döblin seemingly embraced the model of interconnection it represents, with its ability to rupture the sanctity of the whole body, identifying this ability with the disruptive force of organic growth.

Yet it should also be clear that Jünger was not simply reverting to an older model of wholeness. The question of the location of the individual, and the recognition that the level or scale of analysis determined not just the identifiable phenomena but also the epistemological and disciplinary framework necessary to understanding these phenomena—these were important questions of the day, for knowledge production as such, and for biology, in particular.[6] In *The Worker*'s recognition of the level of analysis, in its rejection of both individuality and aggregation in favor of the organically organized collective of the worker, Jünger tries to have it both ways. Organic unities are composed of myriad individuals, and the shifting perspective of the text knows this. Yet, paradoxically, this ceases to matter once the right vantage point has been found, the one that allows the text to identify a meaningful totality, one that is not predicated upon the individual but can instead identify the Gestalt.

At this point, there are two ways we can understand the function of organicism in *The Worker*. On the one hand, it could be working in a reactive, restorative way, as an insistence on wholeness in the face of the kinds of experience and processes of modernization characterized by differentiation, complexity, and fragmentation. This would certainly correspond to much of the organic tradition, and would also fit with the widespread discourse on Gestalt in the early twentieth century, which intensified as a reaction to increasing social differentiation.[7] Nor is the idea that the Germans are the standard-bearers of an organic resistance to the Enlightenment, as described at the beginning of *The Worker*, particularly trailblazing. This picture of *The Worker*, then, would see in its reactionary organicism a refusal of Enlightenment universality, of narratives of progress, and of the social complexity that characterizes modernity, and thus as a fundamentally antimodern text.

Yet to view things in this light perhaps cedes too much to an Enlightenment rationality and liberal narratives of progress, suspicion of which characterized Weimar thought with or without Jünger's help. I am not proposing that we accept (much less like) *The Worker*'s solutions to this conundrum; the way it articulated the problem, however, is instructive. Modernity is not simply something Jünger's text is responding to, but rather something that it is engaged in constructing. In his negative characterization of the bourgeois era in terms of abstraction, fungibility, and a view of history as located along an infinite axis of progress, Jünger develops a self-consciously modernist organicism that allows the present to be both rupture and continuity, newness and teleological fulfillment. Organicism in *The Worker* attempts to account for new aspects of experience which are no longer comprehensible in terms of older paradigms that privileged the autonomous individual; it constitutes Jünger's experiment with newness and rupture, not a return to tradition.

Thus Jünger, like Plessner and Döblin, was engaged in situating the human subject in a world understood as distinctly modern. And here is a key difference between Jünger's organicism and older forms of organicism that derived a harmonious, stable model for society from nature or from the metaphor of the human body: unlike restorative variants of organicism, Jünger sought to locate his vision of the new human within a radically altered, destabilized nature. Developments in nineteenth- and twentieth-century science—thermodynamics, evolution, cell theory, embryology, relativity—had foreclosed the possibility that nature could offer a familiar model for stability or harmony. Responding to this new environment was necessarily a modern project. If Jünger, Döblin, and Plessner re-situated the human subject within nature, it was not to stabilize this subject, but to expand its complexity and intensify its turbulence. With Jünger, history is not just naturalized; nature also becomes an expanded site of human struggle. While *The Worker* arrives (or at least aims) at a teleological stasis, it makes a difference that this stasis is positioned at the end of a turbulent, "total mobilization" that encompasses the global scope of technological and social modernization. Context matters, in other words, and *The Worker*'s ultimate refusal of a disarticulation between subject and object, culture and nature, work and existence is not restorative (as it would be if it understood itself as trying to regain a lost harmony) but forward-looking, in that it attempts to imagine a human future that would be able to transcend a dichotomy of culture and nature. This is why it is insufficient to attribute Jünger's various borrowings from the natural sciences to a refusal of modernity. To reduce the biological or organicist dimension of Jünger to a "nineteenth-century belief in positive science and classification" is to elide the more complex interplay among discourses and epistemological modes that *The Worker* represents.[8] The relationships between development and form, ecology and social structure, level of observation and phenomena observed, and the broader question of the specificity of organic life—these are not the contents of dusty archive drawers, but were rather at the forefront of modern biology as it emerged in the late nineteenth and early twentieth centuries. Jünger's vision of the Gestalt of the worker is not an antimodern project but a paradoxical modernism.

Like Jünger, Döblin offered in *Mountains Seas and Giants* and essays such as "The Spirit of the Naturalistic Age" a diagnostic vision of the twentieth-century present and of a future that would unfold in very different terms than those offered by humanism or narratives of progress. Despite their patent differences in style, focus, temperament, and politics, during the Weimar period both Döblin and Jünger cultivated an antihumanist imaginary that was formulated in explicit opposition to a conception of selfhood built upon notions of the autonomous individual and psychological interiority, and both rejected the dualisms of mind and matter, subject and object, and nature and technology. In so doing, both drew upon specific biological concepts as well as a more diffuse set of metaphors and logics borrowed from organicism, vitalism, and philosophies of nature in order to rethink the human being for an era expressly understood as modern, in the sense of post-humanist and post-bourgeois, among other connotations. Yet the differences in the details of their borrowings show that biological modernism was also a site of contestation that could result in divergent artistic, social, and political visions, even while these cannot be reduced to a restorative desire to escape complexity or fragmentation. Jünger's imagined future in *The Worker* issues in a teleological stasis, and this end state is directly related to his conception of the surplus of a whole over the sum of its parts, a conception formulated in dialogue with the neovitalist idea of entelechy. The future at the end of *Mountains Seas and Giants*, by contrast, is left as open and as subject to change as the bodies dismembered, interpenetrated, and recombined throughout the novel. Döblin's attack on the solidity of the bourgeois individual proceeded by different paths than Jünger's, opting for a dispersion of selfhood throughout materiality, instead of total organization, and these divergent strategies yield the distinct forms of closure found in their narratives of future history. Likewise, the status of death differs from Döblin to Jünger. While it may be striking that both Döblin and Jünger downplay the role of death (in sustained meditations on the organic, of all places), the contours of these elisions are significant. Döblin's deployment of the tropes of "mother liquor" and protoplasm, as well as his sustained riffs on material flows, allow him to sidestep the question of individual death (even as death is portrayed throughout his novel) by decentering the individual organism and the individual body. Jünger, by contrast, diminishes death by subordinating the individual (and the individual phenomenon) to the deeper meanings of the Type and the Gestalt, even as death, in its connection to war, danger,

Conclusion

and elemental forces, is among the forces he sees as rupturing the stability of bourgeois society. Döblin undermines the individual through processes of dissolution, Jünger through integration, subordination, and transcendence. In their reformulation of the human being they were organic and they were modern, and they were so in ways that were fundamentally caught up in their historical moment.

Approaching these texts as paradigmatic of biological modernism also necessarily bears upon how we understand their modernism. Recognizing that both Döblin and Jünger, despite the formal and stylistic differences of their work, to say nothing of their politics, were grappling with questions concerning modernity and the human in similarly transdisciplinary ways may mean foregoing a commitment to modernism as a normative category. To this extent, I would choose to invert Andreas Huyssen's denial of Ernst Jünger's modernism. In his discussion of the relationship between fascism and modernism, Huyssen takes issue with the idea that the fact of Jünger's engagement with modernity makes him a modernist, arguing that it is the nature of this engagement that counts: "Otherwise we run the danger of arriving at the meaningless conclusion that every artist whose work articulates certain aporias of modernity, as Jünger's does, and whose imagination partakes in modernity's phantasmatic constructions is thereby a modernist."[9] This is in fact exactly what this study has posited, and hopefully it has shown why the conclusion "that every artist whose work articulates certain aporias of modernity . . . and whose imagination partakes in modernity's phantasmatic constructions is thereby a modernist" might not actually be meaningless. It is precisely by asking how these figures engaged in constructing an imagined modernity, both reacting to and trying to shape the broad social, imaginary, and conceptual changes of their time—precisely, that is, by reconstructing in their own terms how they imagined modernity, technology, the human, and nature—that we may access features of Weimar modernism that we would otherwise miss, were we guided by a normative approach to modernism. Chief among these are the strong resonance of *Leben* between the sciences and the humanities, and the intricate, dense picture of modernity and modernization that results: the use of the organic and the biological, in other words, to define the technological and the modern. I point this out not to rescue Jünger—indeed, by definition, heuristic inclusion within a non-normative conception of modernism does not indicate praise or approval—but to suggest that a normative understanding of modernism risks flattening the relationship of culture to the life sciences. If organicism or biological borrowings are assumed at the outset to indicate the desire for stable classification or a retreat from the complexities of modern society, then there can be no good way for writers and intellectuals to engage with a different set of disciplines that are also committed to posing questions about development, emergence, and history, about the definition of the individual, and about the relationships between part and whole, materiality and life. Moreover, flattening the transdisciplinary borrowings of what I have here called biological modernism also eclipses the paradoxical and counterintuitive linkages these figures made in order to define modernity in ways that did not rely on an inherited humanist framework they experienced as obsolete, and thus obscures how the organic offered Weimar thinkers a rich site of contestation.

As might perhaps be expected, the very totalizing drive that made these interlinkages among life, the human, and modernity so appealing during the 1920s also indicates the limits (or, less negatively, the context-boundedness) of biological modernism. The intoxicating possibility of collapsing long-held dualisms, at a moment before increasing disciplinary specialization would result in C. P. Snow's "two cultures" and the improbability of intellectuals like Döblin, Plessner, and Jünger who were fluent or at least conversant in both, also offered a promise of boundlessness that now seems dated. If, for example, the human subject is defined according to the same laws that govern materiality, nature, or the universe at large, the risk is that the reverse may also seem true—Döblin's transcendent "I above nature," a principle of selfhood he locates in all matter, and Jünger's claim that atomic vibrations are also a form of work, are but two examples of this paradoxical, cosmic projection of the human as a result of antihumanist projects.

This is why it is necessary to situate this project within its context, as a tendency that emerged at a particular moment, in response to inherited understandings of the human being, of the modern era, and of the relationship between nature and technology. Key parts of this story, such as Döblin's broadside against the idea of the unity of a narrative or personality, or Plessner's attempt to define the human being in a way that can fully reconcile biology and philosophy, might seem perplexing, incoherent, overblown, or passé were they to be attempted today. They are products of their time, in other words. But beyond a more nuanced understanding of this interdisciplinary strain of German modernism, what can biological modernism teach us?

One lesson may be methodological. In so closely integrating ideas about nature, the human, narrative, and art, these texts suggest ways of reading that are attentive to similar kinds of overdetermination, metaphorical transfer, and shared codes. While Döblin's critical exploration of physical closure provides a particularly striking example of a set of parallel re-theorizations—of nature, human subjectivity, narrative, and art—that proceeded precisely by developing shared terms and imagery, and by borrowing prolifically from one domain or discipline into others, it also suggests that similar moves will be found elsewhere in Weimar culture, as well as in texts from other periods, places, and languages.

Other lessons may be more thematically specific to this material. Despite the vast distance in environmental consciousness between the 1920s and the early twenty-first century, these texts continue to provide ecological provocations for thinking about the human. When read as science fiction at our own catastrophic moment of a warming planet and rising tides, for example,

Mountains Seas and Giants and *The Worker* can hone our historical sense for the future, encouraging us to think ourselves into longer, planetary time scales, imagining the ebbs and flows of possible futures that interweave the social, technological, evolutionary, geological, ecological, affective, and elemental strands of human existence. Compared to much other early science fiction, *Mountains Seas and Giants* has aged exceptionally well: its episodic depictions of war, technological advances, resurgent primitivisms, and the clonic human institutions, mythologies, subcultures, and symbolic orders that attempt to make sense of these could usefully be brought into dialogue with Kim Stanley Robinson's future epic *2312*, for example.[10] And Helmuth Plessner's picture of the human being remains a compelling one. Recent accounts of the causal roles played by culture in evolution suggest that a theory like Plessner's, which interprets human specificity within the continuum of life itself, suggest that "eccentric positionality" and "natural artificiality" could be capable of being updated and brought into dialogue with current knowledge.[11]

Furthermore, from the perspectives of the various ecological and material turns that mark our own moment, a century later, much of what these figures wrote seems relevant, even prescient. *Mountains Seas and Giants* could be read as a kind of "cli-fi" (climate fiction) before the fact, and the monist explorations of ensouled materiality in *The I above Nature* evoke present-day theorizations of distributed subjectivity and "vibrant matter."[12] Indeed, reading texts from the 1920s in conjunction with current attempts to articulate a new materialism, object-oriented ontology, or post-humanism could prove fruitful, not least because the different historical context and disciplinary or genre contours of Weimar-era biological modernism could temper present-day anti-dualisms that seek to do away with the boundaries between the human and nonhuman. Döblin's claim that "my stomach, my muscles think" and his location of selfhood on an unbounded material chain, for example, would seem to fit well with the concept of "assemblages," the redefinition of agency, and the general attempt to decenter the human in our understanding of the universe.[13]

And yet it matters that Döblin was polemically responding to the cultural and disciplinary juncture analyzed by Plessner, in which long-held ideas about human uniqueness and the particular state of knowledge production at the time led to an epistemological and representational divide incapable of reconciling different approaches to the human being. We can historicize Döblin's claims about embodied cognition by seeing it as a reaction to dualism, and as a presciently ecological understanding of subjectivity. Starker claims, such as the idea that "I am not I, but rather the street, the lanterns, this and this occurrence, nothing beyond this," which we may not wish to endorse literally, must also be understood in terms of their genre function—in this case, the claim is part of a polemic that explicitly links an idea of the literary work to an idea of the human subject, in order to challenge what Döblin felt was a stale ideology.[14] Current invocations of materiality against subjectivity, by contrast, seem to lack a similar target that would make sense of their polemical force, nor are they involved in the kind of dialogue across genres, media, and disciplines that characterized biological modernism. The distance in environmental knowledge between the 1920s and the present matters as well, since divorcing agency from intention and interest, or blurring all boundaries between natural processes and human action might be said to be particularly unhelpful in an age of anthropogenic global warming.[15] Compared to the radical and diverse attempts of these Weimar intellectuals to draw on nature in order to make sense of modernity, one could historicize some contemporary new materialisms less generously, as a reifying metaphysics of capitalism in environmentalist guise.[16] And Plessner's self-aware historicization of his own project, to give another example, might avoid the pitfalls of a hybridity that perpetuates the dualisms it seeks to overcome.[17]

These are only a couple of ways in which these texts from the Weimar Republic might be able to speak to a very different moment that is rediscovering some of these questions. What links these examples from Weimar culture is their exuberant use of biology, organicism, and life with a critical thrust, aimed against a humanism predicated upon the autonomous individual, which was no longer seen to be capable of locating the human being within modernity. While their context is no longer ours, we may still be able to learn something from the ways in which these texts, read as biological modernism, show that artistic practices and commitments, temporal structures, disciplinary contours, forms of knowledge production, philosophies of nature, and definitions of the human bear upon and shape each other.

NOTES

Introduction

EPIGRAPHS: Aristotle, *Poetics*, trans. Anthony Kenny (Oxford: Oxford University Press, 2013), 26. Alfred Döblin, "Bemerkungen zum Roman," in *Schriften zu Ästhetik, Poetik und Literatur*, ed. Christina Althen (Frankfurt am Main: Fischer, 2013), 124–25, my translation. Bertolt Brecht, "Theatre for Pleasure or Theatre for Instruction," in *Brecht on Theatre: The Development of an Aesthetic*, ed. and trans. John Willett (New York: Hill and Wang, 1992), 70. Original in Bertolt Brecht, "Vergnügungstheater oder Lehrtheater," in *Schriften zum Theater* 3, ed. Werner Hecht (Frankfurt am Main: Suhrkamp, 1963), 53.

1. See especially Bertolt Brecht, "The Modern Theatre Is the Epic Theatre" and "A Short Organum for the Theatre," in *Brecht on Theatre*, ed. and trans. Willett, 33–42 and 179–205.

2. See Wilfred Schoeller, *Alfred Döblin: Eine Biographie* (Munich: Carl Hanser Verlag, 2011), 147–74.

3. "In just the same way a story, since it is the representation of an action, should concern an action that is single and entire, with its several incidents so structured that the displacement or removal of any one of them would disturb and dislocate the whole. If the presence or absence of something makes no discernable difference, then it is no part of the whole." Aristotle, *Poetics*, trans. Kenny, 27–28.

4. Michel Foucault, *The Order of Things: An Archaeology of the Human Sciences* (New York: Vintage Books, 1994), 127–28.

5. Cathryn Carson, "Method, Moment, and Crisis in Weimar Science," in *Weimar Thought: A Contested Legacy*, ed. Peter E. Gordon and John P. McCormick (Princeton, N.J.: Princeton University Press, 2013), 183.

6. Brett Buchanan, *Onto-Ethologies: The Animal Environments of Uexküll, Heidegger, Merleau-Ponty, and Deleuze* (Albany: SUNY Press, 2008).

7. Lynn Nyhart, *Modern Nature: The Rise of the Biological Perspective in Germany* (Chicago: University of Chicago Press, 2009).

8. Nick Hopwood, *Haeckel's Embryos: Images, Evolution, and Fraud* (Chicago: University of Chicago Press, 2015); Lynn Nyhart, *Biology Takes Form: Animal Morphology and the German Universities, 1800–1900* (Chicago: University of Chicago Press, 1995).

9. Nyhart, *Biology Takes Form*. See also Michael North, *Novelty: A History of the New* (Chicago: University of Chicago Press, 2013), 60–112.

10. Carson describes the disciplinary proliferation around the idea of life in Weimar, writing: "The sheer accumulation of empirical knowledge of living systems and mechanisms was stunning. It was overshadowed only by some scientists' conviction that critical questions were scarcely beginning to be framed. The very heterogeneity of the field left some of them disturbed: what unified intellectual

structure could mediate claims about conflicting approaches and meld these disciplines into a coherent scientific view of life? One conspicuous feature of Weimar science was the presence of institutions and forums where problems like these could be argued out." Carson, "Method, Moment, and Crisis," 184. More generally, Georges Canguilhem has described the structuring conflicts that link biological thought to broader questions: "One may notice that biological theory reveals itself to be a thinking that throughout its history has been divided and oscillating. Mechanism and Vitalism confront one another on the problem of structures and functions; Discontinuity and Continuity on the Problem of the succession of forms; Preformation and Epigenesis on the problem of the development of a being; Atomicity and Totality on the problem of individuality." Georges Canguilhem, "Aspects of Vitalism," in *Knowledge of Life*, trans. Stefanos Geroulanos and Daniela Ginsburg (New York: Fordham University Press, 2008), 61.

11. Helmuth Plessner, *Die Stufen des Organischen und der Mensch* (Frankfurt am Main: Suhrkamp, 1981), 140. All translations from this work are mine.

12. Donna Haraway, *Crystals, Fabrics, and Fields: Metaphors That Shape Embryos* (Berkeley, Calif.: North Atlantic Books, 2004), 28–34, 195–97.

13. On the embryological experiments of Roux and Driesch, see Georg Toepfer, "Entwicklung," in *Historisches Wörterbuch der Biologie: Geschichte und Theorie der biologischen Grundbegriffe*, vol. 1 (Stuttgart: Metzler, 2011), 400–401. Plessner's account of the Driesch/Köhler controversy can be found in *Stufen*, 138–49. For further discussion of the mechanism/vitalism debate, as well as a thoughtful reconstruction of Plessner's use of this controversy in the broader context of ideas about biological regulation, see Benjamin Bühler, *Lebende Körper: Biologisches und anthropologisches Wissen bei Rilke, Döblin und Jünger* (Würzburg: Königshausen & Neumann, 2004), 47–88.

14. On the influence of Cartesian dualism on mechanist and vitalist paradigms, see Haraway, *Crystals, Fabrics, and Fields*, especially chapter 1, and, more recently, Jessica Riskin, *The Restless Clock: A History of the Centuries-Long Argument over What Makes Living Things Tick* (Chicago: University of Chicago Press, 2016), especially chapter 2. Haraway: "Needham conceived biology under the new paradigm as a 'manifestation of a great movement of modern thought which sought to base a philosophical world-view on ideas originating from biology rather than from classical physics. It fused once again what Descartes had put asunder.' Not only could organic and inorganic be considered within the same coherent framework, but mind and body no longer contradicted each other." Haraway, *Crystals, Fabrics, and Fields*, 137. See also Plessner, *Stufen*, 78–97.

15. Plessner indicts Cartesian dualism for its disembodied understanding of subjectivity, calling it a "point of view" "that hypostasizes the human being in terms of its specialties, and through this division into spheres of being lost sight of the organic unity [*Lebenseinheit*] so that only a faint 'subject' remained, a bare wire on which existence, reduced to a marionette, executes its dead motions." Plessner, *Stufen*, 77.

16. Plessner, *Stufen*, 83.

17. Riskin, *The Restless Clock*, 3–5.

18. "There is something irrational in all understanding, just as life itself is irrational; it cannot be represented in a logical formula. The ultimate, although quite

subjective, sureness residing in this re-experiencing cannot be replaced by any cognitively tested inferences that explicate the process of understanding. These are the limits placed on the logical treatment of understanding by its very nature." Wilhelm Dilthey, "Drafts for a Critique of Historical Reason," in *Selected Works III: The Formation of the Historical World in the Human Sciences*, ed. Rudolf A. Makkreel and Frithjof Rodi (Princeton, N.J.: Princeton University Press, 2002), 239. On the ways in which Dilthey's conception of *Leben* differed from those of Bergson or Spengler, see Plessner, *Stufen*, 59. On the broader context of historical thought and *Lebensphilosophie* in the Weimar Republic, see Charles Bambach, "The Crisis of Historical Thinking," in *Weimar Thought: A Contested Legacy*, ed. Peter E. Gordon and John P. McCormick (Princeton, N.J.: Princeton University Press, 2013), 133–49.

19. For a helpful reading that explains *Lebensphilosophie* on its own terms while also contextualizing it within its own history as well as that of its appropriations from the Right and the Left, see Nitzan Lebovic, *The Philosophy of Life and Death: Ludwig Klages and the Rise of a Nazi Biopolitics* (New York: Palgrave Macmillan, 2013).

20. "After rebelling against the Enlightenment rationality, *Lebensphilosophie* rebelled against the conventional voice of nineteenth-century historians who depicted history as a clear story line, made up of facts, known events, and a chain of great figures. *Lebensphilosophie*'s version of history argued in favor of a factual but nonlinear and anti-enlightened storyline. During the nineteenth century, then, *Lebensphilosophie* chose the path of resistance to consensual forms of thinking." Lebovic, *The Philosophy of Life and Death*, 17. On the influence of *Lebensphilosophie* on the literature of the 1920s, and particularly the pervasive metaphoric of temporary forms arising from, and dissolving back into a permanent flux, see Martin Lindner, *Leben in der Krise: Zeitromane der Neuen Sachlichkeit und die intellektuelle Mentalität der klassischen Moderne* (Stuttgart: Metzler, 1994).

21. Max Scheler, *Die Stellung des Menschen im Kosmos* (Bonn: Bouvier, 2010), 7, translation mine.

22. Plessner, *Stufen*, 37.

23. Benjamin describes the principle he sees in Blossfeldt's work as "one of the deepest, most unfathomable forms of the creative, on the variant that was always, above all others, the form of genius, of the creative collective, and of nature. This is the fruitful, dialectical opposite of invention: the *Natura non facit saltus* of the ancients. One might, with a bold supposition, name it the feminine and vegetable principle of life." Walter Benjamin, "News about Flowers," in *Selected Writings, Vol. 2: 1927–1934*, ed. Michael Jennings, Howard Eiland, and Gary Smith, trans. Michael Jennings (Cambridge, Mass.: Belknap, 1999), 156–57. For a more detailed discussion of Benjamin's reception of Blossfeldt, see chapter 2 below.

24. Ernst Jünger, *The Worker: Dominion and Form*, trans. Bogdan Costea and Laurence Paul Hemming (Evanston, Ill.: Northwestern University Press, 2017), 146, translation modified. "das Gefühl eines entscheidenden Gegensatzes zwischen mechanischer und organischer Welt . . . , in dem eine letzte Verflachung des alten Gegensatzes zwischen Körper und Seele zu erblicken ist." Ernst Jünger, *Der Arbeiter: Herrschaft und Gestalt* (Hamburg: Hanseatische Verlagsanstalt, 1932), 225.

25. Riskin, *Restless Clock*, 61–62.
26. Riskin, *Restless Clock*, 66.
27. As Riskin has succinctly put it, "The removal of the thinking soul had drained the life from the body-machine." Riskin, *Restless Clock*, 70.
28. Alfred Döblin, "An Romanautoren und ihre Kritiker: Berliner Programm," in *Schriften zu Ästhetik, Poetik und Literatur*, ed. Christina Althen (Frankfurt am Main: Fischer, 2013), 118. My translation.
29. Lorraine Daston and Peter Galison, *Objectivity* (New York: Zone Books, 2010), 37. Robert Brain has also described (and complicated) the assignment of individualism to artists in the nineteenth century, writing: "This domain—art—held a hallowed place in the moral imagination of the nineteenth century as the critical refuge of voluntarism, intentionality, and freedom of the will. Science and art had been cast in a two-cultures divide between allegedly creative individualist artists and communal law-bound scientists, famously expressed in Claude Bernard's famous dictum that 'art is I, science is we.' " Robert Brain, *The Pulse of Modernism: Physiological Aesthetics in Fin-de-Siècle Europe* (Seattle: University of Washington Press, 2015), xiii.
30. "He has some kind friends by whom he is pressed / Entirely in his own interest / To conform with this world and its twists and turns / And give up pursuing his own fishy concerns." Bertolt Brecht, *Man Equals Man*, in *Collected Plays: Two*, ed. John Willett and Ralph Manheim, trans. Gerhard Nellhaus (London: Bloomsbury, 1994), 38. Bertolt Brecht, "Lesebuch für Städtebewohner," in *Gedichte* 1 (Berlin: Aufbau and Suhrkamp, 1988), 157.
31. On the way that Virchow's cell theory seemed to dissolve the individual body, see Monika Fick, *Sinnenwelt und Weltseele: Der psychophysische Monismus in der Literatur der Jahrhundertwende* (Tübingen: Max Niemeyer, 1993), 73. For a historical reflection on the political consequences of cell theory's relationship to individuality, see Georges Canguilhem, "Cell Theory," in *Knowledge of Life*, trans. Stefanos Geroulanos and Daniela Ginsburg (New York: Fordham University Press, 2008), 25–56. On Haeckel's theorization of the relationship between the individual and the organ, see Nyhart, *Biology Takes Form*, 135–36: "in the 1850s, defining the individual was a source of considerable controversy in all realms of biology, and a number of Haeckel's teachers and colleagues had become involved in the discussion." With certain species, Haeckel found that the definition of the individual organism differed depending on whether one took a morphological or a physiological standpoint. "The two views could not be resolved into one; they had to be accepted as two different aspects of individuality. Thus, Haeckel argued, 'the two concepts of the individual and the organ are in nature not nearly so distinct' as one usually assumed: in fact, the decision to call a unit an individual or an organ depended only on the mode of analysis the scientist chose. 'Individual' and 'organ' were not absolute concepts but relative ones." On Braun's use of the "dividual," and Plessner's citation of it, see Georg Toepfer, *Historisches Wörterbuch der Biologie*, vol. 2 (Stuttgart: J. B. Metzler, 2011), 175–76.
32. Alfred Döblin, "Der Geist des naturalistischen Zeitalters," in *Schriften zu Ästhetik, Poetik und Literatur*, ed. Christina Althen (Frankfurt am Main: Fischer, 2013), 180. My translation.
33. Jünger, *The Worker*, 38.

34. Döblin, "Geist," 176.
35. N. Katherine Hayles, "How We Became Posthuman: Ten Years On. An Interview with N. Katherine Hayles," *Paragraph* 33, no. 3 (2010): 322.
36. Hayles, "How We Became Posthuman: Ten Years On," 321.
37. As argued also by Hartmut Rosa in *Social Acceleration: A New Theory of Modernity*, trans. Jonathan Trejo-Mathys (New York: Columbia University Press, 2013), 44.
38. "Their purpose to train is what marks Weimar photographic books as particularly modern. They are not modern in the sense [that] they mimic the experiences of film and modernity." Pepper Stetler, *Stop Reading! Look! Modern Vision and the Weimar Photographic Book* (Ann Arbor: University of Michigan Press, 2015), 13.
39. Stetler, *Stop Reading!* 13.
40. Bruno Latour, *We Have Never Been Modern*, trans. Catherine Porter (Cambridge, Mass.: Harvard University Press, 1993), 11.
41. Elaine L. Graham, *Representations of the Post/Human: Monsters, Aliens and Others in Popular Culture* (New Brunswick, N.J.: Rutgers University Press, 2002), 35.
42. Marshall Berman, *All That Is Solid Melts into Air: The Experience of Modernity* (New York: Penguin, 1988), 5.
43. Berman, *All That Is Solid*, 6.
44. Georg Lukács, *The Theory of the Novel* (Cambridge, Mass.: MIT Press, 1971), 40–41.
45. Döblin, "Geist," 170.
46. I am by no means the first to read Döblin and Jünger together. Benjamin Bühler's pathbreaking 2004 study, *Lebende Körper*, offers a sophisticated discussion of the biological and anthropological knowledge of the early twentieth century—with a focus on the concept of the self-regulating, living body—in order to reread works by Plessner, Döblin, and Jünger, as well as Rilke and Scheler. Peter Sprengel also considers the resonances between Jünger and Döblin in a 2010 article. Peter Sprengel, "Fantasies of the Origin and Dreams of Breeding: Darwinism in German and Austrian Literature around 1900," *Monatshefte* 102, no. 4 (Winter 2010): 458–78.
47. Theodor W. Adorno, "Jene zwanziger Jahre," *Merkur: Deutsche Zeitschrift für europäisches Denken* 167, no. 1 (January 1962): 46–51; Helmuth Plessner, "Die Legende von den zwanziger Jahren," *Merkur: Deutsche Zeitschrift für europäisches Denken* 167, no. 1 (January 1962): 33–46.
48. The quote is from Klaus R. Scherpe, "Zur Faszination des Organischen: Eine Vorbemerkung," in *Faszination des Organischen: Konjunkturen einer Kategorie der Moderne*, ed. Hartmut Eggert, Erhard Schütz, and Peter Sprengel, (Munich: Iudicium, 1995), 10. Scherpe associates organicist discourse with a desire for wholeness, a flight from modernity, as does Walter Gebhard's essay in the same volume. On the *Lebensphilosophie* of Ludwig Klages, see Lebovic, *The Philosophy of Life and Death*.
49. On the influence that Neo-Kantianism's epistemological distinction between historical knowledge and natural-scientific knowledge had on the development of evolutionary thought in Germany, see, for example, Nyhart, *Biology Takes Form*, 332.

50. Carson, "Method, Moment, and Crisis," 183.
51. Nyhart, *Biology Takes Form*.
52. Thomas Pynchon, "Is It O.K. to Be a Luddite?" *New York Times*, October 28, 1984, https://archive.nytimes.com/www.nytimes.com/books/97/05/18/reviews/pynchon-luddite.html.
53. In this, I am following Lynn Nyhart's suggestion that the term "interdisciplinary" is simply anachronistic in some contexts: "This does not mean that the study of form was 'interdisciplinary'; rather, the modern notion of academic disciplines, as they came to be defined by the late nineteenth century, was itself just being molded during this period, and the institutional features that came to mark disciplinary status had not yet been fully established." Nyhart, 1995, 35.
54. Leslie A. Adelson, "Against Between: A Manifesto," in *Zafer Şenocak*, ed. Tom Cheesman and Karin E. Yeşilada (Cardiff: University of Wales Press, 2003), 130–43.

Chapter 1

1. Detlev Peukert, *The Weimar Republic: The Crisis of Classical Modernity* (New York: Hill and Wang, 1992), 126, 216, 233.
2. See Joachim Fischer, *Philosophische Anthropologie: Eine Denkrichtung des 20. Jahrhunderts* (Freiburg: Karl Alber, 2008), 88–111; and Christoph Dejung, *Helmuth Plessner: Ein deutscher Philosoph zwischen Kaiserreich und Bonner Republik* (Zürich: Rüffer & Rub Sachbuchverlag, 2003), 232–33.
3. The last twenty years have seen several important publications on Plessner in German—notable among these are Christoph Dejung's 2003 biography, Benjamin Bühler's discussion of Plessner in *Lebende Körper*, and the extensive work by Joachim Fischer on Plessner. In English, Phillip Honenberger and Jos de Mul have recently published edited volumes on Plessner's Philosophical Anthropology. Jos de Mul, ed., *Plessner's Philosophical Anthropology: Perspectives and Prospects* (Amsterdam: Amsterdam University Press, 2014); Phillip Honenberger, ed., *Naturalism and Philosophical Anthropology: Nature, Life, and the Human between Transcendental and Empirical Perspectives* (New York: Palgrave Macmillan, 2016).
4. Arnold Gehlen, *Gesamtausgabe*, ed. Karl-Siegbert Rehberg, vol. 3, *Der Mensch: Seine Natur und seine Stellung in der Welt* (Frankfurt am Main: Vittorio Klostermann, 1993), 30–35.
5. Joachim Fischer, "Exzentrische Positionalität: Plessners Grundkategorie der Philosophischen Anthropologie," in *Leben und Geschichte: Anthropologische und ethnologische Diskurse der Zwischenkriegszeit*, ed. Thomas Keller and Wolfgang Essbach (Munich: Fink, 2006), 233–35.
6. On the differences between Plessner's approach and those of these figures, see Fischer, *Philosophische Anthropologie*, 572–73.
7. Plessner, *Stufen*, 82. All translations of this work are mine.
8. Plessner, *Stufen*, 81–82.
9. Plessner, *Stufen*, 9.
10. Plessner, *Stufen*, 180.
11. "Jede Zeit findet ihr erlösendes Wort. Die Terminologie des achtzehnten Jahrhunderts kulminiert in dem Begriff der Vernunft, die des neunzehnten im Begriff der Entwicklung, die gegenwärtige im Begriff des Lebens. Jede Zeit bezeichnet

damit etwas Verschiedenes, Vernunft hebt das Zeitlose und Allgemeinverbindliche, Entwicklung das rastlos Werdende und Aufsteigende, Leben das dämonisch Spielende, unbewußt Schöpferische heraus." Plessner, *Stufen*, 37.

12. Fischer, "Exzentrische Positionalität," 235, my translation.
13. Fischer, "Exzentrische Positionalität," 238.
14. Plessner, *Stufen*, 39–40.
15. "In his decision to base 'spirit' [*Geist*] in 'life' [*Leben*], turning the tables on the nineteenth-century passion for dismantling and unmasking, the location of the category of 'eccentric positionality' in the history of philosophy becomes recognizable." Fischer, "Exzentrische Positionalität," 240. By contrast, Gehlen refers to the "impossibility, granted from the outset, of *tracing* 'spirit' [*Geist*] *back* to 'life' [*Leben*]. Gehlen, *Gesamtausgabe*, 3:7.
16. Plessner, *Stufen*, 59.
17. On the intellectual-historical context of *Stages of the Organic* and particularly on the significance of Dilthey for Plessner's project, see Gregor Fitzi, "Anthropologische Hermeneutik als Phänomenologie der menschlichen Lebensform: Helmuth Plessners Programm zur Begründung der Anthropologie und der Vitalismus von Hans Driesch," in *Leben und Geschichte: Anthropologische und ethnologische Diskurse der Zwischenkriegszeit*, ed. Thomas Keller and Wolfgang Essbach (Munich: Fink, 2006), 92.
18. Plessner, *Stufen*, 40.
19. "These developments led to a new appreciation for the complexity of the relation between the human being as 'epistemological subject' and as 'epistemological object,' a distinction that was pivotal to the Kantian epistemological framework." Honenberger, *Naturalism and Philosophical Anthropology*, 13–14.
20. Plessner, *Stufen*, 81.
21. Plessner, *Stufen*, 79–80.
22. Plessner, *Stufen*, 50.
23. Plessner, *Stufen*, 70.
24. Plessner, *Stufen*, 83.
25. Donna Haraway has described the importance of animal studies in undoing the machine paradigm of living organisms. Haraway, *Crystals, Fabrics, and Fields*, 22. For an overview of the importance of animal studies in Germany in the 1920s, see Fischer, *Philosophische Anthropologie*, 50–51. And for an in-depth engagement with the lasting philosophical legacy of ethology in the early twentieth century, see Buchanan, *Onto-Ethologies*.
26. Plessner, *Stufen*, 140.
27. Haraway, *Crystals, Fabrics, and Fields*, 34.
28. Haraway, *Crystals, Fabrics, and Fields*, 194–98.
29. Plessner, *Stufen*, 83.
30. For Plessner, the empirical avoidance of the two-world problem excludes important aspects of reality, particularly forms and patterns: "the vivid, albeit formal, non-sensual components, such as the *Gestalt* character, rhythm, situation ('field structure'), also fall out of what 'actually' exists. What is given can in that case only be sensory data that has taken on an atomistic structure through the omission of all non-sensory, complex-forming relations and functions. But these functions that establish unity are necessary in order to justify the wholeness of the phenomenon." Plessner, *Stufen*, 103–4.

31. Plessner, *Stufen*, 119.
32. Plessner, *Stufen*, 51.
33. Plessner, *Stufen*, 119.
34. Plessner, *Stufen*, 119.
35. Plessner describes the method needed to overcome the impasse in these terms: "The following aims not to overcome the double-aspect as an (unarguable) phenomenon, but rather to eliminate its fundamental status, its influence on the formulation of the question. Everything depends solely on the refutation of this double-aspect as *a principle that rends* scientific labor into natural science, i.e., measurement, and the science of consciousness, i.e., self-analysis." Plessner, *Stufen*, 115.
36. Plessner, *Stufen*, 70.
37. Plessner, *Stufen*, 77.
38. Plessner, *Stufen*, 102.
39. Fischer describes Plessner's strategy in this way: "In order to attain a concept of the human being that thinks the human from the perspective of experience and at the same time explains the doubling of his description, Plessner wants to start operationally with the phenomenon that cannot be understood in terms of the Cartesian alternative of intellect [*Geist*] and physical thing [*körperlichem Ding*]: with 'life.' If a first, deep point of contact between separate factors, between inside and outside, could be shown through a special operation on the category of 'life,' then the phenomenon of 'life,' the pre-rationality of which seemed to function as a basis for dismantling all reason, offered as a site of reversal the condition of possibility for building a foundation out of pre-rational moments." Fischer, "Exzentrische Positionalität," 240–41.
40. Plessner, *Stufen*, 123.
41. "As a result, the thought of a foundation for humanistic, cultural experience necessitates the rolling-out of problems that extend into the sensory-material, physical sphere of 'life,' that is, it necessitates a philosophy of *nature* in the broadest and most originary sense." Plessner, *Stufen*, 61.
42. "Physical objects of contemplation, in which a principally divergent outside-inside relationship objectively appears as belonging to their being, are called *living*." Plessner, *Stufen*, 138.
43. Fischer lucidly summarizes Plessner's discussion of "double-aspectivity" as follows: "Plessner begins within the subject-object relationship, but he starts his explanation of the 'double-aspect' not with the body [*Leib*], in the vicinity of the subject-pole, but rather with the physical [*körperlich*] thing of perception, at the distant object-pole. . . . The 'thing of perception' accordingly only appears as objective [*gegenständlich*] by virtue of a 'double-aspect,' or, more exactly: by virtue of *its*, that is, an *ontological* double-aspect. A thing only appears as objective to the one perceiving because the one 'aspect'—the wreath of really appearing characteristics on the 'outside,' beginning with its positional characteristics in space and time—only appears with reference to an other 'aspect'—the inner substantial core, which is in reality not accessible to experience. This latter aspect is presupposed in experience as the unity of all appearing determinations, which itself never appears." Fischer, "Exzentrische Positionalität," 242.
44. Plessner, *Stufen*, 97.
45. Plessner, *Stufen*, 100–101.

46. Plessner, *Stufen*, 111–12.
47. Plessner, *Stufen*, 154.
48. Plessner, *Stufen*, 154.
49. Plessner, *Stufen*, 180.
50. Plessner, *Stufen*, 154.
51. Plessner, *Stufen*, 212.
52. See especially Plessner, *Stufen*, 258–82. In the 1966 afterword, Plessner briefly takes stock of developments in biology over the nearly four decades since *Stages of the Organic* was published. It is a fascinating, if tantalizingly brief, survey, in which he brings his theory into contact with other important tendencies within biology that sought a non-reductive account of life, and it mentions dialectical materialism (A. I. Oparin) and organicism (J. B. Haldane). Significantly, Plessner updates his theory of the border by comparing it to contemporary understandings of the membrane as "mediating surfaces." Discussing recent research on organic membranes that was not available to him when he wrote *Stages of the Organic*, Plessner describes membranes as fitting his earlier idea of the border—they are not merely the spatial delimitation of an organic body, but are rather a functional interface that determine the relationship between body and medium. Plessner, *Stufen*, 437.
53. In the original text these schematics are K ← Z → M and K ← K → M, respectively.
54. Plessner, *Stufen*, 283, 302.
55. "Being human is not tied to any particular form, and for that reason (to recall a clever speculation of the paleontologist Dacqué) could also occur in various forms that do not coincide with the ones we know." Plessner, *Stufen*, 365.
56. Plessner, *Stufen*, 284–90.
57. Scott Davis, "Plessner's Conceptual Investigations of 'Life': Structural Narratology," in *Naturalism and Philosophical Anthropology: Nature, Life, and the Human between Transcendental and Empirical Perspectives*, ed. Phillip Honenberger (New York: Palgrave Macmillan, 2016), 126.
58. Plessner, *Stufen*, 291.
59. Plessner, *Stufen*, 295–96.
60. Plessner, *Stufen*, 296.
61. *Etymologisches Wörterbuch des Deutschen*, 8th ed., ed. Wolfgang Pfeifer (Munich: Deutscher Taschenbuch Verlag, 2005), 719, 783.
62. Plessner, *Stufen*, 297.
63. Plessner, *Stufen*, 297–98.
64. Plessner, *Stufen*, 298.
65. Plessner, *Stufen*, 296.
66. Plessner, *Stufen*, 297. "Raumhaft" is a term that Plessner defines as a contrast to what is merely spatial (*räumlich*). He defines the difference in this way: "Every physical bodily thing is in space, is spatial [*räumlich*]. As far as its measurement goes, its position exists in relation to other positions and to the position of the observer. Living bodies too, as physical things, are not exempt from this relative order. But . . . living bodies differentiate themselves from non-living bodies as space-claiming, as opposed to merely space-filling, bodies. Every space-filling object is in a place. A space-claiming object is, in contrast, in a relationship to the place of 'its' being by virtue of the fact that it exists beyond and into itself.

Besides its spatiality, it is *into space* or *space-like* [*raumhaft*] and to this extent has its natural place." Plessner, *Stufen*, 186–87.

67. Plessner, *Stufen*, 317–18.

68. Joachim Fischer describes centric positionality in this way: "This life form is granted an inner zone, in which the whole body [*Körper*] is represented once more. The relation of stimulus and reaction occurs via the living subject [*Lebenssubjekt*]. Central positionality implies 'frontality,' being confronted with an environment [*Umwelt*] organized into things, and 'spontaneity,' readiness for action." Fischer, "Exzentrische Positionalität," 247.

69. Plessner, *Stufen*, 332–38.

70. Plessner, *Stufen*, 327–29.

71. Plessner, *Stufen*, 294–95.

72. Plessner, *Stufen*, 74–75.

73. "Its *Körper* has become its *Leib*, that concrete middle through which the living subject [*Lebenssubject*] is connected to its surroundings [*Umfeld*]." Plessner, *Stufen*, 296. "The self and the medium as the Other are in relation only *across a chasm*." Plessner, *Stufen*, 298.

74. Plessner, *Stufen*, 298.

75. Plessner, *Stufen*, 74–75.

76. Plessner, *Stufen*, 298.

77. Plessner, *Stufen*, 299.

78. Plessner, *Stufen*, 299.

79. Plessner, *Stufen*, 385.

80. Plessner, *Stufen*, 384.

81. Plessner says clearly that eccentric positionality, as the full and reflexive unfolding of centric positionality and the closed form of the animal, is necessarily the final positional stage of organic life. Plessner, *Stufen*, 363.

82. For a useful overview of the differences and similarities in the approaches to Philosophical Anthropology of Max Scheler, Helmuth Plessner, Erich Rothacker, Arnold Gehlen, and Adolf Portmann, see Fischer, *Philosophische Anthropologie*, 558–75.

83. Plessner, *Stufen*, 383.

84. Plessner, *Stufen*, 360.

85. Plessner, *Stufen*, 360.

86. Plessner, *Stufen*, 362. For a discussion of how Plessner's category of positionality inverts Fichte's concept of "positing," see Fischer, "Exzentrische Positionalität," 244–45.

87. Plessner, *Stufen*, 362.

88. Plessner, *Stufen*, 362.

89. Plessner, *Stufen*, 364–65.

90. June Hwang, *Lost in Time: Locating the Stranger in German Modernity* (Evanston, Ill.: Northwestern University Press, 2014), 70.

91. Plessner, *Stufen*, 384.

92. "Because [the plant] is dependently involved in its life circuit and is absorbed into it as a part," "weil [die Pflanze] unselbständig in ihren Lebenskreis einbezogen ist und als Teil in ihm aufgeht." Plessner, *Stufen*, 359.

93. Plessner, *Stufen*, 366–67.

94. Plessner, *Stufen*, 367.

95. Plessner, *Stufen*, 372.
96. Plessner, *Stufen*, 375.
97. Plessner locates *Geist* in the *Mitwelt*, the third of the three worlds of eccentric positionality (along with *Außenwelt* and *Innenwelt*). Plessner, *Stufen*, 377–78.
98. Fischer, "Exzentrische Positionalität," 248–49.
99. Plessner, *Stufen*, 385.
100. Plessner, *Stufen*, 383–84.
101. Plessner, *Stufen*, 384–85.
102. Plessner, *Stufen*, 400–401. See also Fischer, "Exzentrische Positionalität," 250–51.
103. Plessner, *Stufen*, 365.
104. On the way that the end of *Stages of the Organic* joins the beginning of the book, see Scott Davis's essay. "Only humans are equipped to do so [i.e., treat the world objectively], in our mediated immediacy, and only we get the aspects and non-appearing core of coherence of the thing. Thus the textual progression of the argument forms a kind of ring and joins itself at beginning and end: this is not *petitio principii* but is a textual icon for how being turns around in consciousness." Davis, "Plessner's Conceptual Investigations," 12.
105. Plessner, *Stufen*, 116.
106. Plessner, *Stufen*, 420–24.
107. Helmut Lethen, *Cool Conduct: The Culture of Distance in Weimar Germany* (Berkeley: University of California Press, 2002), 56.
108. Lethen, *Cool Conduct*, 56. Joachim Fischer (2002) has convincingly shown how the opposite is the case, and how *Grenzen der Gemeinschaft* is in fact Plessner's attempt to unfold his anthropological work as a critical theory of society, rather than an *ex post facto* naturalization of a theory of society.
109. Lethen, *Cool Conduct*, 65.
110. Gehlen, *Gesamtausgabe*, 3:30, my translation.
111. Gehlen, *Gesamtausgabe*, 3:31–32.
112. For the relationship between Gehlen and Plessner, including Gehlen's borrowings from Plessner's theory and his "demonstrative attempt to rid himself of his most recent predecessors by establishing 'Herder as a predecessor,'" see Fischer, *Philosophische Anthropologie*, 176–77, 218–19, 271–72, and 543–44.
113. Fischer, *Philosophische Anthropologie*, 174.
114. Plessner, *Stufen*, 390, 393.
115. Plessner, *Stufen*, 180.
116. Plessner, *Stufen*, 400.
117. The dialectical dimension of Plessner's understanding of organic life is given especial consideration in the section of *Stages of the Organic* where he discusses the processual character of life. He uses a language of becoming and persisting to elaborate on the ontological stakes of the border. Plessner, *Stufen*, 189. Elsewhere, he describes the process of becoming with the figure of the corkscrew, as a synthesis of becoming something different and remaining itself. Plessner, *Stufen*, 196.
118. Plessner, *Stufen*, 217.
119. Plessner writes of the "selves" and "having" of living beings as such, and how these can be differentiated by the positional differences among various stages of the organic. Plessner, *Stufen*, 217, 297.

120. Friedrich Schiller, *The Robbers and Wallenstein*, trans. F. J. Lamport (London: Penguin Books, 1979), 33.
121. Lethen, *Cool Conduct*, 52.
122. Lethen, *Cool Conduct*, 59.
123. Lethen, *Cool Conduct*, 60.
124. For a thorough rebuttal of Lethen's identification of Plessner's concept of the border with armoring, see Joachim Fischer, "Panzer oder Maske: 'Verhaltenslehre der Kälte' oder Sozialtheorie der 'Grenze,'" in *Plessners "Grenzen der Gemeinschaft": Eine Debatte*, ed. Wolfgang Essbach, Joachim Fischer, and Helmut Lethen (Frankfurt am Main: Suhrkamp, 2002), 80–102. Plessner's afterword to *Stages of the Organic*, written in 1966, connects his idea of the border to the understanding of how cell membranes function that had been gained in the interval. As in the original text, it is essential that the border both connects and separates. Plessner, *Stufen*, 437.
125. Lethen writes of the mask in Plessner: "'The maskedness of the public individual' (94), however, not only exists as a formal technique of social intercourse but shelters a precarious inner substance that must not be delivered up defenseless in the public sphere." Lethen, *Cool Conduct*, 63. But as Joachim Fischer has argued, "since the mask is at the same time an artificially constructed phenomenon of protection *and* a genuine phenomenon of expression—everything depends on this for Plessner—an insurmountable barrier separates Lethen's 'armor' from Plessner's 'mask': armor as protection is per se a useful phenomenon that does not have to express anything; a mask only offers protection to the extent that it is also expression, as mediated as it may be.... But Lethen reads 'armor' wherever 'mask' is written, and also understands 'tactics' where Plessner speaks of 'tact.'" Fischer, "Panzer oder Maske," 89. Significantly, Plessner seems to fault Uexküll with a similar one-sidedness for ignoring the fact that an animal's specific environment must always be both a separation from irrelevant or superfluous aspects of the environment and a contact with its relevant aspects; Plessner insists that both separation and contact, "aufgedeckte *und* verdeckte Wirklichkeit," must be understood as a foundation of the closed form of the animal, which already represents the indirect directness and mediated immediacy that come to full realization with the human being. Plessner, *Stufen*, 328–29.
126. Lethen, *Cool Conduct*, 56.
127. "Behavior" (*Verhalten*) is in fact an important term for Plessner, but it has nothing to do with codes of conduct. Rather, Plessner sees *Verhalten* as the kind of behavior that belongs to a *Leib* instead of to a *Körper*. Actions such as walking, lifting, standing up, lying down, and so on cannot merely be reduced to mechanical processes but encompass meaningful unities that Plessner refers to as *Verhaltungsweisen*. It is notable, in the context of Lethen's reading of Plessner, that the latter's deployment of the concept of *Verhalten* arises as a way of conveying a basic meaningful unit of the action of animals, the sense of which dissolves if the action is understood purely mechanistically. This insight is connected to Plessner's work on animal behavior and expression and, contrary to Lethen, does not have so much to do with rigid forms of behavior as with the attempt to provide a framework for thinking about behavior and expression as meaningful units. The terms *Leib* and *Verhaltungsweisen* express an organic unit that exceeds the physical and mechanical properties of thinghood.

See, for example, Plessner's "Die Deutung des mimischen Ausdrucks: Ein Beitrag zur Lehre vom Bewußtsein des anderen Ichs" (1925), especially the section "Die Schicht des Verhalten," in which he describes an overlay of the mechanical *Körper*, which can be analyzed in terms of purely "kinematic" physiological processes, and the living *Leib*, which must be seen in terms of meaningful wholes of expression and behavior. Helmuth Plessner, "Die Deutung des mimischen Ausdrucks: Ein Beitrag zur Lehre vom Bewußtsein des anderen Ichs," in *Gesammelte Schriften VII: Ausdruck und menschliche Natur*, ed. Günter Dux, Odo Marquard, and Elisabeth Ströker (Frankfurt am Main: Suhrkamp, 1982), 77–89.

128. Brett Buchanan's *Onto-Ethologies* (2008) has done much to recover this interdisciplinary constellation by focusing on the theoretical biology of Jakob von Uexküll and its reception in the philosophy of Heidegger, Merleau-Ponty, and Deleuze.

129. Plessner, *Stufen*, 83.

Chapter 2

1. Laura Saltz, "Natural/Mechanical: Keywords in the Conception of Early Photography," in *Photography and Its Origins*, ed. Tanya Sheehan and Andrés Mario Zervigón (London: Routledge, 2015), 195–207.

2. "Born in the midst of massive social and epistemological shifts, photography exemplifies the paradoxical concept of 'the modern' as defined by historian of science Bruno Latour: modern culture simultaneously proliferates hybrids and subjects them to an ongoing project of 'purification,' or the creation of 'distinct ontological zones' of classification through which the possibility of hybridity is repressed." Saltz, "Natural/Mechanical," 197.

3. Stetler, *Stop Reading!* 14–17.

4. "Their purpose to train is what marks Weimar photographic books as particularly modern. They are not modern in the sense [that] they mimic the experiences of film and modernity. . . . In this way, this study defines modern vision as something imagined but never achieved. Whether or not modernity was capable of transforming visual skills and habits, artists central to this study and to the theorization of modern photography *thought* that it was, and this belief motivated their interest in the photographic book. A belief in the potential of new media is what makes Weimar photographic books an important contribution to modernism." Stetler, *Stop Reading!* 13.

5. Daston and Galison, *Objectivity*, 138.

6. Daston and Galison, *Objectivity*, 139.

7. Kurt Korff, "The Illustrated Magazine," in *The Weimar Republic Sourcebook*, ed. Anton Kaes, Martin Jay, and Edward Dimendberg (Berkeley: University of California Press, 1995), 646.

8. Johannes Molzahn, "Stop Reading! Look!" in *The Weimar Republic Sourcebook*, ed. Anton Kaes, Martin Jay, and Edward Dimendberg (Berkeley: University of California Press, 1995), 648.

9. Pepper Stetler's 2015 book *Stop Reading! Look!* which takes its title from Molzahn's essay, explores the ambivalence of the relationship between photographic vision and modernity, and the distinct modes of reading that the new visual media, especially the photobook, sought to teach readers.

10. Albert Renger-Patzsch, "Joy before the Object," in *Photography in the Modern Era: European Documents and Critical Writings, 1913–1940*, ed. Christopher Phillips (New York: Metropolitan Museum of Art, 1989), 108–9.

11. Albert Renger-Patzsch, "Photographie und Kunst," in *Die Freude am Gegenstand: Gesammelte Aufsätze zur Photographie*, ed. Bernd Stiegler, Ann Wilde, and Jürgen Wilde (Munich: Wilhelm Fink, 2010), 83, my translation.

12. Albert Renger-Patzsch, "Aims," in *Photography in the Modern Era: European Documents and Critical Writings, 1913–1940*, ed. Christopher Phillips (New York: Metropolitan Museum of Art, 1989), 104–5.

13. See, for example, Carl Georg Heise's introduction to Renger-Patzsch's *Die Welt ist schön*, in which Heise emphasizes the ways in which photography can expand the category of the beautiful. Albert Renger-Patzsch, *Die Welt ist schön: Einhundert photographische Aufnahmen von Albert Renger-Patzsch*, ed. Carl Georg Heise (Munich: Kurt Wolff, 1928), 13–14.

14. Pepper Stetler, "The Object, the Archive and the Origins of Neue Sachlichkeit Photography," *History of Photography* 35, no. 3 (2011): 281–95.

15. See especially Daniel H. Magilow, *The Photography of Crisis: The Photo Essays of Weimar Germany* (University Park: Pennsylvania State University Press, 2012); Stetler, *Stop Reading!*; and Patrizia McBride, *The Chatter of the Visible: Montage and Narrative in Weimar Germany* (Ann Arbor: University of Michigan Press, 2016).

16. See especially Stefanie Harris, *Mediating Modernity: German Literature and the "New" Media, 1895–1930* (University Park: Pennsylvania State University Press, 2009); Devin Fore, *Realism after Modernism: The Rehumanization of Art and Literature* (Cambridge, Mass.: MIT Press, 2012); Andreas Huyssen, *Miniature Metropolis: Literature in an Age of Photography and Film* (Cambridge, Mass.: Harvard University Press, 2015); and McBride, *Chatter of the Visible*.

17. See Oliver Botar, "Prolegomena to the Study of Biomorphic Modernism: Biocentrism, László Moholy-Nagy's 'New Vision' and Ernö Kállai's 'Bioromantik'" (Ph.D. diss., University of Toronto, 1998); Mia Fineman, "Ecce Homo Prostheticus: Technology and the New Photography in Weimar Germany" (Ph.D. diss., Yale University, 2001); and Juliana Kreinik, "The Canvas and the Camera in Weimar Germany: A New Objectivity in Painting and Photography of the 1920s" (Ph.D. diss., New York University, 2008).

18. August Sander, "From the Nature & Growth of Photography: Lecture 5: Photography as a Universal Language," trans. Anne Halley, *Massachusetts Review* 19, no. 4 (1978): 677.

19. On this lecture, see Anne Halley, "August Sander," *Massachusetts Review* 19, no. 4 (1978): 663–73.

20. On the role of physiognomic discourse in Sander's work, see Liliane Weissberg, "Der Mensch, physiognomisch betrachtet: August Sanders Photographien als politischer 'Übungsatlas,'" in *Humanität in einer pluralistischen Welt?* ed. Christian Kluwe and Jost Schneider (Würzburg: Königshausen & Neumann, 2000), 325–41; and Edward Aiken, "Some Reflections on August Sander and His Physiognomic Portraits," in *Physiognomy in Profile*, ed. Melissa Percival and Graeme Tytler (Newark: University of Delaware Press, 2005), 198–216.

21. Sabine Hake, "Faces of Weimar Germany," in *The Image in Dispute: Art and Cinema in the Age of Photography*, ed. Dudley Andrew (Austin: University of Texas

Press, 1997), 117–47; and Matthias Uecker, "The Face of the Weimar Republic: Photography, Physiognomy, and Propaganda in Weimar Germany," *Monatshefte* 99, no. 4 (2007): 469–84. On the broader physiognomic discourse in Weimar Germany, see Richard Gray, *About Face: German Physiognomic Thought from Lavater to Auschwitz* (Detroit, Mich.: Wayne State University Press, 2004), 177–217.

22. Sander, "Photography as a Universal Language," 678.

23. Sander, "Photography as a Universal Language," 677.

24. For a comparison of Sander's and Günther's physiognomic photography, see Weissberg, "Der Mensch, Physiognomisch Betrachtet," 325–41.

25. Walter Benjamin memorably describes the scenery of earlier studio photography as an "upholstered tropics," writing, "this was the period of those studios—with their draperies and palm trees, their tapestries and easels—which occupied so ambiguous a place between execution and representation, between torture chamber and throne room." Walter Benjamin, "Little History of Photography," in *Selected Writings, Vol. 2: 1927–1934*, ed. Michael W. Jennings, Howard Eiland, and Gary Smith (Cambridge, Mass.: Belknap, 1999), 515.

26. In Baker's compelling reading, this project undermines itself: echoes, doublings, and analogies within and between images disrupt the narrative signification by joining what it means to distinguish. For Baker, the decline shown by Sander's book is not that of modern society, but rather that of the portrait as a specifically bourgeois form. George Baker, "Photography between Narrativity and Stasis: August Sander, Degeneration, and the Decay of the Portrait," *October* 76 (1996): 112.

27. Alfred Döblin, "Faces, Images, and Their Truth," in August Sander, *Face of Our Time* (Munich: Schirmer/Mosel, 1994), 13.

28. "Entire stories could be told about many of these photographs, they are asking for it, they are raw material for writers, material that is more stimulating and more productive than many a newspaper report." Döblin, "Faces, Images," 15.

29. Döblin, "Faces, Images, " 7.

30. Ernst Benkard, *Das ewige Antlitz* (Berlin: Frankfurter Verlagsanstalt, 1927).

31. Döblin, "Faces, Images," 9.

32. Döblin, "Faces, Images," 9.

33. Döblin, "Faces, Images," 10.

34. Döblin, "Faces, Images," 12–13.

35. Döblin, "Faces, Images," 13.

36. Döblin, "Faces, Images," 13.

37. In *Biology Takes Form: Animal Morphology and the German Universities, 1800–1900*, the historian of science Lynn Nyhart reconstructs the institutional and disciplinary contours of the emergence of modern biology. "Comparative anatomy" was an established term for describing the program of evolutionary morphology in the discipline of anatomy. Nyhart, *Biology Takes Form*, 207. On the role of comparative anatomy in the German reception of Darwin's theory, she writes: "To [determine phylogenetic linkages], Haeckel and Gegenbaur relied on a method already available to them: comparison. As Gegenbaur put it in the revised edition (1870) of his *Grundzüge der vergleichenden Anatomie*, 'The task of comparative anatomy lies in explaining the manifestations of form in the organization of the animal body. . . . In this way comparative anatomy offers

evidence for the continuity of entire series of organs.'" Nyhart, *Biology Takes Form*, 150. Georg Toepfer, while situating comparative anatomy in a much longer tradition, also indicates the connection in the nineteenth century between comparative embryonic anatomy and development, which would culminate in Haeckel's "biogenetic law." Georg Toepfer, "Anatomie," in *Historisches Wörterbuch der Biologie: Geschichte und Theorie der biologischen Grundbegriffe*, vol. 1 (Stuttgart: Metzler, 2011), 17–19.

38. Thanks to Christina Althen's painstaking recent reconstruction of Döblin's studies, we know that Döblin took "Darwinian Theory" with Bernhard Rawitz and "Human Anatomy" with Wilhelm Waldeyer in the 1900–1901 winter semester at Berlin, and "General Anatomy" with Oscar Hertwig in the following semester. Christina Althen, "Alfred Döblins medizinische Ausbildung dargestellt anhand von Quellen," in *Internationales Alfred-Döblin-Kolloquium Zürich 2015: Exil als Schicksalsreise: Alfred Döblin und das literarische Exil 1933–1950*, ed. Sabina Becker and Sabine Schneider (Bern: Peter Lang, 2017), 30–32. Rawitz links comparative anatomy to evolutionary questions in his popularizing 1903 work *Urgeschichte, Geschichte und Politik*. Bernhard Rawitz, *Urgeschichte, Geschichte und Politik: Populär-naturwissenschaftliche Betrachtungen* (Berlin: Leonhard Simion, 1903), 36. Likewise, Hertwig's approach to anatomy was "less strictly medical and more evolutionary" than Waldeyer's (Nyhart, *Biology Takes Form*, 230).

We also know that Döblin took "Hegel's Theory" and "Anatomy of the Brain" in the 1901 summer semester and "Seminars on Kant's *Critique of Pure Reason*" and "Treating Syphilis" in the 1902–1903 winter semester, academic constellations that intimate deeper realms of modernism than the present study is equipped to sound. Althen, "Alfred Döblins medizinische Ausbildung," 30–31.

39. Nyhart, *Biology Takes Form*, 220.
40. Döblin, "Faces, Images," 13.
41. Daston and Galison, *Objectivity*, 63, 23.
42. See chapter 3.
43. Döblin, "Faces, Images," 10.
44. See, for example, Bertolt Brecht, "Fotografie," in *Werke: Grosse Kommentierte Berliner und Frakfurter Ausgabe, Schriften I*, ed. Werner Hecht, Jan Knopf, Werner Mittenzwei, and Klaus-Detlef Müller (Berlin: Aufbau, 1988), 265; and Benjamin, "Little History of Photography," 520. On Benjamin's view of photography as physiognomic training, see Miriam Bratu Hansen, *Cinema and Experience: Siegfried Kracauer, Walter Benjamin, and Theodor W. Adorno* (Berkeley: University of California Press, 2012), 158.
45. Benjamin, "News about Flowers," 156.
46. See Hansen, *Cinema and Experience*, 157–58.
47. Benjamin, "Little History of Photography," 512.
48. Stetler, *Stop Reading!* 115. On the reception of Blossfeldt, see also Annika Baacke, "Fotografie zwischen Kunst und Dokumentation" (Ph.D. diss., Freie Universität Berlin, 2014), 93–96; and Fineman, "Ecce Homo Prostheticus," 111–24.
49. Fineman, "Ecce Homo Prostheticus," 93–94
50. See Gert Mattenklott, "Karl Blossfeldt—Photographs," in *Art Forms in Nature*, by Karl Blossfeldt (Munich: Schirmer/Mosel, 1999), 14; Baacke, "Fotografie Zwischen Kunst und Dokumentation," 89–96; and Fineman, "Ecce Homo Prostheticus," 91–96.

51. Fineman, "Ecce Homo Prostheticus," 89.
52. Baacke, "Fotografie zwischen Kunst und Dokumentation," 89–90.
53. Baacke, "Fotografie zwischen Kunst und Dokumentation," 84.
54. Benjamin, "News about Flowers," 157.
55. Karl Blossfeldt, *Karl Blossfeldt: Working Collages*, ed. Ann Wilde and Jürgen Wilde (Cambridge, Mass.: MIT Press, 2001), 7.
56. As Ulrike Meyer Stump writes in her introduction to *Working Collages*, "In order to extract these art forms from nature, Blossfeldt sometimes dissected specimens with the scalpel so radically that they are no longer botanically identifiable. At a later stage, he sometimes retouched undesirable features, removing them from a print. . . . Damaged emulsion, dust particles, and other blemishes on prints were cleaned up, and visible shadows were occasionally deleted from contact prints by hand." Blossfeldt, *Working Collages*, 12.
57. On the manipulation of the plant specimens in *Art Forms in Nature*, see Stetler, *Stop Reading!*; and Kreinik, Baacke, and Meyer Stump. Kreinik reads these manipulations as being performed in the service of an "evidentiary aesthetic," whereby the technical control of the camera and the similarity to scientific codes of representation help advance the argument about *Urformen*. Kreinik, "The Canvas and the Camera," 257–63. Stetler too reads Blossfeldt's photographic practice in the context of Meurer's functional forms: "Like his mentor [Meurer], Blossfeldt seems to have conceived of photography as a process of manipulation and modification rather than the *sachlich* approach that he would be associated with in the 1920s." Stetler, *Stop Reading!* 125. Baacke meanwhile sees these manipulations in the context of Jugendstil, such that Blossfeldt's manipulations served to bring out an aesthetic idea inherent in nature. See Baacke, "Fotografie zwischen Kunst und Dokumentation," 137.
58. Kreinik, "The Canvas and the Camera," 252–63.
59. Kreinik, "The Canvas and the Camera," 262.
60. For more on the category of the *type* in truth-to-nature, see Daston and Galison, *Objectivity*, 69–70. It is also noteworthy that botany is the example that Daston and Galison give for a scientific "discipline in which truth-to-nature persisted as a viable standard in the realm of images." Daston and Galison, *Objectivity*, 105.
61. Daston and Galison, *Objectivity*, 58, emphasis added.
62. "Tracing and strict measuring controls could also be enlisted to the cause of mechanical objectivity, just as photographs could conversely be used to portray types. What was key was neither the medium nor mimesis but the possibility of minimizing intervention, in hopes of achieving an image untainted by subjectivity." Daston and Galison, *Objectivity*, 43.
63. Daston and Galison, *Objectivity*, 151.
64. Daston and Galison, *Objectivity*, 42.
65. Daston and Galison, *Objectivity*, 187.
66. And Albert Renger-Patzsch. See Carl Gelderloos, "Simply Reproducing Reality: Brecht, Benjamin, and Renger-Patzsch on Photography," *German Studies Review* 37, no. 3 (October 2014): 549–73.
67. Daston and Galison, *Objectivity*, 42. See also their discussion of eighteenth-century botanical illustrations: "The type was truer to nature—and therefore more real—than any actual specimen." Daston and Galison, *Objectivity*, 60.

68. On the various valences of *Sachlichkeit* for the visual arts, see Kreinik, "The Canvas and the Camera," 21–22.
69. Benjamin, "News about Flowers," 156.
70. Benjamin, "News about Flowers," 156–57.
71. Jacques Rancière, *Aisthesis: Scenes from the Aesthetic Regime of Art* (London: Verso, 2013), 99.
72. Describing Mallarmé's new idea of fiction, Rancière writes: "The new fiction is this pure display of forms. These forms can be called abstract because they tell no stories. But if they get rid of stories, they do so in order to serve a higher *mimesis*: through artifice they reinvent the very forms in which sensible events are given to us and assembled to constitute a world. . . . What is imitated, in each thing, is the event of its apparition." Rancière, *Aisthesis*, 100.
73. Rancière's discussion of Art Nouveau is also strikingly relevant to Blossfeldt's work. For Rancière, Art Nouveau is not a "temporary decorative style" evocative of plant and machine forms alike, but the attempt to represent "potentials and forms anterior to these specifications [of material and process]." Rancière, *Aisthesis*, 106.
74. Rancière, *Aisthesis*, 107.
75. Siegfried Kracauer, "Photography," in *The Mass Ornament: Weimar Essays*, ed. Thomas Y. Levin (Cambridge, Mass.: Harvard University Press, 1995), 48.
76. Kracauer, "Photography," 48.
77. Kracauer, "Photography," 47.
78. Kracauer, "Photography," 58.
79. The status of individuality, seriality, and repetition within the chorus line, and the deeper historical and philosophical connections between these and capitalist rationality, are of course the subject of one of Kracauer's best-known essays, "Mass Ornament."
80. Kracauer, "Photography," 47. "*So* sieht die Filmdiva aus." Siegfried Kracauer, "Die Photographie," in *Das Ornament der Masse* (Frankfurt am Main: Suhrkamp, 1977), 21, italics added.
81. Kracauer, "Photography," 52.
82. Hansen, *Cinema and Experience*, 30.
83. Kracauer, "Photography," 55.
84. Kracauer, "Photography," 56.
85. Kracauer, "Photography," 58.
86. Kracauer, "Photography," 52.
87. McBride, *The Chatter of the Visible*, 115. In her reading of Kracauer's essay, Patrizia McBride has linked Brecht's and Kracauer's critiques of photography's claims, within the context of the mass media of the 1920s, to a superior representation. McBride draws on Clive Scott's elaboration of Peirce's semiotics to show how Kracauer's essay indicts the contemporary overconfidence in photography's indexical dimension at the expense of a fuller consideration of its iconic and symbolic functioning.
88. Kracauer, "Photography," 61–62, translation modified.
89. Siegfried Kracauer, "Calico World," in *The Mass Ornament: Weimar Essays*, ed. Thomas Y. Levin (Cambridge, Mass.: Harvard University Press, 1995), 282.
90. Kracauer, "Calico World," 282, 285, 287.
91. Kracauer, "Calico World," 287.

92. Kracauer, "Photography," 62.
93. Kracauer, "Photography," 55.
94. Stetler, "The Object, the Archive, and the Origins of Neue Sachlichkeit Photography," 290.
95. Kracauer, "Photography," 61.

Chapter 3

1. Alfred Döblin, "An Romanautoren und ihre Kritiker: Berliner Programm," in *Schriften zu Ästhetik, Poetik und Literatur*, ed. Christina Althen (Frankfurt am Main: Fischer, 2013) 118. All translations of Döblin's texts in this chapter are mine.
2. "Die Geschlossenheit der alten Romanform spiegelt die vermeintliche der Persönlichkeit wider." Kracauer is playing with the multiple senses of "Geschlossenheit" in German—when referring to a literary plot, it can mean "tight construction." Siegfried Kracauer, "Die Biographie als neubürgerliche Kunstform," in *Werke 5.3: Essays, Feuilletons, Rezensionen 1928–1931* (Berlin: Suhrkamp, 2011), 265.
3. Döblin, "An Romanautoren," 118.
4. Döblin, "An Romanautoren," 119.
5. Döblin, "An Romanautoren," 120.
6. "Swept away by the psychological mania, one has placed the single human being in an exaggerated way at the center of novels and novellas. One has invented thousands of particular, highly exaggerated characters in whose complexity the author basked. Behind a pernicious rationalism, the whole world with its multiple dimensions has completely vanished; these authors have truly been working in a closed chamber." Döblin, "An Romanautoren," 121.
7. Döblin, "An Romanautoren," 120.
8. "One should learn from psychiatry, the only science that deals with the whole of the mental person; it has long recognized the naive aspect of psychology, restricts itself to noting processes and movements—with a shake of the head and a shrug of the shoulders for anything beyond this and for the 'why' and the 'how.'" Döblin, "An Romanautoren," 119–20. As Veronika Fuechtner has shown, Döblin's early training in psychiatry was challenged by his encounter with war neuroses in the years after he wrote "An Romanautoren." Over the course of the 1920s, his medical practice in Berlin and his encounter with the Berlin Psychoanalytic Institute and especially with Ernst Simmel helped encourage an embrace of psychoanalysis over a purely physiological approach. See Veronika Fuechtner, *Berlin Psychoanalytic: Psychoanalysis and Culture in Weimar Republic Germany and Beyond* (Berkeley: University of California Press, 2011), 18–64. What I hope to show is that the material, embodied dimension of the psyche remained a strategy Döblin used to critique older notions of individuality and art, even after he had abandoned as a medical practice the kind of psychiatry he describes in "An Romanautoren."
9. The critique of domains of knowledge that claim to objectively represent reality while ignoring their own epistemic constraints, while indeed fetishizing the idea of objectivity, seems to have been a persistent one for Döblin. He made a similar critique of academic history's "manic ideal of objectivity" (*wahnhafte Objektivitätsideal*) a couple of decades later in the essay "Der historische Roman

und wir." Alfred Döblin, "Der historische Roman und wir," in *Schriften zu Ästhetik, Poetik und Literatur*, ed. Christina Althen (Frankfurt am Main: Fischer, 2013), 303.

10. Döblin, "An Romanautoren," 122.

11. For an in-depth study of the relationship between the crises in historiography and narrative, see Ulrich Kittstein, *"Mit Geschichte will man etwas": Historisches Erzählen in der Weimarer Republik und im Exil (1918–1945)* (Würzburg: Königshausen & Neumann, 2006). For a discussion of the debates in contemporary historiography, see Charles Bambach, "Weimar Philosophy and the Crisis of Historical Thinking," in *Weimar Thought: A Contested Legacy*, ed. Peter E. Gordon and John P. McCormick (Princeton, N.J.: Princeton University Press, 2013), 133–49.

12. As Gregor Streim specifies, with regard to the "crisis of the novel" in the 1920s: "But it was not the novel as such that was challenged, but rather just a certain kind of novel: namely, the psychological-realistic novel of the nineteenth century based on the belief that the totality of life can be represented in the form of a closed narrative." Gregor Streim, *Einführung in die Literatur der Weimarer Republik* (Darmstadt: Wissenschaftliche Buchgesellschaft, 2009), 68, my translation.

13. Lukács, *The Theory of the Novel*, 30–39, 65–69.

14. Alfred Döblin, "Bemerkungen zum Roman," in *Schriften zu Ästhetik, Poetik und Literatur*, ed. Christina Althen (Frankfurt am Main: Fischer, 2013), 124–25.

15. Döblin, "Bemerkungen zum Roman," 124.

16. Alfred Döblin, "Der Geist des naturalistischen Zeitalters," in *Schriften zu Ästhetik, Poetik und Literatur*, ed. Christina Althen (Frankfurt am Main: Fischer, 2013), 180. "Die Städte sind Hauptorte und Sitze der Gruppe Mensch. Sie sind der Korallenstock für das Kollektivwesen Mensch."

17. Döblin, "Geist," 168–70.

18. Döblin, "Geist," 170. "Was ist das biologisch gesehen?"

19. Döblin, "Geist," 171.

20. Peter Sprengel, "Künstliche Welten und Fluten des Lebens oder: Futurismus in Berlin: Paul Scheerbart und Alfred Döblin," in *Faszination des Organischen: Konjunkturen einer Kategorie der Moderne*, ed. Hartmut Eggert, Erhard Schütz, and Peter Sprengel (Munich: Iudicium, 1995), 92–93.

21. For a broad analysis of the role of masses in Döblin's work and poetics, see Sabina Becker, "'Korallenstock' Moderne: Alfred Döblins Poetologie der Masse," in *Internationales Alfred-Döblin-Kolloquium: Berlin 2011: Massen und Medien bei Alfred Döblin*, ed. Stefan Keppler-Tasaki (Bern: Peter Lang, 2014), 33–50.

22. On the biological basis of Döblin's thought about (and depictions of) "masses," see also David Midgley, "'Wie die Bienen sind sie über den Boden her': Zu den biologischen Bezügen der Massendarstellungen in Döblins Romanen," in *Internationales Alfred-Döblin-Kolloquium: Berlin 2011: Massen und Medien bei Alfred Döblin*, ed. Stefan Keppler-Tasaki (Bern: Peter Lang, 2014), 51–65.

23. Döblin, "Geist," 185.

24. Döblin, "Geist," 173–74.

25. Döblin, "Geist," 174–75.

26. Döblin, "Geist," 176.

27. Döblin, "Geist," 172.
28. "Two things fill the mind with ever new and increasing admiration and reverence, the more frequently and persistently one's meditation deals with them: *the starry sky above me and the moral law within me.*" Immanuel Kant, *Critique of Practical Reason*, trans. Werner S. Pluhar (Indianapolis, Ind.: Hackett, 2002), 203.
29. Alfred Döblin, "Der Bau des epischen Werks," in *Schriften zu Ästhetik, Poetik und Literatur*, ed. Christina Althen (Frankfurt am Main: Fischer, 2013), 226.
30. Döblin, "Der Bau," 227–28.
31. Döblin, "Der Bau," 228.
32. Anton Kaes, Nicholas Baer, and Michael Cowan, eds., *The Promise of Cinema: German Film Theory, 1907–1933* (Berkeley: University of California Press, 2016), 551–52.
33. Harris, *Mediating Modernity*, 180 n. 63.
34. Harris, *Mediating Modernity*, 114.
35. On the ways in which Döblin's engagement with media shaped his conception of literature, see Harris, *Mediating Modernity*, 95–132; and Becker, "'Korallenstock' Moderne," 33–50.
36. Döblin, "Der Bau," 233.
37. Döblin, "Der Bau," 236–38.
38. On Döblin's philosophy of nature, see Barbara Belhalfaoui-Köhn, "Alfred Döblins Naturphilosophie—Ein Existentialistischer Universalismus," *Jahrbuch der Deutschen Schillergesellschaft* 31 (1987): 354–82; Ursula Elm, *Literatur als Lebensanschauung: Zum ideengeschichtlichen Hintergrund von Alfred Döblins Berlin Alexanderplatz* (Bielefeld: Aisthesis Verlag, 1991); Helmuth Kiesel, *Literarische Trauerarbeit: Das Exil- und Spätwerk Alfred Döblins* (Tübingen: Niemeyer, 1986), 165–68; and Peter Sprengel, "Fantasies of the Origin and Dreams of Breeding: Darwinism in German and Austrian Literature around 1900," *Monatshefte* 102, no. 4 (winter 2010): 474–75. On the reception of Gustav Fechner's monism and panpsychism around 1900, see Monika Fick, *Sinnenwelt und Weltseele: Der psychophysische Monismus in der Literatur der Jahrhundertwende* (Tübingen: Niemeyer, 1993). On Döblin, Haeckel, and the monist idea of an *Urkraft*, see Sander's editorial notes to *Mountains Seas and Giants*, in Alfred Döblin, *Berge Meere und Giganten* (Munich: Deutsche Taschenbuch Verlag, 2006), 756.
39. Alfred Döblin, "Das Wasser," *Die neue Rundschau* 33, no. 2 (1922): 854–55.
40. Alfred Döblin, *Das Ich über der Natur* (Berlin: Fischer, 1927), 22–23.
41. "Eigentlich führen die Nervenfasern gar nicht ins Innere, sie führen ins Gehirn, etwa in die Rinde, fasern sich da auf, bilden Verbindungsfasern mit anderen Bahnen, und weiter ist nichts. Was habe ich eigentlich erwartet? Ein Loch für die denkende Seele?" Döblin, *Das Ich über der Natur*, 114–15.
42. Alfred Döblin, "Die Natur und ihre Seelen," *Der neue Merkur* 6 (1922): 9. This passage is reprinted nearly verbatim five years later in *Das Ich über der Natur*, 126.
43. Döblin, "Die Natur," 7–9.
44. Döblin, *Berge Meere und Giganten*, 517.
45. Alfred Döblin, *Briefe*, ed. Heinz Graber (Munich: Deutscher Taschenbuch Verlag, 1988), 122–23.

46. I am grateful to Elcio Cornelsen for pointing to the importance of this letter in understanding Döblin's philosophy of nature. For more, see his essay in the collection of essays from the 2017 International Alfred Döblin Colloquium in Cambridge, edited by David Midgley and Steffan Davies (Bern: Peter Lang, forthcoming). For a discussion of Döblin's debts to Mauthner, see Devin Fore, "Doblin's Epic: Sense, Document, and the Verbal World Picture," *New German Critique* 33, no. 3 (fall 2006): 171–207. For the importance of Spinoza to Döblin's monism, see Klaus Müller-Salget, *Alfred Döblin: Werk und Entwicklung* (Bonn: Bouvier Verlag, 1972), 236. For a reconstruction of Döblin's early philosophical development and influences, see David Midgley, "Metaphysical Speculation and the Fascination of the Real: On the Connections between Döblin's Philosophical Writings and His Fiction before Berlin Alexanderplatz," in *Alfred Döblin: Paradigms of Modernism*, ed. Steffan Davies and Ernest Schonfield (Berlin: de Gruyter, 2009), 7–27.

47. Döblin, *Das Ich über der Natur*, 121.

48. Döblin, *Das Ich über der Natur*, 126.

49. For an early work that identifies a radical change in Döblin's view of the *Ich*, see Müller-Salget, *Alfred Döblin*.

50. Döblin, "Die Natur," 10–11.

51. Döblin, *Das Ich über der Natur*, 122. This view supports Peter Sprengel's claim that, far from demonstrating Döblin's futurist-influenced turn to the inorganic world of technology, *Berge Meere und Giganten* and Döblin's work in general represent instead the assimilation of organic and inorganic nature. See Sprengel, "Künstliche Welten und Fluten des Lebens."

52. Döblin, *Das Ich über der Natur*, 12.

53. Döblin, *Das Ich über der Natur*, 122.

54. Döblin, "Die Natur," 9.

55. Döblin, "An Romanautoren," 121.

56. The common genre term in early twentieth-century German literature for works of science fiction was *Zukunftsroman*, or "novel of the future"; the engineering novel (*Ingenieurroman*) was a related subgenre. On the relationship of early *Zukunftsromane* to the *Ingenieurroman* and its strong-willed protagonist, see Dina Brandt, *Der deutsche Zukunftsroman 1918–1945: Gattungstypologie und sozialgeschichtliche Verortung* (Tübingen: Niemeyer, 2007), 14, 69–71, and 117–21. For an overview of the formal and thematic characteristics of early German science fiction, see Roland Innerhofer, *Deutsche Science Fiction 1870–1914: Rekonstruktion und Analyse der Anfänge einer Gattung* (Vienna: Böhlau, 1996), 20–29. For a discussion on the thematic and political differences between *Berge Meere und Giganten* and contemporary nationalist *Zukunftsromane*, see Peter Fisher, *Fantasy and Politics: Visions of the Future in the Weimar Republic* (Madison: University of Wisconsin Press, 1991), 151–56. For a detailed consideration of *Berge Meere und Giganten* in relation to the contemporary science fiction market and its deserved place within a science fiction canon, see Evan Torner, "A Future-History Out of Time: The Historical Context of Döblin's Expressionist Dystopian Experiment, *Berge Meere und Giganten*," in *Detectives, Dystopias, and Poplit: Studies in Modern German Genre Fiction*, ed. Bruce B. Campbell, Alison Guenther-Pal, and Vibeke Rützou Petersen (Rochester, N.Y.: Camden House, 2014), 53–54 and 57–62.

57. Roland Dollinger, "Technology and Nature: From Döblin's *Berge Meere und Giganten* to a Philosophy of Nature," in *A Companion to the Works of Alfred Döblin*, ed. Roland Dollinger, Wulf Koepke, and Heidi Thomann Tewarson (Rochester, NY: Camden House, 2003), 95; Gabriele Sander, *Alfred Döblin* (Stuttgart: Reclam, 2001), 154; Irmgard Hunt, "Utopia, Anti-Utopia, and the Role of Technology in Two Futuristic Novels: Paul Gurk's *Tuzub 37* and Alfred Döblin's *Berge Meere und Giganten*," in *The Image of Technology in Literature, the Media, and Society* (Pueblo, Colo.: Society for the Interdisciplinary Study of Social Imagery, 1994), 65; Ritchie Robertson, "Alfred Döblin's Feeling for Snow: The Poetry of Fact in *Berge Meere und Giganten*," in *The Critical Reception of Alfred Döblin's Major Novels*, ed. Wulf Koepke (Rochester, NY: Camden House, 2003), 216.

58. Döblin, *Berge Meere und Giganten*, 7–8.

59. While Döblin commonly uses the term "das Ich," the development of his terminology from "To Novelists and Their Critics" makes it appropriate, in my opinion, to speak of subjectivity in a broader sense to characterize his ideas on this score. Part of the thrust of such programmatic essays, as well as of *Berge Meere und Giganten*, is to undermine atomistic notions of the "Ich," in order to create a picture of subjectivity, perception, embodiment, and environment as entwined concepts. Thus, when I refer to "subjectivity," this is not meant to be taken in a dualistic sense, but refers to the way that Döblin situates the "Ich," the self, and the subject in the dispersed relationships that connect the individual unit to the surrounding environment.

60. Thus, although Döblin's narrating I writes by hand, the scene offers a different model than that described by Friedrich Kittler, in which the "continuous and coherent flow of ink" is the "material substrate of all individuals and indivisibilities." Friedrich A. Kittler, *Grammophone, Film, Typewriter*, trans. Geoffrey Winthrop-Young and Michael Wutz (Stanford, Calif.: Stanford University Press, 1999), 193.

61. Plessner, *Stufen*, 291–302.

62. See chapter 1.

63. Plessner, *Stufen*, 295–98.

64. Torsten Hoffmann has convincingly shown how, in the 1910s, Döblin poses the problem of bodily instrumentality, such that the body is both the instrument and the object of a protest of *Geist*. Döblin thus explores the potential autonomy of the human body as a response to the inflated role of *Geist* in German expressionism. By drawing on Döblin's early literary publications and his medical writings, Hoffmann suggests that Döblin's notion of the human is not to be understood as "antipsychological," but as involving a "radical centering on the body," which would make the conception of subjectivity compatible with contemporary medical knowledge. Hoffmann's reading of the autonomy of bodily organs in Döblin in relation to the author's medical writings, his critique of the dualist subject, and his philosophy of nature can also illuminate the relationship among these terms in Döblin's work from the 1920s. Torsten Hoffmann, "'Inzwischen gingen seine Füße weiter': Autonome Körperteile in den frühen Erzählungen und medizinischen Essays von Alfred Döblin und Gottfried Benn," in *Alfred Döblin: Paradigms of Modernism*, ed. Steffan Davies and Ernest Schonfield (Berlin: Walter De Gruyter, 2009), 46–73.

65. In a sense, Plessner's anthropology is predicated on the primacy of the individual organism. Döblin, on the other hand, radically unsettles the automatic centrality of the individual by insisting that the individual is one level among many, and is nothing more than an arbitrary, heuristic organizing principle. This is a motif of his work from "To Novelists and Their Critics" to *The I above Nature*.

66. As Döblin writes, "you think you are writing and you are spoken, or you think you are writing and you are written." Döblin, "Der Bau," 243–44.

67. Döblin, *Berge Meere und Giganten*, 84. For an exposition of the various scientific and medical discourses that facilitated Döblin's focal shift from the organism to the organ, see Annette Ripper, "Überlegungen zur Aneignung des Körpers und zum Aspekt der Bio-Macht in Alfred Döblins Berge Meere und Giganten," *Musil-Forum* 30 (2007): 194–220.

68. Döblin, *Berge Meere und Giganten*, 87–88.

69. The word is significant—*Wirrsal*, also *Wirrnis*, indicates a chaos or confusion, and derives from the adjective *wirr*, which means tangled, confused, or tousled, itself originally deriving from the verb *wirren*, which originally meant to confuse, mix up, disturb. It is a root favored by Döblin, and one which, like the trope of the *Mutterlauge*, allowed him to connect his understanding of subjectivity to his theory of the epic. I have elsewhere traced the relationship between these tropes in more detail. See Carl Gelderloos, "'Ersticken Im Stofflichen': Characters as Collectives in Alfred Döblin's Wallenstein and His Theoretical Writings," in *The German Historical Novel since the Eighteenth Century: More Than a Bestseller* (Newcastle, Eng.: Cambridge Scholars, 2016), 97–125, and Carl Gelderloos, "Döblins 'Mutterlauge' vom Expressionismus bis zur Schicksalsreise: Laufbahn einer interdisziplinären Denkfigur," in *Internationales Alfred-Döblin-Kolloquium Zürich 2015: Exil als Schicksalsreise: Alfred Döblin und das literarische Exil 1933–1950*, ed. Sabina Becker and Sabine Schneider (Bern: Peter Lang, 2017), 287–97.

70. Döblin, *Berge Meere und Giganten*, 88. "Auch sie waren umgeben von einem Wirrsal von Drähten und Röhren. Sie waren gespalten, angebohrt; in die Kronen Stämme Wurzeln führten Leitungen."

71. Döblin, *Berge Meere und Giganten*, 93.

72. Döblin, *Berge Meere und Giganten*, 301–5.

73. Döblin, *Berge Meere und Giganten*, 138.

74. Döblin, *Berge Meere und Giganten*, 139.

75. Döblin, *Berge Meere und Giganten*, 139.

76. Döblin, *Berge Meere und Giganten*, 141.

77. Döblin, *Berge Meere und Giganten*, 143.

78. Döblin, *Berge Meere und Giganten*, 142.

79. Döblin, *Berge Meere und Giganten*, 274–75.

80. Thanks to a travel grant provided by the American Friends of Marbach in the summer of 2013, I was able to access the manuscripts. For more on the characteristic features of the manuscript, see Gabriele Sander, "Alfred Döblins Roman 'Berge Meere und Giganten'—aus der Handschrift gelesen: Eine Dokumentation unbekannter textgenetischer Materialien und neuer Quellenfunde," *Jahrbuch der deutschen Schillergesellschaft*, vol. 45, (2001): 39–69. For a compelling reading of *Berge Meere und Giganten* as a work of Expressionist science fiction, see Torner,

"A Future-History Out of Time," which recovers a key tension in the novel between the generic expectations of Expressionist prose and those of science fiction.

81. In his study of Döblin's engagement with Fritz Mauthner's theory of language, Devin Fore argues that the shift in Döblin's prose that culminates in *Berlin Alexanderplatz* should be seen as the adaptation of a "verbal" over a "substantival" world picture that is "oriented not toward ontology (*Sein*, a word that Mauthner despised) but toward morphology (*Werden*), toward transformation and mutability, toward time and action." Fore, "Döblin's Epic," 202.

82. Döblin, *Berge Meere und Giganten*, 487–88.

83. Döblin, *The I above Nature*, 40.

84. "Es war als wenn ein Adergeflecht nach allen Seiten ausschoß von den Knochenresten, als wären sie Kristalle, Keimpunkte in der übersättigten Lösung ~~der Mutterlauge~~." From the papers of Alfred Döblin in the German Literature Archive in Marbach, Signatur A:Döblin, Alfred: Manuskripte Prosa, Berge Meere und Giganten. Roman (Drucktitel). Reproduced with permission of Stephan Döblin. Copyright © DLA Mabach.

85. "Flüssigkeit, die nach dem Auskristallisieren einer Verbindung aus einer Lösung zurückbleibt." Günther Drosdowski, ed., *Duden: Das große Wörterbuch der deutschen Sprache in sechs Bänden* (Mannheim: Duden, 1978), 4:1836.

86. On the idea of "Proteus Döblin," see Klaus Müller-Salget, *Alfred Döblin: Werk und Entwicklung* (Bonn, 1972), 1.

87. Alfred Döblin, *Schicksalsreise: Bericht und Bekenntnis* (Munich: Deutscher Taschenbuch Verlag, 1996), 285.

88. Martin Lindner, *Leben in der Krise: Zeitromane der Neuen Sachlichkeit und die intellektuelle Mentalität der klassischen Moderne* (Stuttgart: J. B. Metzler, 1994), 5.

89. Alfred Döblin, "Epilog," in *Schriften zu Leben und Werk* (Olten: Walter-Verlag, 1986), 305.

90. Döblin, "Der Bau," 236–37.

91. Alfred Döblin, "Von der Freiheit eines Dichtermenschen," in *Schriften zu Ästhetik, Poetik und Literatur*, ed. Christina Althen (Frankfurt am Main: Fischer, 2013), 132.

92. Döblin, "Von der Freiheit," 131.

93. Döblin, "Epilog," 305.

94. For a more detailed reading of the trope of the *Mutterlauge* in Döblin's work, see Gelderloos, "Döblins 'Mutterlauge' vom Expressionismus bis zur Schicksalsreise." In this article I consider the implications of this trope for understanding Döblin's conversion to Catholicism, and argue that we should see an underlying continuity in Döblin's thought from his early avant-garde leanings to his later turn to mysticism.

95. Döblin, *Berge Meere und Giganten*, 502.

96. Döblin, *Berge Meere und Giganten*, 515. "Das fürchterlich Zerstörende dieser Gewalt wurde bei den Versuchen klar: sie zersprengte jeden Zusammenhang, trieb Teile hervor, unter Vernichtung des Organismus."

97. Döblin, *Berge Meere und Giganten*, 516.

98. Döblin, *Berge Meere und Giganten*, 517. "Sie waren oft im Begriff, ihren Geist und ihr Menschenwesen aufzugeben und ins bloße Wuchern und Wachsen einzudämmern."

99. Döblin, *Berge Meere und Giganten*, 517–18.

100. "His sharp pale face, bushy brows, stiff bristly mustache, sprinkled by the mutilated regiments of a generation; slipping down, they held onto the buttons of his green doublet, onto his belt. Each one of his knobbly fingers marked the annihilation of cities; with every joint a dozen eradicated villages were designated. The bodies of the slaughtered Turks, French, inhabitants of the Palatinate shuffled, flounced over his shoulders, and yet he was supposed to appear with all this before Judgment one day, together with their horses and dogs, which hung over him this way and that, one in front of the other, over the other, a monstrous burden, so that his head along with his little hat disappeared beneath them. The torn-open red and chapped necks, stomachs with white lively colors, veined, trickling over the slit arms pushing back and the bending legs. Loops of intestines on the long mesentery, which tangled him up, bellying and wobbling over bracing, leather-clad knees, an immensely long, soft, vermicular trickling train, at which he jerked, tore, gasped as he walked. A mammoth, he burdened the ground; but icily he maintained himself, did not hear the people yelling, the bloodcurdling screams, shrill whistling of the horses that all held onto him, wanted to draw their life from him, out of the finest capillary tubes of his hair; horse necks reaching around, nostrils quivering, brindled, black; dogs, who had been shot, who sniffed at his mouth, his nose, eagerly slurped his breath. He must have long been emptied, they sucked at brittle wood, he rattled inside and they did not make him fall." Alfred Döblin, *Wallenstein* (Frankfurt am Main: Fischer, 2008), 292–93.

101. For a more detailed version of this argument, see Gelderloos, "'Ersticken Im Stofflichen.'"

102. Döblin, *Das Ich über der Natur*, 44.

103. Döblin, *Das Ich über der Natur*, 93.

104. In this regard, I follow Hannelore Qual's reading of the novel. Qual has demonstrated the linkages in the novel between Döblin's philosophy of nature and his political and social thought, arguing that *Berge Meere und Giganten* advances an ecologically minded anarchism in the spirit of Gustav Landauer and Pyotr Kropotkin. Rather than being a fundamentally pessimistic or fatalistic work, Döblin's novel would thus represent an open, dynamic utopianism that supports a view of human society as ultimately perfectible. See Hannelore Qual, *Natur und Utopie: Weltanschauung und Gesellschaftsbild in Alfred Döblins Roman "Berge Meere und Giganten"* (Munich: Iudicium, 1992).

105. The significance of the cultural geography of the novel lies outside the scope of this chapter. For an illuminating discussion of how Döblin's depiction of the relationship between Europe and Africa invokes such key themes as technological development, modernization, colonialism, and cultural conflict, decline, and borrowings, see Gabriele Sander, "'Der uralte noch immer traumverlorene Erdteil': Die Afrika-Thematik in Alfred Döblins Roman *Berge Meere und Giganten*," in *Alfred Döblin: Paradigms of Modernism*, ed. Steffan Davies and Ernest Schonfield (Berlin: Walter De Gruyter, 2009), 229–44.

106. Döblin, *Berge Meere und Giganten*, 547.

107. Döblin, *Berge Meere und Giganten*, 548. "Mann und Weib zueinander. Dazu hatte man Füße und Knie, konnte gehen, sich nähern. Blicke zueinander, Hände zueinander, Münder zueinander. Und nicht nur Münder. Man hatte einen Leib; das einzige Wühlen. Was man tastete umfing: daß man nicht Wasser war, um

mit ihm zusammenzuschmelzen. Daß man sich hielt, diese Beruhigung Besänftigung: dies Stieren und Vergehen im Feuerschein."

108. Döblin, *Berge Meere und Giganten*, 572. Döblin's novel has been read as drawing on parallel dualisms, so that the supposed domination of nature by technology is coded in gender terms. See especially Dollinger, "Technology and Nature," and Nezvat Kaya, "'Tellurische' Rationalitätskritik: Zur Weiblichkeitskonzeption in *Berge Meere und Giganten*," in *Internationales Alfred Döblin-Kolloquium Bergamo 1999*, ed. Torsten Hahn (Bern: Peter Lang, 2002), 131–40. To be sure, a profusion of power struggles is presented, often as battles between the sexes, and there are enough instances of male engineers and politicians and subversive female figures to give this reading ample traction, especially considering the many episodes that fall outside the scope of this study. Yet what such an alignment may also occlude is the extent to which the novel destabilizes such dichotomies, particularly the dichotomy between nature and technology, precisely by frustrating a focus on the individual, gendered body. Döblin's molecular exploration of the relationship between particle and mass and his agglomeration of human, plant, and animal bodies complicate an assessment of the role of gender in those places where one has tended to pursued it: feminized nature, the armored male ego, the dissolute and feminized masses, the vamp in the machine, the conquest of nature by technology. Gender in Döblin's novel seems to function according to more diffuse and less certain codes. The potentiality of nature in Döblin certainly seems feminine at times (the character of Venaska would support this idea), yet at other times, in, for example, Döblin's evocation of "Das Tausendnamige" in the dedication or in the "Ich" that permeates nature in *The I above Nature*, a force of generation and inchoate potential is depicted as neuter or hermaphroditic more than anything else. For a recent psychoanalytic account of the gendering of nature in Döblin's early work, including *Mountains Seas and Giants*, see Larson Powell, *The Technological Unconscious in German Modernist Literature: Nature in Rilke, Benn, Brecht, and Döblin* (Rochester, N.Y.: Camden House, 2008).

109. Döblin, *Das Ich über der Natur*, 202.

110. Döblin, *Berge Meere und Giganten*, 631.

111. Döblin, *Das Ich über der Natur*, 119–20. "Da bin ich Eiweiß, Protoplasma, Zellmasse—bin Wasser, Kalk, Kohle, Salz, Phosphor, Eisen, Magnesium, Silizium, die sich überall draußen regen. . . . Das bin ich alles, und das ist weither gekommen, Prärie, Berg und Tal, Sintflut, offene Natur."

112. Döblin, *Berge Meere und Giganten*, 631.

113. The quote is from Thomas Huxley. Quoted in Frances Emily White, "Protoplasm," *Popular Science Monthly*, July 1882, 367. On the history of protoplasmic theory across experimental physiology in the nineteenth century, see Brain, *The Pulse of Modernism*, 37–63. For a survey of the history of protoplasm in the context of cell theory, see Toepfer, *Historisches Wörterbuch der Biologie*, vol. 3, 770–71.

114. Brain, *The Pulse of Modernism*, 39.

115. Gabriele Sander, "Alfred Döblins Roman 'Berge Meere und Giganten'— aus der Handschrift gelesen: Eine Dokumentation unbekannter textgenetischer Materialien und neuer Quellenfunde," *Jahrbuch der deutschen Schillergesellschaft* 45 (2001): 66. See also Sander's excellent apparatus to the 2006 critical edition of *Mountains Seas and Giants*, especially 762.

116. "Der Träger des Lebens ist das Protoplasma, wie man den lebendigen Stoff genannt hat." Mathias Jacob Schleiden, *Das Meer* (Hamburg: Severus Verlag, 2012), 117.

117. Brain, *The Pulse of Modernism*, 54.

118. Brain, *The Pulse of Modernism*, xxix.

119. For other scenes that represent life as persisting in material flows that continue after the death of the organism, see Döblin, *Berge Meere und Giganten*, 85–86, 302, and 621, for example.

120. On the broader influence of monism in modern German thought, see Eric Paul Jacobsen, *From Cosmology to Ecology: The Monist World-View in Germany from 1770 to 1930* (Bern: Peter Lang, 2005).

121. Charles Bambach, "Weimar Philosophy and the Crisis of Historical Thinking," in *Weimar Thought: A Contested Legacy*, ed. Peter E. Gordon and John P. McCormick (Princeton, N.J.: Princeton University Press, 2013), 136.

122. And for Kracauer, recall: "The closed construction of the old novel form mirrors the presumed closure of personality." Kracauer, "Biographie," 265.

123. "This form of fluidity cannot be grasped." Döblin, *Das Ich über der Natur*, 25.

124. Helmut Lethen, *Verhaltenslehren der Kälte: Lebensversuche zwischen den Kriegen* (Frankfurt am Main: Suhrkamp, 1994), 133–34. (The translation in *Cool Conduct* of the same passage, found on 101–2, does not attempt to translate "Entmischung," subsuming it instead under the idea of polarity.)

125. Lethen, *Cool Conduct*, 23.

126. Lethen, *Cool Conduct*, 101–2.

127. Merchant elaborates: "Its [i.e., monistic vitalism's] emphasis on the life of all things as gradations of soul, its lack of a separate distinction between matter and spirit, its principle of an immanent activity permeating nature, and its reverence for the nurturing power of the earth endowed it with an ethic of the inherent worth of everything alive. Contained within the conceptual structure of vitalism was a normative constraint." Carolyn Merchant, *The Death of Nature: Women, Ecology and the Scientific Revolution* (New York: HarperCollins, 1989), 253–54. On monism and panpsychism in Döblin, Scheerbart, and Fechner, see Peter Sprengel, "Künstliche Welten."

128. In his open letter to Marinetti, Döblin accuses the Italian Futurist of precisely such a tediously mimetic techno-fetishism: "But you don't think there is only one reality, and identify the world of your automobiles, airplanes, and machine guns with the world, do you? . . . Or even attribute an absolute reality to the angular, audible, colorful world, which we would have to approach reverently, as minute-takers?" Alfred Döblin, "Futuristische Worttechnik: Offener Brief an F.T. Marinetti," in *Schriften zu Ästhetik, Poetik und Literatur*, ed. Christina Althen (Frankfurt am Main: Fischer, 2013), 113.

129. Stefan Davies and Ernest Schonfield, eds., *Alfred Döblin: Paradigms of Modernism* (Berlin: De Gruyter, 2009), 6.

Chapter 4

1. *The Worker* is seen in the scholarship as the culmination of Jünger's work of the 1920s and, to a certain extent, as the summation of his writing about the experience of the First World War; it thus marks a caesura and a turning point in his

work. See Harro Segeberg, "Technikverwachsen: Zur 'organischen Konstruktion' des 'Arbeiters' bei Ernst Jünger," in *Faszination des Organischen: Konjunkturen einer Kategorie der Moderne*, ed. Hartmut Eggert, Erhard Schütz, and Peter Sprengel (Munich: Iudicium, 1995), 212–13, 217; Bernd Stiegler, "Technik," in *Ernst Jünger Handbuch: Leben—Werk—Wirkung*, ed. Matthias Schöning (Stuttgart: J. B. Metzler, 2014), 351–52; Jürgen Brokoff, "*Der Arbeiter: Herrschaft und Gestalt* (1932)," in *Ernst Jünger Handbuch: Leben—Werk—Wirkung*, ed. Matthias Schöning (Stuttgart: J. B. Metzler, 2014), 105; and Helmuth Kiesel, *Ernst Jünger: Die Biographie* (Munich: Pantheon Verlag, 2009), 384.

2. Ernst Jünger, *The Worker: Dominion and Form*, trans. Bogdan Costea and Laurence Paul Hemming (Evanston, Ill.: Northwestern University Press, 2017), 69.

3. Jünger, *The Worker*, 69. When referring to Jünger's concept of *Typus*, "Type" will be capitalized. The 2017 translation renders it as "typus," which I use when quoting; otherwise it will be "Type."

4. Walter Gebhard has described the long prehistory of organicism as a longing for harmony that arose as a response to modernizing processes, especially to social differentiation. See Walter Gebhard, "Die Erblast des 19. Jahrhunderts: Organismusdiskurs zwischen Goethes Morphologie und Nietzsches Lebensbegriff," in *Faszination des Organischen: Konjunkturen einer Kategorie der Moderne*, ed. Hartmut Eggert, Erhard Schütz, and Peter Sprengel (Munich: Iudicium, 1995), 13. As Horst Denkler writes, the restorative, simplifying, explanatory valences of the organic were important for the National Socialists' embrace of the metaphor. For a discussion of the commonalities and differences between Jünger's "organic construction" and the use of the organic that prevailed in Nazi discourse, see Horst Denkler, "Organische Konstruktion: Natur und Technik in der Literatur des 'Dritten Reiches,'" in *Faszination des Organischen: Konjunkturen einer Kategorie der Moderne*, ed. Hartmut Eggert, Erhard Schütz, and Peter Sprengel (Munich: Iudicium, 1995), 278–80.

5. Brokoff, "*Der Arbeiter*," 105.

6. Brokoff, "*Der Arbeiter*," 105.

7. Bernd Stiegler locates Jünger's treatment of technology in *The Worker* between Spenglerian pessimism and Soviet Constructivism. Jünger inverts Spengler's pessimism into a radical optimism while preserving (and welcoming) the broad trajectory of the decline of the bourgeois era; but rather than associating technology with alienation, he sees "a reconciliation of the human being and nature by means of technology." Bernd Stiegler, "Technik," in *Ernst Jünger Handbuch: Leben—Werk—Wirkung*, ed. Matthias Schöning (Stuttgart: J. B. Metzler, 2014), 352, translation mine.

8. Jünger, *The Worker*, 5, 94.

9. Helmuth Kiesel's biography situates Jünger's early revolt against bourgeois society within the authoritarian social context of the Wilhelminian school system; in this context, Jünger was not alone among contemporaries in rejecting the discipline and strictures of that world. See Kiesel, *Ernst Jünger,* 44–58. Nor was Jünger's valediction to bourgeois society in the last years of the Weimar Republic unique. Again, Kiesel: "Of course Jünger was not alone in taking leave of the bourgeois. This was among the obsessions and commonplaces of the era and can even be found among declared representatives of bourgeois culture." Kiesel, *Ernst Jünger*, 387, translation mine.

10. On the role of the First World War in signaling the end of an era, Bernd Stiegler writes: "Everything regarding technology, which was still mostly treated implicitly in these [earlier] texts, then finds its theoretical elaboration in *The Total Mobilization* and *The Worker*. Here the First World War appears as a historical caesura, as a 'steel bath' in which the bourgeois dies and out of which the new technical human rises. The bourgeois era met its end in the World War and the Worker, as a new historical configuration, had its origin." Stiegler, "Technik," 351–52, translation mine. Similarly, Jürgen Brokoff, describing *The Worker*, writes that "more than any other event, the First World War ushered in the decline of bourgeois society." Brokoff, "*Der Arbeiter*," 107, translation mine.

11. Jünger, *The Worker*, 33.
12. Jünger, *The Worker*, 69.
13. Jünger, *The Worker*, 69.
14. "So the individual can no longer don the dignity of a person, any more than he can appear as individuum, or the mass as a sum, as a countable set of individuals. Wherever the mass may be encountered, another structure is unmistakably beginning to find its way into it." Jünger, *The Worker*, 63. Elsewhere, he writes that the "totality of individuals, *insofar as they appear as a mass*, cannot escape the process of dissolution to which the single individual is subject." Jünger, *The Worker*, 71, emphasis added.
15. Jünger, *The Worker*, 141.
16. Jünger, *The Worker*, 141.
17. The articulation of a specifically German *Kultur* opposed to a (French) *Zivilisation* is best known from Thomas Mann's essay "Betrachtungen eines Unpolitischen" (1918), a text that influenced Jünger at the beginning of the Weimar Republic. On Mann's essay as representative of an assessment of the war that was important for Jünger, see Kiesel, *Ernst Jünger*, 95–102. On the relationship between the pairs culture/civilization and community/society in Jünger, see Steffen Martus, *Ernst Jünger* (Stuttgart: J. B. Metzler, 2001), 90–91.
18. Jünger, *The Worker*, 89.
19. Lethen's discussion of *The Worker*'s reliance on tropes of fluidity, particularly as a contrast to the Type of the worker, is insightful: "This blurring of contours strikes the cool persona as a provocation—and truly so when it turns up inside the state apparatus and in the 'amorphous body of the masses,' becoming conspicuous in the commotion of Sundays and holidays, in the tumult of the streets, or in the 'gray hordes of demobilization' as the 'ferment of decomposition' (110). The outlines of the worker-soldier type, which Jünger juxtaposes to partisans and lumpen proletarians, never blur." Lethen, *Cool Conduct*, 160.
20. Jünger, *The Worker*, 71.
21. Jünger, *The Worker*, 72.
22. Jünger, *The Worker*, 12.
23. Jünger, *The Worker*, 10–11.
24. Jünger, *The Worker*, 73.
25. Jünger, *The Worker*, 73.
26. Jünger, *The Worker*, 69.
27. Lethen, *Cool Conduct*, 160.
28. Lethen, *Cool Conduct*, 160, emphasis added, translation modified. The key passage in the original reads: "Jünger führt ihn in 'kentaurischen' Bildern vor, in

der Verschalung von Maschine und Körper, als 'organische Konstruktion.' . . . Durch Funksignale erfahren wir, daß da noch ein Organismus in der metallischen Schale hockt—oder täuscht das Funkgerät seine Anwesenheit nur vor?" Lethen, *Verhaltenslehren der Kälte*, 202.

29. Jünger, *The Worker*, 20, emphasis added.

30. Jünger, *The Worker*, 18.

31. Referring to the first half of the twentieth century, Haraway writes: "The period is a time of basic crisis in which the age-old dichotomy between mechanism and vitalism was reworked and a fruitful synthetic organicism emerged, with far-reaching implications for experimental programs and for our understanding of the structure of organisms." Haraway, *Crystals, Fabrics, and Fields*, 2. See 197–98 for an elaboration of the difference between vitalism and organicism.

32. As Annette Simonis has written, "Gestalt" was a buzzword around the turn of the century, serving as a holistic reaction to increasing social differentiation. The Gestalt psychology of Christian von Ehrenfels, for example, understood perception in terms of totalities, rather than as an accumulation of sense data. Yet the relationship between Gestalt and organic life extends back, as she writes, to Schiller and Goethe. And while the term was pervasive in psychology and cultural criticism of the early twentieth century, its connection to ideas of wholeness and immediacy had a special appeal for figures on the Right: Eric Michaud has described how "Gestalt" frequently occurred in the titles and subtitles of texts written by Nazi ideologues. Eric Michaud, *The Cult of Art in Nazi Germany* (Stanford: Stanford University Press, 2004), xiii. Yet Jünger's use and transformation of the concept took it beyond its existing range of meanings and functions, as Annette Simonis has shown. Annette Simonis, "Gestalt," in *Ernst Jünger Handbuch: Leben—Werk—Wirkung*, ed. Matthias Schöning (Stuttgart: J. B. Metzler, 2014), 325–27.

33. The German context may have been especially receptive to the idea of a connection between the organization of the individual and the evolution of the species. Seen in *The Worker*'s linkage between the characteristics of the new Type and the historical development that Type represents, this connection is perhaps best known from Ernst Haeckel's recapitulation theory, the idea that the embryonic development of the organism (ontogeny) recapitulates the evolutionary development of its species (phylogeny). Lynn Nyhart explains the specificity of the German context of *Entwicklung*: "While in English the ideas of evolution and individual development came to mean quite separate things, the Germans never lost the connection between the two. At least until the end of the century, descent was considered one facet of the more general phenomenon of development. This German understanding of evolution also explains why Haeckel's neologisms 'ontogeny' and 'phylogeny' were promptly accepted by German scientists: these terms permitted a clear and concise distinction between the two kinds of development while preserving the long-held belief in their essential similarity by defining both as subsets of development." Nyhart, *Biology Takes Form*, 139.

34. Haraway, *Crystals, Fabrics, and Fields*, 18–19, 137.

35. Jünger, *The Worker*, 71.

36. Jünger, *The Worker*, 19.

37. Jünger, *The Worker*, 86.

38. Jünger, *The Worker*, 50, translation modified.

39. Jünger, *The Worker*, 90, translation modified. The original reads: "Die Gestalt ist nicht zu erfassen durch den allgemeinen und geistigen Begriff der Unendlichkeit, sondern durch den besonderen und *organischen Begriff* der Totalität." Jünger, *Der Arbeiter*, 139, emphasis in original.

40. "The Gestalt does not exclude development; rather, it includes it as a projection on the plane of causality—just as form appears as a new focus for the writing of history." Jünger, *The Worker*, 86.

41. Driesch took up a position at the University of Leipzig in 1921; Jünger studied there between 1923 and 1926. Thomas Löffler, "Ernst Jüngers organologische Verwindung der Technik auf dem Hintergrund der Biotheorie seines akademischen Lehrers Hans Driesch," in *Titan Technik: Ernst und Friedrich Georg Jünger über das technische Zeitalter*, ed. Friedrich Strack (Würzburg: Königshausen & Neumann, 2000), 57.

42. On *Ganzheitskausalität*, entelechy, embryology, and neovitalism in Driesch, see Georg Toepfer, *Historisches Wörterbuch der Biologie: Geschichte und Theorie der biologischen Grundbegriffe*, vol. 1 (Stuttgart: J. B. Metzler, 2011), 400–401, 696–98, and 706. On the development of Driesch's neovitalism out of his embryological experiments, see Riskin, *The Restless Clock*, 283–95; and Bühler, *Lebende Körper*, 59–72.

43. On the differences between Driesch's entelechical "Ganzheitskausalität" and Köhler's use of the Gestalt, see Plessner, *Stufen*, 138–49; Bühler, *Lebende Körper*, 75–88; and the entry on "Ganzheit" in Toepfer, *Historisches Wörterbuch der Biologie*, vol. 1, especially 697–700.

44. Löffler, "Ernst Jüngers organologische Verwindung der Technik," 64, my translation.

45. Löffler, "Ernst Jüngers organologische Verwindung der Technik," 64.

46. Haraway describes the difference between Driesch's vitalism and organicism thus: "the German embryologist Hans Driesch was instrumental in breaking the limits of a too simple mechanism in biology and in precipitating the crisis leading to a nonvitalist organicism. But he violated the mandate of the concretization paradigm in postulating an entelechy as the director of developing form. He relapsed into the ideal, and if anything, weakened the aesthetic appeal of his explanations." Haraway, *Crystals, Fabrics, and Fields*, 13. See also 23, 37. For an institutional history of Driesch's work and its role within the development of modern biology, see Nyhart, *Biology Takes Form*, especially 306–37.

47. For further discussions of the figure of the "organische Konstruktion," see Bühler, *Lebende Körper*, 268–70; and Löffler, Pekar, and Segeberg in *Faszination des Organischen,* ed. Eggert et al.

48. Jünger, *The Worker*, 115–16, translation modified.

49. The mechanical appears in a pejorative sense as an inadequate perception of history (Jünger, *The Worker*, 9); more broadly, the category of the mechanical frequently appears without being named as such, in the sense that the historical dominance of a mechanist view of matter—the paradigm of "discrete bits of matter in blind motion" (Haraway *Crystals, Fabrics, and Fields*, 19)—is both the context within which and the target against which many passages in *The Worker* argue.

50. Harro Segeberg has described this aspect of *Der Arbeiter* as the transformation of the organic into a guiding category of modernization: "Jünger aggressively

attempts to transform the category of the organic into the guiding category of a *modernization*, the 'organic construction' of which is distinguished by achieving a kind of naturalness [*Selbstverständlichkeit*], raised to the level of a natural grace, in its use and the aesthetic presentation of technical means. For Jünger it is not the human being *alienated* from its individual or species-nature by a technical existence, but rather the *symbiotic* human being, tightly fused with its technical means of power, that characterizes the signature of a modernity which first announced itself on the battlefields of the First World War." Harro Segeberg, "Technikverwachsen: Zur 'organischen Konstruktion' des 'Arbeiters' bei Ernst Jünger," in *Faszination des Organischen: Konjunkturen einer Kategorie der Moderne*, ed. Hartmut Eggert, Erhard Schütz, and Peter Sprengel (Munich: Iudicium, 1995), 212, my translation.

51. Jünger, *The Worker*, 140, translation modified, emphasis added.

52. "This value-based distinction between mechanical and organic world is characteristic of the weakened existence that will be put down by assaults from a life as integrated with its means as an animal simply and securely manages its organs." Jünger, *The Worker*, 147.

53. Jünger, *The Worker*, 146.

54. Lethen, *Cool Conduct*, 160.

55. Jünger, *The Worker*, 125. The original reads, "Technik und Natur sind keine Gegensätze—werden sie so empfunden, so ist dies ein Zeichen dafür, daß das Leben nicht in Ordnung ist." Jünger, *Der Arbeiter*, 193.

56. Jünger, *The Worker*, 135.

57. Jünger, *The Worker*, 104.

58. Jünger, *The Worker*, 113, translation modified.

59. "The perfection of technology is nothing other than *one* of the signs of the end of the total mobilization that has us in its grip. Therefore it may well be capable of raising life to a higher level of organization, but not to a higher level of value, as promised by progress." Jünger, *The Worker*, 110, emphasis in original.

60. Jünger, *The Worker*, 115.

61. Jünger, *The Worker*, 110–11.

62. Jürgen Brokoff argues that the seeming contradiction between Jünger's scathing rejection of the bourgeois need for security, on the one hand, and the "deeper security" that Jünger attributes to the closure inaugurated by the work-state is actually consistent. See Brokoff, "*Der Arbeiter*," 113.

63. Jünger, *The Worker*, 40.

64. Jünger, *The Worker*, 91.

65. Jünger, *The Worker*, 93.

66. Jünger, *The Worker*, 73.

67. Jünger, *The Worker*, 73–74.

68. Jünger, *The Worker*, 91.

69. Jünger, *The Worker*, 69.

70. Jünger, *The Worker*, 40.

71. The status of the individual in *Der Arbeiter* is ambiguous, among other reasons, because individuality plays a role on both sides of the critique of the bourgeois era: it is the "heroic consciousness" that can instrumentalize its body but it is also, within the new, technological, totally mobilized world, a relic of an obsolete subjectivity that must make way for forms of activity and collectivity characterized as integration rather than as the acts of an individual will. For

Jünger, this ambiguity of the individual had become acute in the experience of the war and can be seen in his war writings from the 1920s, where emphases on the primacy of technology and of the heroic individual exist side by side. On this ambiguity of individual will and the subordination of the individual to technology, see Kiesel, *Ernst Jünger*, 164. Conceptually, this experience and the ambiguous status of the individual correlates to Jünger's reception of Nietzsche, and his gradual abandonment of the latter's "will to power." See Kiesel, *Ernst Jünger*, 143–46.

Another relevant context, when considering the role of the individual in *Der Arbeiter*, would be that of the tension in Jünger's oeuvre at this point between observation and polemics, avant-gardism and the autonomous privilege of the writer. See Schöning, ed., *Ernst Jünger-Handbuch*, 16.

72. Jünger, *The Worker*, 93.
73. Jünger, *The Worker*, 94.
74. Jünger, *The Worker*, 6.
75. Thomas Löffler has argued that Jünger, in adopting Driesch's entelechy as a model of history, mistook the organicist heuristic construction that thereby resulted for an ontological truth. Löffler, "Ernst Jüngers organologische Verwindung der Technik," 64–65. Yet Georg Toepfer has pointed out that, even for Driesch, wholeness came to stand for a real causality rather than a conceptual construct. See Toepfer, *Historisches Wörterbuch der Biologie,* vol. 1, 706–7.
76. Jünger, *The Worker*, 42.
77. Jünger, *The Worker*, 43.
78. Jünger, *The Worker*, 45.
79. Jünger, *The Worker*, 45, emphasis added.
80. Jünger, *The Worker*, 106, emphasis in original.
81. Jünger, *The Worker*, 106.
82. Jünger, *The Worker*, 9.
83. Jünger, *The Worker*, 39–40.
84. Ernst Jünger, *Typus Name Gestalt* (Stuttgart: Klett, 1963), 8, translation mine. "Das Thema ist einfach, und darin liegt seine Schwierigkeit. Einfache Dinge sind schwieriger zu beschreiben als komplizierte, weil sie dem Namenlosen näher liegen und der Beschreibende auf den Grund der Sprache zurückgreifen muß. Eine komplizierte Maschine mit ihren Einzelteilen und deren Zusammenwirken läßt sich in einer Vorschrift mit absoluter Genauigkeit darstellen. Weit einfachere und überall prägende Formen wie Typen und Gestalten sind schwieriger zugänglich."
85. Jünger, *The Worker*, 38, emphasis in original. This rejection of an additive vision, while it fits with the contours of Jünger's project in *The Worker*, also shows how this project resonated with contemporary discourses—in this case, the Gestalt psychology of Christian von Ehrenfels, which stressed the holistic, rather than additive, nature of perception. See Simonis, "Gestalt," 325.
86. Jünger, *The Worker*, 18.
87. On one level this indicates the pivotal role that *Der Arbeiter* has in Jünger's oeuvre, as the text in which he distances himself from his earlier nationalism. On another level, Germany's role in the text is interestingly complex; while Jünger's discussion of the Germans' constitutional unsuitability for the bourgeois era and its abstract notion of freedom fits into a long and illiberal tradition pitting civilization against culture, one may also identify, in the terms of his discussion of

the Germans' unique role, an early articulation in *The Worker* of the critique of fungibility and abstraction. Jünger, *The Worker*, 5–7.

88. Jünger, *Typus Name Gestalt*, 82–83.

89. Jünger, *Typus Name Gestalt*, 78–79, 83–84. On the relationships that Jünger draws among the *Urpflanze*, the Gestalt, and the worker, see Simonis, "Gestalt," 326–27.

90. Ernst Jünger, "Der Baum," in *Bäume: Photographien schöner und merkwürdiger Beispiele aus deutschen Landen*, by Albert Renger-Patzsch (Ingelheim am Rhein: C.H. Bohringer Sohn, 1962), 7.

91. Jünger, *Typus Name Gestalt*, 88.

92. On this dual vision, see Brokoff, "*Der Arbeiter*," 105.

93. See Beltran-Vidal's discussion of *désinvolture* in Schöning, ed., *Ernst Jünger-Handbuch*, 321–22.

94. Lethen, *Cool Conduct*, 157.

95. For an overview of how these associations arose as part of a Cartesian legacy, see Riskin, *The Restless Clock*, 54–76.

Conclusion

1. "Let us now conceive this city from a greater distance than we have yet been able to do—let us observe it as if through a telescope on the surface of the moon. From such a great distance, the different goals and purposes dissolve into one another. The observer participates at once more coldly and yet more searingly, but in any case differently from the relationship the individual down there has as a part within the whole. What is seen perhaps is the image of a particular structure, and we can work out from various indications that it is nourished by the sap of a great life force." Jünger, *The Worker*, 38.

2. Jünger, *The Worker*, 38.

3. Döblin, "Geist," 180.

4. Döblin, "Faces, Images," 11.

5. On the similarities between Jünger's organic construction and Döblin's *Mountains Seas and Giants*, see Sprengel, "Fantasies of the Origin," 475.

6. For example, Lynn Nyhart describes how, in the nineteenth century, Ernst Haeckel came to the conclusion that "individual" and "organ" were relative terms. Nyhart, *Biology Takes Form*, 135–36.

7. See Gebhard, "Die Erblast des 19. Jahrhunderts," 13–36; and Simonis, "Gestalt," 325–27.

8. Andreas Huyssen, *Miniature Metropolis: Literature in an Age of Photography and Film* (Cambridge, Mass.: Harvard University Press, 2015), 239.

9. Andreas Huyssen, "Fortifying the Heart—Totally: Ernst Jünger's Armored Texts," *New German Critique* 59 (1993): 5.

10. Kim Stanley Robinson, *2312* (New York: Orbit, 2013).

11. On the generative roles played by culture, language, and social learning in human evolution, see, for example, Eva Jablonka and Marion J. Lamb, *Evolution in Four Dimensions: Genetic, Epigenetic, Behavioral, and Symbolic Variation in the History of Life* (Cambridge, Mass.: Bradford, 2014); Kevin N. Laland, *Darwin's Unfinished Symphony: How Culture Made the Human Mind* (Princeton, N.J.: Princeton University Press, 2017), and Michael Tomasello, *Becoming Human: A Theory of Ontogeny* (Harvard: Harvard University Press, 2019).

Assessing the relevance of Plessner for present-day approaches to anthropology, evolution, culture, and technology, as well as bringing Plessner's thought into dialogue with that of evolutionary anthropologists such as Tomasello, are the guiding threads of three recent works: the 2014 collection *Plessner's Philosophical Anthropology: Perspectives and Prospects*, edited by Jos de Mul; the 2016 collection *Naturalism and Philosophical Anthropology: Nature, Life, and the Human between Transcendental and Empirical Perspectives*, edited by Phillip Honenberger; and Joachim Fischer, *Exzentrische Positionalität: Studien zu Helmuth Plessner* (Weilerswist: Velbrück, 2016).

12. Jane Bennett, *Vibrant Matter: A Political Ecology of Things* (Durham, N.C.: Duke University Press, 2010).

13. Döblin, *Das Ich über der Natur*, 84–90; Bennett, *Vibrant Matter*, 23–24. See also the editorial introduction to Diana Coole and Samantha Frost, eds., *New Materialisms: Ontology, Agency, and Politics* (Durham, N.C.: Duke University Press, 2010), 1–39.

14. Döblin, "An Romanautoren," 121.

15. Andreas Malm, *The Progress of This Storm: Nature and Society in a Warming World* (London: Verso, 2018), 78–118.

16. Andrew Cole, "Those Obscure Objects of Desire," *Artforum* 53, no. 10 (June 2015): 323.

17. Malm, *Progress*, 48–51.

INDEX

Adelson, Leslie A., 20
Adorno, Theodor, 19
anatomy, 19; comparative, 7, 21, 70, 78, 79, 80–81, 199n37; in Jünger, 156
animals, 4, 58; "deficient being" theory and, 53–54; as machines, 9, 11; in Plessner, 27, 28–29, 33, 37, 39–48, 54–55, 196n125; psychological studies of, 43
anthropocentrism, 110, 183
anthropology, 26, 50, 52, 57, 208n65; Scheler on, 10. *See also* Philosophical Anthropology
Aristotle, 3–4, 5, 142, 159
armor (and armoring), 14, 28, 176; Döblin and, 121, 143, 144, 145, 153–54; Jünger and, 149–50, 153–54, 155, 174; Plessner and, 52, 56, 58, 196n125
art and science relationship, 12, 61, 63
atlases, 79, 89

Baker, George, 69, 75, 199n26
Bakhtin, Mikhail, 105
Benjamin, Walter, 62, 80, 98, 199n25; on Blossfeldt, 11, 81, 82, 83, 89–91, 187n23
Benkard, Ernst, 77
Bentley, Wilson, 88
Bergson, Henri, 31
Berman, Marshall, 16
biology, reformulations of, 5–13, 33–34, 175, 185n10, 186n14
Blossfeldt, Karl, 5, 11, 21, 66, 67, 81–92, 99–100, 175, 176; background of, 82–83; form in, 79–80, 81–83, 88–91; New Objectivity and, 81, 83, 87, 88–89, 91; working methods of, 87, 201nn56–57

WORKS: *Art Forms in Nature*, 62, 64, 81–91; *Working Collages*, 87
borders and boundaries, 16, 19, 62, 91, 113, 150, 184; Blossfeldt and, 81–82; Döblin and, 120–21, 125, 126, 131, 136, 143, 183; Lethen on, 56; Plessner and, 16, 25, 28, 37–41, 46–47, 50, 52, 54–56, 58, 120, 193n52, 195n117, 196n124
bourgeois humanism. *See* humanism
bourgeois subject, 22, 109, 150, 173. *See also* subjectivity
Brain, Robert, 141, 188n29
Braun, Alexander, 13
Brecht, Bertolt, 3–4, 5, 12, 62, 80
Brokoff, Jürgen, 148, 214n10, 217n62
Buchanan, Brett, 197n128
Buddha, 114
Bühler, Benjamin, 150, 189n46
Bütschli, Otto, 27
Buytendijk, Frederik Jacobus Johannes, 27

Canguilhem, Georges, 186n10
Carson, Cathryn, 6–7, 185n10
"cold persona" of Weimar era, 52, 56–57, 143–44, 155, 174, 214n19
Cornelsen, Elcio, 206n46
cybernetics, 14

Darwinism. *See* evolution; social Darwinism
Daston, Lorraine, 12, 63, 79, 87–89, 201n60, 201n62, 201n67
Davis, Scott, 195
"deficient being" (*Mängelwesen*) theory, 26, 27, 50–56, 58, 176
degeneration, 7
Denkler, Horst, 213n4

221

Index

Descartes, René, 7, 8, 10, 11, 27, 28. *See also* dualism
Dilthey, Wilhelm, 9, 27, 30, 31, 34
disciplines, interdisciplinarity, and transdisciplinarity, 18, 20, 22, 25, 27, 31, 58, 62, 67, 80, 99, 143, 145, 173, 175, 181–82, 190n53
Döblin, Alfred, 10, 17, 103–46, 175–82; background of, 107, 125, 200n38, 203n8; closure in, 103–4, 106–8, 117, 137, 143, 173, 180, 182; "collective being" in, 109–10, 111, 135–36; "confusion" in, 122, 208n69; earthworm imagery of, 3–5, 6, 9, 106; gender in, 211n108; instrumental body in, 117, 118–21, 123, 127, 133–35, 143, 207n64; Jünger and, 18, 149, 152, 153–54, 162, 173, 174, 176–77, 180–81; monism of, 22, 82, 100, 104, 106, 107, 108, 111, 114, 126–27, 141–42, 144, 183; "mother liquor" trope in, 129–33, 142, 145, 180, 208n69, 209n94; on novel form, 3–4, 104–7, 116, 117, 142; paratactic style of, 125–27, 132; protoplasm in, 129, 139–41, 180; psychiatry and psychology and, 105, 106, 108, 117, 203n203n6, 203n8; on Sander and photography, 21, 62, 64, 68, 70, 75, 76–81, 89, 91; on the soul, 113–14; utopian vision of, 137, 143, 144, 145, 210n104. *See also under* armor; dualism; epic poetics; individuality; interiority; nature; organicism; selfhood; subjectivity; type and/or mass
  WORKS: *Berlin Alexanderplatz*, 22, 105, 107, 117, 142, 209n81; "Comments on the Novel," 3, 106; "The Construction of the Epic Work," 107, 108, 111–12, 131; *Destiny's Journey*, 130–31; "Faces, Images, and Their Truth," 64, 70, 76–78, 177; *The I above Nature*, 22, 107, 113, 115–16, 119, 120, 129, 136, 138, 139–41, 143, 177, 182, 183; *Mountains Seas and Giants*, 14, 15, 16, 18, 21, 22–23, 103–4, 107, 108, 113, 114, 116–46, 153, 175, 177, 180, 183, 210n104, 211n108; "Nature and Its Souls," 107, 108, 114–16, 139; "Observations on *Mountains Seas and Giants*," 118; "Of the Freedom of a Writerperson," 131–32; "The Spirit of the Naturalistic Era," 10, 107, 109, 110–11, 114, 177, 180; "To Novelists and Their Critics," 103, 104–5, 107, 108, 113, 114, 115–16, 119, 126–27, 136, 142; *Wallenstein*, 107, 135–36, 142; "Water," 107, 112–13, 115
Dollinger, Roland, 117
Driesch, Hans, 8, 27, 34, 141, 150, 159, 216n41, 216n46, 218n75
dualism, 8–9, 10–11, 14, 17–18, 19, 59, 175, 176, 180; Döblin and, 108, 123, 162; Jünger and, 11, 149, 157, 160–61, 162, 165, 166, 173; Plessner and, 28, 32–38, 58, 120, 157, 162, 165, 186n15

ecology and climate change, 7, 33, 182–84
Ehrenfels, Christian von, 157, 215n32, 218n85
embryology, 7, 19, 27, 33, 57, 159
empiricism, 6, 8, 10, 21, 26–35
entelechy, 8, 34, 129, 157, 159–60, 167, 176, 180, 216n46, 218n75
Enlightenment thought, 9, 10, 14, 147, 178–79
epic poetics: Bakhtin and, 105–6; Brecht and, 4; Döblin and, 3–4, 12, 22–23, 62, 75, 76, 80, 100, 103–4, 105–6, 108, 111–12, 116, 130, 131–32, 143; Lukács and, 106
ethology, 7, 27, 33, 56, 57–58
eugenics, 7
evolution, 7, 28, 54, 78, 82, 91, 142, 183, 200n38, 215n33
Expressionism, 125, 131–32, 208n80

fascism, 19; Jünger and, 148. *See also* Nazism
film theory, 62, 63, 65, 97–98
Fineman, Mia, 82
Fischer, Joachim, 26, 30, 49, 192n39, 192n43, 194n68, 196n125
Fore, Devin, 209n81

Index

Foucault, Michel, 6
fragmentation, 4, 5, 13, 15, 61, 63, 122, 124, 178, 180; Kracauer and, 97–98
Freud, Sigmund, 7
Frölich, Paul, 72, 73
Fuechtner, Veronika, 203n8
Fuller, Loïe, 90

Galison, Peter, 12, 63, 79, 87–89, 201n60, 201n62, 201n67
gaze: of Jünger's worker, 147, 151, 155; medical, 151; photographic, 65, 72
Gegenbaur, Carl, 78, 199n37
Gehlen, Arnold, 26, 27, 46, 51, 53–54, 55
Geist. See life, spirit, and reason, the relationship between
German Idealism, 27, 29, 30, 49
Gestalt, 8, 215n32; Jünger and, 148, 154, 155, 157–60, 162–64, 167–73, 177–78, 180, 216n40
Goethe, Johann Wolfgang von, 171, 215n32
Gunning, Tom, 63
Günther, Hans, 70

Haeckel, Ernst, 13, 78, 82, 142, 188n31, 199n37, 215n33
Hake, Sabine, 69
Hansen, Miriam Bratu, 95
Haraway, Donna, 8, 34, 156–57, 160, 215n31
Harris, Stefanie, 111
Hayles, N. Katherine, 14
Hegel, Georg Wilhelm Friedrich, 27, 29, 36, 200n38
Heidegger, Martin, 25
Herbst, Curt, 27
Herder, Johann Gottfried, 53
Hindemith, Paul, 70–71
Hoffmann, Torsten, 207n64
Hofmannsthal, Hugo von, 119
humanism, 13, 14, 111, 145, 184; bourgeois, 5, 9, 11, 14–15, 19, 107, 109, 110, 114, 116, 175
humanities and sciences, relationship between, 6, 9–10, 12, 19–20, 181; Plessner and, 21, 26, 33, 57–58
Hunt, Irmgard, 117
Husserl, Edmund, 34

Huyssen, Andreas, 181
Hwang, June, 47–48

individuality, 12–14, 188n29, 188n31, 202n79; Döblin and, 14, 103, 106, 109, 127, 138–39, 144, 155, 203n8; Jünger and, 14, 23, 147, 149–51, 153–55, 157–58, 166, 172–74, 178, 214n14, 217n71
information theory, 14
interiority, 6, 13, 18, 19, 180; Döblin and, 22, 104, 106, 108, 111, 116, 135–37, 144; Jünger and, 147, 149, 150, 152, 173, 174; Plessner and, 28, 32, 33, 35–38, 59
intermediality, 80, 98, 111

Jünger, Ernst, 5, 10, 11, 100, 147–74, 175–83; abstraction rejected by, 149, 167–69, 171, 172, 179; background of, 213n9, 216n41; *désinvolture* in, 173–74; Döblin and, 18, 149, 152, 153–54, 162, 173, 174, 176–77, 180–81; fascism and, 148; freedom and, 148, 157, 166–67, 168; fusion in, 150, 161, 163, 165–66, 167, 168, 172, 173, 174; on Germany, 171, 218n87; instrumental body in, 151–52, 166; on living body vs. corpse, 156–57, 163; "organic construction" and, 18, 150, 153, 161–63, 166, 172, 174, 216n50; on work, 165, 166. *See also under* armor; dualism; gaze; Gestalt; individuality; interiority; organicism; subjectivity; technology; type WORKS: *Storms of Steel*, 148; "The Tree," 171–72; *Typus Name Gestalt*, 170, 171; *The Worker*, 10, 14, 15, 21, 23, 147–81, 183, 212n1

Kant, Immanuel, 110, 200n38, 205n28
Karolus cell, 111–12
Kiesel, Helmuth, 213n9
Klages, Ludwig, 9
Köhler, Wolfgang, 8, 43, 141, 157
Kopp, Guido, 72, 74
Korff, Kurt, 65
Kracauer, Siegfried, 103, 175; "Calico World," 97–98; "Photography," 21, 62, 64, 68, 92–99, 202n87

Kreinik, Juliana, 87
Kultur vs. *Zivilisation*, 109, 152, 214n17

Landauer, Gustav, 144
Lask, Emil, 27
Latour, Bruno, 16, 61, 197n2
Lavater, Johann Casper, 69
Leben, status of, 29–31, 141, 142–43, 163
Lebensphilosophie, 7, 9, 19, 27, 29–31, 49, 105, 187n20
Lethen, Helmut, 17–18, 143, 144; on Jürgen, 155, 164, 174, 214n19; on Plessner, 51–57, 196n125, 196n127. See also "cold persona" of Weimar era
life, concept of. *See* biology; *Leben*
life, spirit, and reason, relationship between, 29–30, 31, 49, 192n39
Lindner, Alois, 72, 74
Lindner, Martin, 131
Locke, John, 33
Löffler, Thomas, 150, 157, 159–60, 218n75
Lombroso, Cesare, 69
Lukács, Georg, 16, 105–6

Mach, Ernst, 33
machines, 4, 63, 66, 91, 125, 143, 155, 170, 178; body as, 151, 153, 188n27
Mallarmé, Stéphane, 90, 202n72
Mann, Thomas, 214n17
Marinetti, F. T., 212n128
Marx, Karl, and Marxism, 71, 169
materialism, 8, 11, 14, 30, 114, 158, 174, 183–84
Mauthner, Fritz, 114, 209n81
McBride, Patrizia, 96, 202n87
mechanism vs. vitalism debate, 7–9, 11, 27, 29, 33–34, 141–42, 215n31
Meurer, Moritz, 82
mimesis, 87, 89–91, 96, 201n62, 202n72
modernism/modernity, definitions of, 15–16, 61, 100, 173, 181, 197n2
Moholy-Nagy, László, 99
Molzahn, Johannes, 65
montage, 3–4, 67, 98, 106
morphology, 19, 33, 54, 80
Mühsam, Erich, 72, 74

Müller-Salget, Klaus, 118
Musil, Robert, 119

natural artificiality. *See under* Plessner, Helmuth
natural history, photography and, 21, 62, 64, 68, 70, 75–76, 78, 80, 92, 96–97
nature, philosophy of: Döblin and, 12, 22, 100, 103–4, 106, 107, 108, 110–16, 117–18, 129–30, 141–42; Plessner and, 25, 29, 36
Nazism, 4–5, 9, 19, 25, 213n4
"new human" in Weimar culture, 13–15, 104, 176
New Objectivity, 21, 56, 66–67, 100; Blossfeldt and, 81, 83, 87, 88–89, 91
Nierendorf, Karl, 82
Nietzsche, Friedrich, 9, 30, 218n71
nominalism vs. realism, 64, 76–78, 79, 89
novel, crisis of the, 105–6, 204n12. *See also* epic poetics
November Revolution, 5, 25
Nyhart, Lynn, 78, 190n53, 199n37, 215n33

objectivity, 27, 35, 82, 87–89, 203n9; machines and, 63; photography and, 64, 66, 67, 87. *See also* empiricism
organic growth, 11, 22, 41, 70, 161; Döblin and, 104, 120, 123, 124, 127, 141, 143, 178
organicism, 5–6, 17–18, 213n4, 216n46; definitions of, 5, 147; in Döblin, 140–41, 142, 143, 154, 178; in Jünger, 23, 147–50, 154, 156–57, 172–74, 178–79; Nazi and political Right uses of, 4–5, 18–19, 100, 213n4; photography and, 67

panpsychism, 112, 115, 141–42
Pekar, Thomas, 150, 157
phenomenology, 27, 28, 35, 51
Philosophical Anthropology, 10, 26–27, 29, 31, 36, 46, 51
photobook genre, 62–63, 67–68, 79, 87, 89, 98, 197n4
photography: genres of, 62; halftones in, 93–94; memory and, 93–95, 98; modernity and, 61–65; nature and culture and, 61, 63; speed and

Index

exactitude of, 64–67, 91, 92; theory and practice of, 20–22, 61–101
physiognomy, 69, 70, 75, 77, 78, 80–81
physis, 90–91
Plessner, Helmuth, 5, 10, 12, 25–59, 175, 179, 182, 183, 191n30, 208n65; behavior in, 196n127; "double-aspectivity" in, 35, 36, 48, 51, 192n35, 192n43; "eccentric positionality" of humans in, 14, 25, 27, 29, 30, 36, 40, 46–52, 54–55, 58–59, 120, 175–76, 183, 194n81; interiority and exteriority in, 28, 32–33, 35–38; *Körper* vs. *Leib* in, 38–45, 46, 48–49, 51, 54, 120; on mechanism/vitalism debate, 7; mediated immediacy in, 50, 54–55; on natural artificiality of humans, 18, 21, 26, 27, 50, 52–56, 58, 100, 183; subjectivity in, 33–35, 37; on three basic anthropological laws, 50; utopian standpoint in, 50. *See also* animals; borders and boundaries; dualism; interiority; vitalism
WORKS: "Die Legende von den zwanziger Jahren," 19; *The Limits of Community*, 195n108; *The Stages of the Organic and the Human Being*, 10–11, 15, 18, 20, 21, 25–59, 193n52
Portmann, Adolf, 26
posthumanism, 14, 183
Pynchon, Thomas, 20

Qual, Hannelore, 210n104

Rancière, Jacques, 90–91, 202nn72–73
Renger-Patzsch, Albert, 62, 65–66, 99, 171
representation, 12, 49; Döblin and, 80, 105, 106; photography and, 20, 21–22, 62, 64–66, 67, 76, 87, 91, 92, 96, 99–100
Rilke, Rainer Maria, 119
Riskin, Jessica, 9, 11, 188n27
Robertson, Ritchie, 117–18
Robinson, Kim Stanley, 183
Roh, Franz, and Jan Tschichold, 99
Rothacker, Erich, 26
Roux, Wilhelm, 8, 159

Saltz, Laura, 61
Sander, August, 5, 12, 21, 66, 67, 68–81, 89, 91–92, 99–100, 175, 176; Döblin on, 21, 62, 64, 70, 75, 76–81, 91; physiognomy and, 68–69
WORKS: *Face of Our Time*, 64, 68–76, 78, 81, 83, 89, 91; "From the Nature & Growth of Photography," 68–69
Sander, Gabriele, 117, 141
Scheerbart, Paul, 144
Scheler, Max, 10, 25, 26, 46
Schleiden, Mathias Jacob, 141
science fiction genre, 22, 103, 117, 183, 206n56. *See also* Döblin, Alfred (works): *Mountains Seas and Giants*
Segeberg, Harro, 150, 216n49
selfhood, 11–13, 23, 34, 180; Döblin and, 104, 106, 108, 111–12, 114–16, 119, 123, 127, 135, 139, 141, 144, 145, 177–78, 180, 182, 183; Plessner and, 32, 35
Semper, Gottfried, 82
Simmel, Georg, 9, 30
Simonis, Annette, 215n32
Snow, C. P., 20, 182
social Darwinism, 7
Spengler, Oswald, 7, 9, 30, 31, 69, 75, 80–81, 142, 213n7
Spinoza, Baruch, 114
Sprengel, Peter, 109, 206n51
Stetler, Pepper, 15, 63, 66, 99, 201n57
Stiegler, Bernd, 213n7, 214n10
Streim, Gregor, 204n12
Stump, Ulrike Meyer, 201n56
subjectivity: Döblin and, 12, 103, 104, 106, 107–8, 110, 111, 113–14, 116, 119–20, 130, 132–33, 136–39, 142, 143, 144, 207n59; Jünger and, 12, 147, 149, 152, 154, 172–74

Talbot, William Henry Fox, 61
technology, 5–6, 15–19, 21–23, 58–59; Döblin and, 104, 107, 109–12, 117, 121–23, 127, 144; Jünger and, 16, 21, 22, 147–48, 161–63, 165, 168–69, 174, 217n59; photography and, 61–62, 63, 65–66, 81; Plessner and, 27, 50, 58
Toepfer, Georg, 218n75

Tri-Ergon process, 111–12
Troeltsch, Ernst, 27
type and/or mass, 12–13, 57, 176; Döblin and, 13, 17, 68, 77, 89, 108, 109–11, 113, 138, 152, 154; Jünger and, 13, 17, 68, 147, 150–56, 158, 161, 170, 171, 180, 214n19, 215n33; photography and, 21–22, 63, 67–70, 75, 77–82, 88–89, 100, 201n62

Uecker, Matthias, 69
Uexküll, Jakob von, 27, 42, 43, 196n125

Virchow, Rudolf, 13
vitalism, 5, 7–9, 11, 27, 31, 33, 144, 156, 160, 212n127; Döblin and, 112, 126, 141, 145; Haraway on, 34, 215n31, 216n46; in Jünger, 23, 156; photography and, 67; in Plessner, 30, 34, 52
Volkelt, Hans, 43

Windelband, Wilhelm, 27
World War I, 214n10, 217n50; Döblin and, 5; Jünger and, 148, 149, 150, 218n71

www.ingramcontent.com/pod-product-compliance
Lightning Source LLC
Chambersburg PA
CBHW032033290426
44110CB00012B/789